BECOMING MANNY

Inside the Life of Baseball's
Most Enigmatic Slugger

JEAN RHODES
and SHAWN BOBURG

SCRIBNER

New York London Toronto Sydney

SCRIBNER
A Division of Simon & Schuster, Inc.
1230 Avenue of the Americas
New York, NY 10020

First Scribner hardcover edition March 2009

SCRIBNER and design are registered trademarks of The Gale Group, Inc.,
used under license by Simon & Schuster, Inc., the publisher of this work.

For information about special discounts for bulk purchases,
please contact Simon & Schuster Special Sales:
1-800-456-6798 or business@simonandschuster.com

The Simon & Schuster Speakers Bureau can bring authors to your live event.
For more information or to book an event, contact the Simon & Schuster
Speakers Bureau at 866-248-3049 or visit our website at
www.simonspeakers.com.

Text set in Caledonia

Manufactured in the United States of America

3   5   7   9   10   8   6   4   2

Library of Congress Control Number: 2009002348

ISBN-13: 978-1-4165-7706-5
ISBN-10: 1-4165-7706-8

All photographs not listed otherwise are courtesy of the Ramirez family.

To Carlos "Macaco" Ferreira, Mel Zitter,
and every coach who has made a difference.

Contents

Contents

Foreword

By Leigh Montville

It probably is fair to say that more words have been written, more opinions delivered, more beery pronouncements made about the residents of a small stretch of grass in the left corner of Fenway Park during the past one hundred or so years than about anyone at any other address in the city of Boston, Massachusetts. Not mayors, not governors, not Cabots nor Lodges nor Kennedys, not even the assorted members of the Wahlberg family of Dorchester, have come under the same unrelenting scrutiny as the men who have played left field for the Boston Red Sox.

Hemmed in by a thirty-seven-foot wall behind them, the encroaching grandstand to the right, and the consistent expectations for greatness on all sides, a succession of publicly tortured souls has stood in this space, each athlete famous and proud yet ultimately vulnerable, naked as a person could be in a full suit of baseball clothes. Every move has been dissected. Every failing has been exposed. The men of left field, Fenway Park, have been loved and hated (emotions sometimes changed in a flash, then changed back in another flash), talked about, typed about, psychoanalyzed, put on grand pedestals, and often humbled.

None more so than Manuel Aristides Ramirez.

He arrived in the spring of 2001, left in the summer of 2008, a total of seven and a half seasons in a Red Sox uniform. He was a subject of controversy from the moment he signed his eight-year, $160 million contract (an ungodly figure at the time) until he ultimately wriggled his way out of the last restrictions of that contract in its final season. (To be eligible for an even more ungodly figure for his next contract.)

He was cheered and chided, poked and prodded. He was the subject of grand speculation and flat-out gossip. Boston, like every other city in the country besides New York and Los Angeles, operates on a celebrity deficit. Manny Ramirez! Superstar! He was as big as a person could be within local boundaries, where baseball is the king of sports, the Red Sox a well-organized religion. An appearance at, say, a local super-market to buy food was cause for great excitement. Call your relatives. Tell them the news. Film at eleven.

When things went well, as they did in 2004 and 2007 when his team ended an eighty-six-year drought and won a pair of world championships, he was seen as a sweet-swinging wonder, a force of baseball nature, his face and statistics suitable for framing, hung from the nearest refrigerators. When things did not go well, when he didn't run out ground balls or disappeared from the lineup with curious maladies, sounds of displeasure were heard from the stands and the talk shows, questions raised about everything from his latest haircut to his fundamental attitude.

His predecessors in left field, subjected to similar pressures, had reacted in negative ways. Ted Williams, the most famous of the lot (1939 to 1960), arguably the best hitter in history, fought an open battle with the forces around him, snarled at the fans, spit toward the press box, was a man in constant conflict against anyone who might say the word "boo." Carl Yastrzemski (1961 to 1983) always seemed haunted by his situation as he gritted his teeth, squeezed his Louisville Slugger into sawdust, went through all movements with an enormous boulder of *responsibility* attached to his back. Jim Ed Rice (1974 to 1989) retreated, said little, snarled when he did choose to speak.

Manny Ramirez was different. He gave little public display of angst. To the contrary, he smiled and clowned, acted as if nothing mattered. He resembled nothing so much as a big, goofy puppy dog, especially when he played the outfield or ran the bases. Think Marmaduke of the comic strips. Think Marley of *Marley and Me*. He ran and fetched. Or sometimes ran and didn't fetch. He knocked over baseball conventions as if they were many lamps or end tables in a living room. His hat fell off all the time.

Oh, you Marmaduke . . .

Oh, you Manny . . .

The dog lovers in the crowd were charmed. They thought he was different, sweet, simply a lot of fun. "Manny being Manny" was the public refrain. His ability to hit a baseball, his greatness in that one act, gave him latitude for anything else he might do. The nondog lovers were not amused. They mostly saw him pissing on the carpet. "Manny being Manny" was not a great thing.

For all the talk, though, all the words in the newspapers, all the public conjecture, not a lot was known about him. The biographical details of his past and present were sketchy. He offered little to fill in the blanks. Like many of the present stars of Major League Baseball, he came from a Spanish-speaking culture, spoke limited English, and mostly spoke not at all. Less was known about him than about Williams, about Yastrzemski, even Rice, less than about certain utility infielders and middle relief pitchers. It was a curious situation. The constant debate had very few facts.

Who was this guy, this character in front of us? Why did he act the way he did? What (on earth) was he thinking?

Now, at last, some answers to those questions have arrived.

Dr. Jean Rhodes, a psychologist at the University of Massachusetts at Boston, in tandem with Shawn Boburg, has written this well-researched examination of Manny Ramirez's life. They have fused a pile of interviews with psychological insights. We learn about his family, his rocky beginnings, about the serious drumbeat that works underneath all of those magic moments and pratfalls we see on the public stage. It is fascinating stuff.

Wow.

Manny, as we say around here in good-bye, we hardly knew ye . . .

BECOMING MANNY

Selfish Slugger?

Who is Manny Ramirez?

Reduce Manny to a series of stats, and it's easy to see who he is: one of the best batters in history. A twelve-time All-Star and nine-time Silver Slugger, Manny ranks seventeenth in career home runs and eighth in career slugging as of this writing. The only players above him on both lists are Babe Ruth, Jimmie Foxx, and Barry Bonds. Manny is also second all-time in gram slams, behind only Lou Gehrig, and has hit more postseason home runs than anyone in the history of professional baseball. He still appears to have several years of baseball ahead of him.

But if you skip the stats, the question "Who is Manny?" gets confusing, controversial, and cultural. A favorite target of reporters and talk show pundits, Manny's every misstep is exhaustively analyzed and then reduced to "Manny being Manny." This oblique phrase has come to provide a shared wink of explanation for a player whose laser-beam focus at home plate seems irreconcilable with his periodic gaffes (or "Manny Moments") in left field and outside the ballpark.

The history of the phrase "Manny being Manny" in the popular press provides a series of thumbnail portraits of Manny at his most bizarre and intriguing, and a catalogue of the baseball world's struggles to understand him.

Its first mention in a major publication came in 1995, when Cleveland Indians' manager Mike Hargrove was asked about the young slugger's carefree-bordering-on-careless approach to money.

How do you explain Manny and Dominican teammate Julian Tavarez asking a Cleveland sportswriter to loan them $60,000, so they could buy a Harley-Davidson motorcycle? And what about forgetting a paycheck in a pair of boots he left behind in the Texas Rangers visiting clubhouse?

"That's just Manny being Manny," Hargrove told a *Newsday* reporter.

Several years later, a Cleveland sportswriter used the phrase to account for why Manny's old New York City neighborhood still adored him—because of how he showed up at his old high school cafeteria unannounced almost daily in the off-seasons to eat lunch with kids, and in spite of how he forgot promises to childhood friends to leave game tickets at the stadium box offices. But the phrase became less clearly defined after Manny moved to the Boston Red Sox in 2000, and its use grew with the city's fascination and ultimate disillusionment with their star slugger.

It has been invoked in print and online tens of thousands of times since 2000 as a shorthand explanation for Manny's mysterious injuries, his absences, his tardiness, his indiscriminate use of other players' bats and clothing, his silence in the clubhouse, his quiet acts of kindness to friends, his choice of an expletive-riddled song to play over Boston's Fenway Park sound system, his childlike playfulness, his midinning break inside Fenway's left-field wall, his failure to show up at the White House to meet President George W. Bush after the Red Sox won the world championship, and, yes, his towering home runs and unparalleled work ethic.

Manny is partly to blame for the mystery. He rarely grants interviews, and reporters who manage to breach his defenses are rewarded with little more than clichés or incendiary one-liners.

So, with little to go on but fielding miscues, baggy uniforms, flowing dreadlocks, big hits, and tired anecdotes, the public is left with caricatures of Manny as a carefree goofball and spoiled superstar.

Yet the question of who Manny really is endures, baffling his most ardent admirers and even some of his teammates. In fact, it was never more pressing than during the 2008 season, in the days before the Boston Red Sox traded Manny to the Los Angeles Dodgers, his third team in seventeen years as a professional. Manny's dispute with Red Sox ownership over his future—and questions about his commitment to the team—convinced many once-adoring fans that he was selfish.

The day after the trade, Red Sox third baseman Mike Lowell told the *Providence Journal*, "For me, he's a sure first-ballot Hall of Famer, and when he gives his speech, he'll probably give it via satellite because he'll be in Brazil. That's him and that'll be perfect. He'll be wearing a Brazilian National Team hat when he does it."

Lowell's distinction between malice and oddity is insightful. On many levels, Manny and Boston were a mismatch from the start. Nothing excuses Manny's shoving of sixty-four-year-old traveling secretary Jack McCormick, and perhaps Manny didn't give the Red Sox his best in 2008. Still, there were reasons for his frustration. And one could argue that if Manny had behaved this way in 2004, the Red Sox front office, not yet emboldened by two championships in four seasons, would have found a way to weather the storm.

If Manny had finished his career in Boston—or simply departed under more amicable circumstances—the grandchildren of today's vociferous fans might have even driven through the Manny Ramirez tunnel. That may sound farfetched, but

Manny's comments in advance of his exit are comparable to those of Red Sox legend Ted Williams, whose name graces the recently constructed highway that runs under Boston Harbor.

In fact, Williams was so embittered by his years of acrimony with the Boston press, Red Sox management, and fans that he refused to even tip his cap after his final hit. Manny's "enough is enough" comment, directed to the Red Sox management in the middle of the 2008 season when tensions were at their peak, was less acerbic than Williams's vituperations. As Leigh Montville described in *Ted Williams*:

> [Williams] said he wanted to be traded. He said he hated Boston, hated the fans, hated the newspapers, hated the trees, hated the weather, hated, just hated. The word "fuck" or some derivative was woven into most sentences. He wanted out. And for most of Williams' tenure on the team, Boston hated him right back.

Manny's badmouthing was mild by comparison. Moreover, there is consistency in his teammates' and coaches' characterizations of him as a hardworking team player. He was, according to the Cleveland *Plain Dealer*, "everybody's little brother" in his early years and, recently, has been more of a role model and source of support to younger players than he's generally credited for. "He was a mentor to me," says Red Sox shortstop Julio Lugo, three years his junior. "When I went through tough times, he knew that I had trouble sleeping so he would call me early in the morning, when he knew I'd be awake, and he'd say, 'Look, don't worry about it, man. You're going to do good today.' That meant a lot to me. There's no one like Manny."

"To be honest," says Pedro Martinez, "I don't have enough kind words to say about Manny. I think he's misunderstood."

But Manny's teammates are not the only ones capable of

shedding light on the vexing question of who Manny is. Conversations with Manny and his coaches, agents, mentors, parents, wife, sisters, and childhood friends, as well as side trips to his neighborhoods, show that he cannot be reduced to a caricature. They illuminate a nuanced, if inscrutable, man who defines himself by what he is least known as—a dedicated athlete, a well-regarded teammate, and a beloved father, husband, and son.

Among the mentors in Manny's life were his sandlot coach, Mel Zitter, and his then Triple-A manager, Charlie Manuel. But none have been more influential than his former Little League coach, Carlos Ferreira. In his neighborhood, Ferreira is endearingly known as "Macaco"—Spanish for little monkey. A thoughtful, charismatic man who left a medical career in the Dominican Republic to immigrate to the U.S. in 1979, Macaco, now fifty-nine, has coached several Little League teams in the baseball-crazed Washington Heights neighborhood of New York City. He was—and he remains—a de facto father to many aspiring Dominican players.

The story of how Manny came to rely on this gentle, unassuming coach—from their first encounter in the basement of a Washington Heights housing project to their ongoing, daily conversations—is a window into Manny's development and his hidden essence: his vulnerabilities, his values, his uncomplicated worldview, and what it really means to be Manny.

But to understand the story of Manny and Macaco, we first need to understand another story: that of Manny's early life with his parents, Aristides and Onelcida, and his three sisters.

CHAPTER 1

Manny at the Plate

The year was 1993, and Manny and his Double-A team, the Canton Indians, were playing the last-place New Britain Red Sox in their home-opening series at Beehive Field, about nine miles south of Hartford, Connecticut. Manny, twenty, was on deck, immersed in his warm-up ritual. This has always been Manny's zone—a place where his unrivaled power of concentration seems to create its own force field. He rhythmically twisted his torso from left to right, pushed down the top of his helmet, and lowered his eyes, face expressionless as he prepared for his chance to bat.

The setting sun shone brightly into the stadium's west-facing press box, where Don Bardlow, New Britain's blind radio commentator, ran his fingers over Braille sheets, with Gizmo, his five-year-old black Labrador guide dog, at his feet. Taking a cue from his radio sidekick, Bardlow introduced Manny, two years into his minor league career, to listeners: "The legend about this man is that when he hits the ball, it sounds different than when anybody else hits it."

Below Bardlow, thousands of fans were packed into the modest aluminum and cinder-block stadium, eager to soak in the familiar quirks that returned to Beehive every April: the man in the shabby bee costume who floated around the bleachers; the organist who played "La Cucaracha" when Hispanic players were announced; the silly billboard advertisements, such as the local hotel that suggested, "Have your next affair here." And, of course, there was the baseball. Beehive had seen its share of greats: Roger Clemens, Ellis Burks, and Jody Reed made their professional debuts here.

But, for Manny, this might as well have been a sandlot, any empty field, or an echo chamber. "Manny would prefer to hit in an empty stadium," observes former agent Gene Mato. Even as a young man, Manny had an ability to shut out the commotion in a baseball stadium, to ignore the exultations and insults, to remain emotionally neutral regardless of time or location.

But during this at-bat, there was a surprise that snapped Manny out of his spell: the voice of his mother, Onelcida. Oblivious to the sanctity of the on-deck circle, Onelcida marched purposefully along the wooden planks of the bleachers toward the aluminum railing that separated fans from the field. "Manny! *Hola*, Manny!" she chirped, waving her arms and grinning broadly. Behind her were Manny's father, Aristides, as well as his three sisters and first agent.

Despite all of Manny's prior successes, this was the first time Onelcida and his three sisters had ever set foot near one of his games. Baseball and family—two things Manny cared about deeply—had always been kept separate in Manny's world. Baseball was a game. Life outside the ballpark was something quite different. Manny's mother was occupied with providing and caring for her family, working long hours at a textile factory for $187 a week. She gave him money for gloves and spikes. His father, Aristides, would occasionally sit in the stands but never seemed that interested in the sport. And Manny did little to involve them. He assumed they had more consequential concerns. He also feared their presence would unnerve him. "You know, my mom was always working. She had to wake up at five or six in the morning and then come home at five in the evening. Because of that, going to a game wasn't easy for her," explains Manny. "It's not like other people who have parents who are professionals and have a good income and can say, 'This weekend I'm going to watch my son play.'"

That Manny's family was not involved in his baseball pursuits makes his accomplishments even more impressive. It also explains why Manny has clung to baseball mentors, who have helped bolster his confidence and hone his skills throughout his adolescence and into adulthood. In high school, Manny's successes as a star third baseman remained hidden from his family. In 1991, when Manny was nineteen, his family had no idea he had been named New York City Public School High School Player of the Year. (He batted .650 his senior year and belted fourteen home runs in twenty-one games.) Manny's high school coach Steve Mandl remembers that reporters would ask Manny before big games if his parents would be watching. "And he'd say, 'Why would they come? What are they going to see?'" He was a first-round pick (thirteenth overall) in the amateur draft. He nearly won the rookie-level triple crown in 1991. And he would be named *Baseball America*'s 1993 Minor League Player of the Year. Yet through it all, Onelcida had never seen her son play.

The plan to take the hundred-mile journey from Washington Heights to New Britain, Connecticut, was hatched by Manny's then-agent, a young Cuban lawyer named Jaime Torres. During one of Torres's many visits to the Ramirezes' apartment on 168th Street in Washington Heights, he learned that neither Manny's mother, nor his grandmother, nor any of his sisters for that matter, had ever seen him play. Torres made a mental note. As soon as Manny was within driving distance, he made arrangements.

The impromptu family reunion rattled Manny. His two worlds collided. Given the choice, he would have discouraged the visit. Glancing at his exuberant mother, Manny surrendered the trace of a smile. Then he resumed his preparations, stepping into the box. That night Manny had three hits and an RBI.

After the game, Manny walked to the stands for a few minutes of conversation before disappearing into the clubhouse. For nearly half an hour the Ramirez family, dressed in their Sunday best, awaited his return. As the stands thinned out, their disappointment grew. Torres rounded them up and offered to treat them to dinner at a nearby Chinese restaurant. "That was a complete waste of time," groaned Aristides Ramirez, who is now seventy, as the cramped car pulled out of the empty lot. "He barely even spoke to us."

But all these years later the first memory of her son on the baseball field still shines brightly for Onelcida, now sixty-two. "*Sí, sí, el primer juego*" (yes, yes, the first game), Onelcida recalls joyfully, unaware of how unusual, by American middle-class standards, it is to have missed her son's previous games.

Manny's oldest sister, Rossy, first saw him play in a Cleveland Indians uniform at Yankee Stadium. "Growing up, we never got to see him play," she says. "We knew it was one of the things he liked. But we were all into studying and doing our things in school."

"Let me tell you this," adds his next-older sister, Evelyn. "When we found out that Manny was drafted, we had no idea. I mean, nobody knew about it. Somebody called us and told us to turn on the television. They told us that there was gonna be this big news. I remember, it was the six o'clock news. So my sister and I, we all sat down there in my grandmother's apartment and watched Manny on the news. We knew he loved to play baseball, but we had no idea."

"I honestly don't remember Manny playing baseball in high school," says sister Clara, just eighteen months older than Manny. "We never went to any of his games. It was just something he did. That was just his stuff, and he never talked about it. He was just like a regular kid. He never invited anyone to see him play, never said anything about it. Once in a while he'd say, 'Mom, I'm going to buy you a really nice house someday,' and he got up early to do his exercises. But nobody paid it any attention."

Paying attention to his exercises would have been difficult under any circumstances: In high school, Manny's alarm rang at 4:30 A.M. every day. He rose regardless of the weather and heedless of sleep deprivation. In the dark, Manny dragged himself off his sofa bed and felt around on the linoleum floor for his gear: sweatpants, a sweatshirt, running shoes, and a set of old headphones that invariably pulsed merengue.

Sometimes a teammate or two joined him, but usually Manny ran alone. His route took him up Fort George Avenue, past closed bodegas, restaurants, bakeries, and electronic stores and up the forty-five-degree, half-mile stretch of road that climbed Fort George Hill. It was also nicknamed Snake Hill for its serpentine path, which wound past an abandoned lot and hillside apartment buildings resting on stilts.

Before ascending, Manny roped a twenty-pound tire around his waist, which would drag behind him for added resistance. The residents, although mindful of ubiquitous drug dealers, soon began to recognize the ambitious boy as he struggled against the pull of the city streets, determined to reach the top.

CHAPTER 2

Dominican Roots

Like an overwrought Hard Rock Café, Onelcida Ramirez's airy, Spanish-style home in Pembroke Pines, Florida, is a memorabilia-packed tribute to her only son. Framed newspaper articles, going back to his early days with the Indians, and photos of Manny with his three sisters, wife, and babies cover the walls of the library. But perhaps the most striking tribute is the glass coffee table, the base of which is a life-sized, plaster baseball player, sliding into home plate. Onelcida (whose nickname is Kiru) purchased it when she was living with Manny in Cleveland. After Manny autographed the plaster player's shirt, she had his number blazoned on the helmet.

Manny's father, Aristides, also advertises his son's number, in the form of a diamond-encrusted medallion, which often rests against his ribbed, sleeveless T-shirt. Aristides is modest in stature, particularly compared with his son, and his fair-skinned face is framed by two clouds of white hair and a neatly trimmed mustache.

Aristides occupies himself refurbishing a 1954 Buick that squats in the circular driveway. Meanwhile, Onelcida and her mother, Pura, a spry eighty-year-old, display countless laminated newspaper articles mailed to them from Dominican friends. Onelcida's face beams as she points to the dramatic headlines in Latin American newspapers. The articles are more like a hodgepodge of Manny's triumphs than a frame-by-frame narrative of his career. This hodgepodge mirrors the family's perspective on Manny's actual career; to them, his fame and fortune arrived not as a long-sought culmination, but all at once—out of left field, as it were.

Pura emerges from her bedroom with a stack of weathered photo albums. *"Mis tesoros"* (my treasures), she says, spilling them gently onto the kitchen table. She turns the pages in search of her favorite: a photo of the smiling one-year-old Manny with chubby little legs, standing backward in his high chair, a mischievous look in his eyes.

Other photos depict Manny's grandmothers, mother, and sisters at their fifteenth birthdays—a special ceremony called *quinceañeras,* honoring the passage to adulthood. Large gatherings of extended family embrace and dance—men and boys in blue pastel suits and women in ornate dresses, snug at the top, with bell-shaped, floor-length skirts.

Still more photographs show Manny doted on by his older sisters; leaning comfortably against his mother's lap; or sitting on the front steps, surrounded by neighborhood friends.

The broad strokes that have been applied to Manny's Dominican childhood—impoverished and living in barrios— tell one story. But the sum total of these photos and his grandmother's, mother's, and sisters' collective memories tell a richly layered story of a Dominican family whose seasons of love, separations, and, of course, baseball both connect and distinguish it from others.

The family matriarch, Pura, was born in 1928 in Haina, a port city in the southern Dominican Republic, about twelve miles west of the capital, and hometown to Red Sox designated hitter David Ortiz. The only child of a tropical fruit farmer, she still remembers the sweet taste of her father's freshly harvested mangoes, passion fruit, and plantains. The fruit was profitable, enabling her father to acquire adjacent land and hire day laborers. He eventually sold the farm to an oil refinery, and the family moved to a middle-class neighborhood in Santo Domingo. With her daughter nearly grown and time on her hands, Pura's mother began caring for the children of the country's tyrannical dictator, Rafael Leonidas Trujillo. Pura has little to say of these days, or her Dominican childhood under Trujillo's and his brother's bloody rule, as if uttering his name might still somehow evoke brutal retribution. She says only that her family "was not critical of him, so we didn't have any trouble."

Pura met her husband (and Manny's namesake), Manuel Sanchez Polonio, while she was still a high school student in Santo Domingo. Although Polonio began his career as a shoemaker, he eventually saved and borrowed enough money to buy a tank truck with which he transported gasoline across the island. As the years went by, Polonio made enough money to buy more trucks. He acquired one after another until he held a small fleet. His company is still in operation today.

Meanwhile, Pura, living with Polonio and his mother, had retired from a short-lived teaching career and given birth to Onelcida, her only child. But Polonio—according to Pura—was a bit of a mama's boy. His allegiance to his mother, who constantly carped at Pura, drove Pura away. She found a new teaching job and was remarried to a barber, Hermodenes Soto. In 1974, Pura and her second husband immigrated to Washington Heights.

It was hard to imagine that the Washington Heights section of Manhattan in which Pura and her husband arrived in the mid-1970s had once been home to many of New York City's wealthy elite. Naturalist John Audubon drew inspiration from the waterfowl that nested on his twenty-four-acre summer estate, which stretched from 153rd Street to 160th Street and from the Hudson River to what is now Amsterdam Avenue. It remained home to the white and wealthy through the early 1920s. In *The Great*

Gatsby, narrator Nick Carraway writes, "We went on, cutting back again over the Park toward the West Hundreds. At 158th Street the cab stopped at one slice in a long white cake of apartment-houses. Throwing a regal homecoming glance around the neighborhood, Mrs. Wilson gathered up her dog and her other purchases, and went haughtily in."

By the late 1920s, however, the extension of the IRT west side train had begun to open the area to Irish, Greek, and German-Jewish immigrants living in cramped quarters on the Lower East Side. The neighborhood's German-Jewish population increased again in the thirties and forties as refugees fled Nazi Germany.

Washington Heights was also home to many African-Americans, including Duke Ellington, Thurgood Marshall, W. E. B. DuBois, and Ralph Ellison. By the early 1960s, many of the European groups had moved to the suburbs, replaced in turn by waves of Puerto Rican, Cuban, and African immigrants. The Dominican diaspora began in the late 1960s and 1970s and, to this day, Washington Heights remains home to the world's second largest Dominican population, outside Santo Domingo. Corner groceries sell plantains, and a stretch of St. Nicholas Avenue has been renamed Juan Pablo Duarte Boulevard, after the founding father of the Dominican Republic.

A *New York Times* article from August 1976, entitled "Spanish Influx Felt in Washington Heights," captures the anxieties and ethnic profiling of the era. Reporter Richard Severo wrote that the Dominican immigrants had brought with them "the liabilities that contributed to the decline of the neighborhoods they left. These include poor education, a lack of marketable skills, and children who may cause trouble if left unattended." The article continued:

> The melting pot cools and a feeling of apartness asserts
> itself. At 608 W 187th Street, there is a hand-lettered sign

advertising a room to rent. On either side of it are two stars of David. It does not say "Hispanic People need not apply." For Latinos it doesn't have to.

But what may have been delightful to the casual observer is something else for New Yorkers who are wary of "changing neighborhoods," since "changing" has become a euphemism for "declining." It is disquieting to see the brownstone brick buildings along Audubon and Amsterdam Avenues that seem undecided whether to end up as unredeemed tenements or rehabilitated apartment buildings.

Amid this icy but evolving sociocultural climate, Pura and Soto settled into their third-floor walkup in a brownstone on 168th Street and Amsterdam Avenue. It was the same building to which she later brought her daughter, Onelcida, and, eventually, young Manny and his sisters.

Within a few weeks, Pura was commuting to a sewing factory on the Bowery. Meanwhile, back in Santo Domingo, Onelcida, now in her late twenties, was creating her own family with a man she had met years earlier, while a teenager in Catholic school. It was while waiting for a bus to school that she first laid eyes on Manny's father, Aristides Ramirez.

He was not among the fellow students with whom she stood in blue and white uniforms under the palm trees each morning. Nor was he a neighbor or family friend. No, Aristides, who had grown up in the Santiago barrios, was an ambulance driver. A slightly older, slightly dangerous, very handsome ambulance driver. And, to the everlasting dismay of her parents and grandparents, he worked his charm on her. "They didn't like him. Yes, he was handsome, but they wanted better for me. He was poor," recalls Onelcida.

To this day, Pura has not accepted Aristides as worthy of her only child. Nor has Pura ever resisted the urge to insult Aristides as a ne'er-do-well, even though Pura herself was once the subject of a mother in-law's scorn. "It's funny," says Manny's sister Clara, "but my dad will drive my grandma somewhere and, as soon as he leaves the room, she'll complain about him. 'Can you believe he said this? Can you believe he did that?'"

Manny's parents are still married after forty-one years, but this longevity is partly attributable to their willingness to take breaks from each other. Onelcida spent many a night in her mother's third-floor apartment during rough patches in New York, and now takes refuge by moving in with Manny for periods of time. Aristides, for his part, takes frequent trips to Santo Domingo when he needs to get away.

Despite their skirmishes, there is no mistaking the bond that remains between them. When Aristides unexpectedly sits down to lunch, a visibly pleased Onelcida doles out a choice helping of her homemade soup. His amusing little remarks evoke her gentle laughter. But still, Pura stares at him in stony silence.

CHAPTER 3

Shy Slugger

Onelcida and Aristides married just after Onelcida finished Catholic school. She worked the desk at the Dermatological Institute in Santo Domingo, while Aristides gave up ambulances to drive tank trucks for his father-in-law. By 1969, their first child, Rossy, arrived. Then came Evelyn. Clara followed the next year, and on May 30, 1972, the family welcomed Manuel Onelcida Aristides Ramirez.

Manny was born at the right time, into a tight-knit family with three sisters who, as the photos reveal, were all too happy to take turns holding him. He was the only son of a loving mother who had already suffered three miscarriages on her way to having her cherished son. Researchers have noted that many Latino mothers continue to have children *until* they have a son, regardless of their health or their financial ability to support additional children. In one study, low-income Latino mothers reported wanting an average of 2.8 sons but only 0.1 daughters. "Boys," according to a study in *Family Planning Perspectives*, "are typically more valued in Hispanic families; sons often become 'little kings,' whose needs and opinions are placed above those of female family members."

This was definitely the case for Manny. Everyone loved and spoiled "Nando," as he was nicknamed. He was the male baby, and he was Manny—exuberant, goofy, and determined. In the

Dominican Republic, it was common to consult quasi-spiritual books that revealed the hidden significance of birth dates—even years after the baby in question was born. "When we finally looked up Manny's," recalls Evelyn, "it said 'King.'"

"For me, he was like a doll," recalls Rossy. "I would bathe him, play with him, tell him stories to calm him down." She recalls how he would toddle off—from the pediatrician's waiting room, the grocery store, or anywhere—if they turned their heads. "My mom was very patient, though. She just doted on him. Remember, he was her only son."

As he grew older, he would spend his time at school playing, and then come home, looking for more fun. His sisters remember him crashing whatever games they were playing, even dolls, demanding to be included.

But that's not all he crashed. Aristides, while working for his father-in-law, took young Manny in the tank trucks, often leaving him to wait in the idling truck as he and gas station attendants arranged the logistics of the delivery. Never one to sit idly, Manny once managed to grab hold of the stick shift and lunged the tanker into a parked car. Onelcida chuckles, searching for the laminated coverage. "Yes, even as a baby, he was doing crazy things that got him into the newspaper."

By the time Manny was five years old, his family had moved into a brand-new housing project in Santo Domingo. The neighborhood, El Brisal, consisted of uniform rows of two-bedroom cinder-block units, piled onto each other like military barracks. Although its decaying structures now epitomize some of the most entrenched poverty in the Caribbean, it was, at the time, a symbol of upward mobility for poor families. Such public-housing initiatives, begun in the late 1950s, targeted families and individuals making at least the minimum wage—the more stable segments of the working class.

What mattered to Manny was a vacant dirt lot with a playing

field that stood (and remains) directly across the street from his unit. From the start, the field was an open extension of Manny's floor plan. "He would go out there before school to play with neighborhood kids," recalls his mother. Aristides has vivid memories of his wife taking meals out to Manny on the field. Sometimes Manny would come home, but only long enough to have his mother prepare his favorite drink: *morir soñando* (to die dreaming), a concoction of orange juice, sugar, evaporated milk, and ice. "I don't remember much about those times," says Manny, "but I do remember that my mom would get upset, because I never came home in time to eat at the table with the rest of the family. I was always at the field playing."

Manny eventually joined a team. "There was a Little League called Las Americas, and we would play on a field behind the Dario Contreras hospital. We also played in the street, with a stick and a bottle cap," Manny says. "In the Dominican," explains Manny, "you play baseball for the sake of playing. You don't grow up thinking I want to be this or that. What happens, all the kids in the neighborhood, just like when I got to New York, they all play baseball. So you go with them and play." But Onelcida remembers it differently. By the time he turned seven, Manny had informed her that he was going to be a professional baseball player.

Consistent with this ambition, Manny begged his grandmother to send him a baseball, cleats, and a glove from New York City. "I was a big fan of the Dodgers," recalls Pura, "so I bought him a Dodgers uniform, number 30, with his name sewn onto it." She recounted this story in March 2008—four months before Manny got traded to the Dodgers and started wearing number 99.

Manny wore his number 30 uniform night and day—to the field, to practices, even to school. "Thirty is still his favorite number," Clara says, laughing. And, on the day Manny was traded to the Dodgers, his sisters all invoked Manny's first uniform. One day he left it on the field and could not find it when he returned to look. Crying, he went home to his mother, begging for another. Never mind that money was tight. When Manny wanted something, he cried for it. "I remember when yo-yos were in style, and Manny wanted one," recalls Clara. "He just started crying to my mom: 'Kiru, I want a yo-yo. I want it.'"

Rossy recalls Manny's temper tantrums if he didn't get what he wanted—or if Onelcida punished him by confiscating his baseball. "He would throw himself on the ground and just have a fit. I would try to comfort him by telling him stories or telling him that Daddy would be back soon to play with him."

Although Manny dominated his close-knit family, traces of shyness and anxiety began to surface. Shyness presents an interesting paradox. Because it is most acutely experienced in unfamiliar settings, it can remain unnoticed in the inner circle. A socially anxious child can be perfectly relaxed and talkative at home, yet hold his mother's arm in a death grip at the threshold of an unfamiliar preschool.

Such was the case with Manny. Onelcida remembers the dichotomy between the carefree Manny at home and the Manny she would hear about on his Little League team. "One day his coach saw me and said, 'Why is he so quiet? Why does he stay to himself?'"

In future years, Manny's coaches would also notice. Macaco recalls, "When we had games, all the kids would sit on the bench, teasing each other and throwing gloves at each other. He was the kid who sat at the end of the bench with a very serious look." Manny's high school coach, Steve Mandl, adds, "He was shy, unless he was around close friends. Then he'd laugh and open up. But otherwise, you'd never hear a sound out of him."

It seems that Manny inherited this shy temperament from his grandfather Manuel. "My mother's father was a lot like Manny," explains Clara. "He was so shy. If he came home from work and heard people in the house, he'd sneak in a back door so he wouldn't have to visit with them."

Psychologists can identify this sort of social inhibition at remarkably early ages. For example, Harvard researcher Jerome Kagan found that shy infants become perturbed when presented with a series of colorful animal characters. Whereas some babies coo and smile as each animal is introduced one by one onto a mobile over their cribs, others see them as unwelcome intruders. They become agitated, arch their little backs, fret, and cry. Two years later, the same babies who shunned the animal characters were less relaxed in social situations. Similarly, children who had been classified as shy at age two were retested at ages seven, eleven, and fifteen. More than a third of the shy children turned into cautious, serious, and quiet seven-year-olds, and these behavior patterns continued into the teenage years.

"The infants' reaction of thrashing and crying occurred because they were hypersensitive to unexpected and unfamiliar events, due in part to the chemistry of the amygdala," explains Kagan. "[As they got older] they still had unrealistic worries— the future, new cities, crowds." The amygdala, the part of the brain that triggers the fear reaction, is thought to be more easily activated in shy children. Others have pointed to right frontal lobe activity, or lower levels of serotonin and dopamine. Whatever the physiology, there is no mistaking the thread of shyness that runs through Manny as well as his sister Clara, who guiltily admits to once climbing out her bedroom window to avoid unexpected houseguests.

Another early sign of his anxiety was Manny's intense fear of the dark. The ubiquitous power outages, which still plague the Dominican Republic, often left Manny and his friends stranded after dark. Manny would go so far as to pay an older boy a few pesos to take him home from the field rather than brave it alone.

"I'd say, Manny, why you always so scared of the dark?" recounts his mother lovingly. "He'd say, because, Mama, I'm a scaredy cat." Manny has done a good job of masking his shyness. But, where his avoidance of the press (even of the president, whose White House invitation to the world champion Red Sox was rebuffed by Manny) might look like aloofness, it could also be merely a strategy to manage his social anxiety—the public equivalent of entering a back door or climbing out a window. But shyness is only one dimension of his temperament. Although shy and sensitive, Manny was a very cheerful, active boy whose passion for baseball was fueled by his natural intensity.

According to Manny, "By age twelve, my routine still hadn't changed much—to the field in the morning, to school in the afternoon, and back to the field in the evening." What *had* changed, however, was his family. Manny's oldest sister, Rossy, had moved in with their grandfather, Manuel, who still lived with his mother. Manuel continued to employ Aristides as a driver. Meanwhile, Manny's sister Evelyn went to live with Pura in New York, at Onelcida's behest. Onelcida knew that she would be joining her mother and daughter in New York before long. Pura had already set the paperwork in motion. Although this fostering of children might appear to be something from the pages of a Dickens novel, it is in keeping with the fluid boundaries of many Caribbean families.

With Rossy and Evelyn out of the house, Manny and his sister Clara got the lion's share of Onelcida's attention—until Onelcida and Aristides immigrated to Washington Heights in the summer of 1983, leaving young Manny and Clara behind. Pura had seized on a vacant apartment on the sixth floor of her Washington Heights building, and arranged a job for Onelcida as a seamstress at the Royal Craft sewing factory. Aristides also took a job in a factory that manufactured dietary supplement products from royal jelly, a honeybee secretion.

Manny and Clara joined their sister Rossy in their grandfather and his new wife's house. Manny and Clara struggled to adjust to the stricter rules of this new household: homework immediately after school, no baseball after dinner, and regular Sunday mass. Before bed, their grandmother would kneel the three children in front of the bed to recite prayers and sing a hymn. "We couldn't go out at night because we had a 7:00 P.M. curfew," says Rossy. "We had to be home when my grandfather returned from work so he could check whether we had done the work we were supposed to."

In some ways, Manny's ability to buck his grandfather's rules foreshadowed how his free-spirit antics would challenge the behavioral standards set by his future employers. On one occasion, Manuel drove his three wards to a resort in La Romana, a tourist city on the southeast coast. As soon as Manuel had finished checking in, he realized that twelve-year-old Manny was missing. After a frantic search, they found him almost drowning in the hotel swimming pool. His arms flailed and he was struggling for air. According to Rossy, "He didn't wait till we got in the room. He didn't change his clothes. He just ran to the pool. At first the lifeguard thought he was joking. But he couldn't swim."

Or course, it was a painful transition for Onelcida, too. Although reunited with her mother and her second-oldest daughter, Evelyn—and relieved to have some distance from her overbearing father, Manuel—she suffered a deep longing for her other children, Clara, Rossy, and Manny. As she walked Washington Heights' bustling streets each morning, she thought of them. Tears welled up in her eyes if she saw a boy of Manny's age on the trains. "It was very hard for me because Manny was so little when we moved, and he was very attached to me." She burned through phone cards, which she purchased after each paycheck. "I didn't understand, you know," recalls Manny, "but there is a common idea of the United States in Santo Domingo.

Because everyone wants to come here. I knew they were trying to get papers for me to join them. You know that we Dominicans, many of us, come here to the United States for a better life. There's more work, you earn more money."

This leaving behind (or sending ahead) of one's children is common practice. In their five-year study of immigrant families, researchers Carola and Marcelo Suarez-Orozco found that 90 percent of Dominican children had experienced some period of separation from parents during the transition. Such separations have become part of the narrative of sacrifice and opportunity that surrounds the immigration process.

Eighteen months later, Manuel's mother passed away. A bereft Onelcida quit her job and journeyed back to the Dominican Republic for the funeral. After several weeks of mourning, Onelcida returned to the United States—this time, with all of her children.

So it was in December 1985 that the entire Ramirez family was united in their two-bedroom walk-up on 168th Street. Evelyn and Pura had spent the week in anxious preparation. For Clara and Manny, they had equipped the apartment's second bedroom with a bunk bed, purchased from a neighbor. On each sleeping surface they placed hats, mittens, and winter coats, with the tags still attached.

Manny's memory of the flight up the Atlantic coastline—his first time on a plane—is vivid. "We arrived at night," he says. "It was great to see all the lights. I was really excited!"

Manny's sister Rossy, who was seventeen at the time, remembers it differently. "As we drove up to our apartment, I saw a huge ugly building. I thought to myself, this place is horrible. This is nothing like the DR. I thought, 'Oh, my God, this can't be it.' There was a laundromat on one side of the building and a bunch of Dominican guys standing around on the sidewalk, just looking at us."

Their arrival coincided with a devastating spike in neighborhood crack commerce, facilitated by the convergence of several major interstate highways and bridges in the area. The notorious Zulu Nation street gang claimed Manny's neighborhood as its turf. Manny recalls passing drug dealers on every street corner as he walked to school. The neighborhood's police precinct recorded the second-highest murder rate in the city, logging more than one hundred homicides during Manny's senior year of high school. And it was in this neighborhood that former mayor Rudolph Giuliani and former U.S. senator Alfonse D'Amato dressed as Hells Angels, in an attention-grabbing stunt to demonstrate the ease with which one could buy crack cocaine on the streets.

But Manny only had eyes for baseball. At Highbridge Park, just a short walk from the apartment, he met a crop of like-minded Dominican boys and learned of the upcoming Little League registration. It was at that registration that Manny met Macaco, the man who would forever change his life.

CHAPTER 4

Enter Macaco

The boys came holding oversized leather baseball gloves, perhaps passed down from older brothers or on loan from an
uncle who still lived out his own childhood dreams on the
neighborhood softball teams that filled the dusty parks along
Amsterdam Avenue on weekends. They came with their fathers,
whose banter about Dominican players like George Bell and
Tony Fernandez betrayed hopes for their adolescent sons. These
boys, and their fathers, came for Little League baseball.

The small man sitting behind a steel desk in the corner of the
basement beckoned them with a crescent smile. He introduced
himself as Coach Carlos Ferreira to the few boys who did not
already know him by his nickname, shouted on summer
evenings by neighborhood kids who chased the fly balls he hit to
them in Highbridge Park. Macaco, as he was known in the
neighborhood, shook hands with each boy's father, a practice
that Ferreira made a prerequisite for playing in the league. It
was a rule that rarely needed mentioning, for almost all the boys
who entered the basement were accompanied by a parent—
except one. This thirteen-year-old boy—thin, yet taller and more
physically imposing than the other boys—came alone to register
for a baseball team.

Approaching the registration table, he timidly asked the
coach for an application. "What's your name?" asked Ferreira.

"Manuel Aristides Ramirez," the boy replied.

"All right, Manuel," said Ferreira in Spanish, handing him an application. "Take this to your house and tell your mom or dad to bring it back to me so I can meet them."

One week later, Manny brought the complete application back. But again, he came alone. "Where are your parents? I only need to meet one. Just one. Tell them to come and meet me," Ferreira told him.

Weeks passed. Manny's parents never came. But Manny always showed up to practice.

Ultimately, years would pass before Macaco met Manny's parents. By the time Macaco finally laid eyes on them, in 1995, Manny was at the plate in Yankee Stadium, as a Cleveland Indian. By then, Macaco had become a father figure, friend, and hitting advisor to the rising star. In many ways, Macaco is an unlikely confidant to one of professional baseball's highest-paid stars. A nurse who still works the overnight shift at Columbia Presbyterian Hospital in Washington Heights, Macaco spends his working hours running errands for emergency room staff.

Here's a typical night in the life of Macaco: He walks through the hospital doors, flashing his badge, and makes his way through the labyrinth of hallways and stairs to the cardiology unit. It was through nearby hallways that former president Clinton took short strolls as he recuperated from a quadruple-bypass operation in September 2004. Macaco remembers how Clinton was set apart from the rest of the staff, patients, and visitors, and how additional members of the hospital's security staff were assigned to stand vigil with the Secret Service. Thousands of cards, fruit baskets, flowers, and overnight packages were dispatched to the hospital, each carefully screened before being sequestered in a storage room.

Macaco's little piece of fame, however, is Manny. Even in his scrubs, he can't contain his pride. A signed Red Sox skullcap covers his head and he proudly flashes his sparkling new iPod, a recent gift from Manny. Although his mostly young, mostly female, occasionally dreadlocked, Afro-Caribbean coworkers are happy to indulge his tales, their interest is distant and polite—the sort of attention they might give to a grandfather.

Macaco rests on the vinyl sofa in the staff lounge, gathering his strength for the shift. His nights here are filled with muted conversations and microwaved Hot Pockets. His occasional moments of sleep are interrupted by emergencies requiring hasty preparation of operating rooms. Macaco and his coworkers ready the rooms before patients and surgeons arrive.

One of the more physically demanding aspects of the job involves Macaco's runs to the blood bank. Hospital workers smile and move aside as Macaco jogs through the dimly lit corridors. But Macaco is growing weary of this routine. His feet ache and his knees give him trouble. Plans for retirement occupy his thoughts and conversations. In just six years, Macaco figures, he will be able to retire. He'll live on his monthly pension of $1,174. "I can easily survive on that," he asserts, "especially in Santiago."

Despite the manifest contrast in their earnings and lifestyles, Manny and Macaco have remained bonded through their love of baseball. In May 2008, during Manny's final season with the Red Sox, Macaco sits in Fenway Park. "Every time he goes to the plate, I look at his mechanics and speed of his swing," says Macaco, as he watches Manny walk from the dugout to the on-deck circle.

At the plate, Manny is the picture of relaxation. His dreadlocks rest on his shirt, which is only partially tucked into his baggy pants. He pulls at the top of his shirtsleeves before lowering his head. His head stays down and his hands stay back until, shifting his weight forward, he whips his bat through the zone, ending with it high in the air.

Macaco has been analyzing that swing for twenty years,

beginning when Manny debuted on his Little League team in 1985. Through the years, Macaco kept watching, as Manny starred for the George Washington High School Trojans. It was this mindful watching that laid the foundation for Macaco's role in Manny's life. Macaco showed up, he watched, and, with time, he earned Manny's trust. We once asked Manny how he came to trust Macaco's batting advice. "I think of all the time he put in. We were building our relationship when I was young, and he used to come to my games. I was always working harder than anybody, and he saw something in me that nobody else saw."

Over the years, this batting-coach-to-pupil relationship became something more. Macaco became Manny's mentor—a lifelong companion whose steady influence enabled Manny to avoid the mistakes that have derailed so many other talents.

The term "mentor" dates back to Homer's *Odyssey*; before leaving on his long journey, Odysseus asked a close friend named Mentor to watch over and guide his son. Today, mentoring stands as a valuable tool that can help young people—especially those born into poverty and difficult circumstances—make the most of their lives.

Macaco's techniques are a radical contrast to the tough-love school of coaching. He is a far cry from, say, a hard-ass martinet like Ken Carter of Richmond High School in California, whom the actor Samuel L. Jackson portrayed in the 2005 film *Coach Carter*. Carter enforced a strict code of dress, behavior, and grades for his basketball team. Likewise, Macaco's approach would never be confused with that of Coach Fitz, Michael Lewis's high school baseball coach in New Orleans, whom Lewis profiled in *Coach: Lessons on the Game of Life*. Fitz was a master at spewing well-intentioned verbal abuse onto his players each spring.

Then there's Steve Mandl, Manny's baseball coach at George Washington High School. Mandl is from the Carter-Fitz school, and seems right out of central casting. An imposing man who characterizes himself as quiet and stern, Mandl proudly describes how his players are "petrified" of him before they get to know him. Mandl's coaching has, in fact, proven to be the salvation of many students. But what Manny also needed—and found in Macaco—was understanding, comfort, and trust.

Trust is perhaps a defining feature in Manny's most important relationships. Manny's riches have complicated his ties with high school friends; to Manny, those interactions feel tinged with opportunism. He doesn't feel that way about his interactions with Macaco. His faith in the purity of Macaco's intentions is what sets their relationship apart. Manny explains his conception of Macaco's purity a few days before the trade to the Dodgers: "You can tell when people are real and want to be there for you. You come across a thousand people who say 'Put your money here' or 'Put your money there,' but it's not common to find a person you can really trust. There are three people in my life who I can really trust: Juliana [Manny's wife], my mom, and Macaco. [Macaco is] a person who is honest, who tells you how it is. He won't say one thing to you and say something else to somebody else. There are a lot of people like that. It hurts me that the world is like that but it is, so you have to have someone you can trust. Someone who calms you and helps you move forward.

"He's like my father. When you're young, you need to have someone next to you, someone who is going to push you. You need people who are positive by your side. I'm just blessed to have a coach who was always there to give me support. I'm just blessed to have somebody like Carlos next to me all my career.

"We like to dance and listen to music and have cookouts and have a few drinks. He's like my lucky charm. Every time he goes to the stadium, me and David [Ortiz] always hit home runs. He was with me in the World Series, playoffs, the regular season. And I call him every day. We talk about the game and when stuff is not going real good he always talks to me and says 'hey, just be patient. It's not how you start, it's how you finish.'"

Macaco, a thin man who stands five-foot-seven, is now fifty-nine. He has a soft, round face with a wide mouth and brown, smiling eyes. Despite his ever-present baseball cap, he also has a sun-baked complexion. Most days, he dresses like a coach, with a pair of clean, white sneakers, jeans, and a track jacket. Instead of a coach's whistle, however, Manny's 1999 All-Star ring hangs proudly from a chain around his neck.

How does Macaco characterize their relationship? "We talk like father and son," he says as he sits on the couch of his spartan, subsidized housing unit, which he shares with his mother, sister, and adopted nephew.

The aroma of fresh plantains wafts from the hallway-sized kitchen adjoining the living room. A plastic-covered floral sofa sits under a window, which frames a spectacular view of the George Washington Bridge. It was through that window that Macaco's mother, Angela, saw the first plane on 9/11, flying ominously low, prompting her to call her son at work.

Macaco's coaching awards hang prominently above a coffee table. Alongside the awards are newspaper clippings and old photographs featuring his famous protégé. We ask Macaco how he benefits from his bond with Manny. He gazes past the windowsill and says: "It's really made me whole. It's given me a full life instead of just half. Still, my life is not perfect. I work very hard. But it makes me—it's like when someone takes medicine for an illness. It's like if you have a failure in your heart and you need medicine to make it regular. When I'm with him, I feel different. I feel more relaxed because of the way we can talk and the respect he has for me. Sometimes I ask myself, 'Why is he asking me for help? I'm not a professional.' The answer to that question I don't know. But in my heart, Manny is my son."

•   •   •

Carlos "Macaco" Ferreira was born August 20, 1949, the second of four children. His mother, a nurse practitioner, instilled a strong work ethic in her children, all of whom attended college. Macaco's father, a private driver for Santiago's political elite, bestowed on his son a love of baseball. Each winter, they watched Santiago's team in the Dominican Winter Baseball League, Las Aguilas Cibaenas, battle longtime rival Los Tigres del Licey. In spring, they watched Sunday night rebroadcasts or listened to Spanish radio coverage of major league games.

As Macaco's father sat smoking at the kitchen table, young Macaco stood with bat in hand, enacting each play. He wore socks from his mother's nursing uniform pulled up over his pants and a latex glove on his right hand. He also played baseball outdoors quite frequently. It was during those games that his playmates nicknamed him Macaco. "Probably 90 percent of people don't know my real name is Carlos."

When he was seventeen, Macaco tried out for the Instituto de Agronomia, a team analogous to a Double-A team in the United States. But his dreams were always more robust than his frame. So, in 1967, at age eighteen, he turned to medical care. By day, he took preparatory courses for a career in medicine; by night, he tended to street children in the state-run Arturo Grullon Children's Hospital. Often, he sutured deep cuts on children's feet. They had been walking barefoot in the streets, unable to afford shoes. Macaco found that he liked working with children. Furthermore, his night shift gave him time to play and coach during the day.

Macaco coached—and, without knowing the term, mentored—a team of fifteen Santiago-area teenagers in the Luis Vera League. The boys played on hard dirt fields. Macaco drew the baselines in charcoal. He bought cracked bats for a peso from Dominican leagues and repaired them with white hospital tape. Some of the boys he coached carved their own bats from the timber of adjacent forests. Other boys fashioned their own mitts from pieces of canvas torn from the roofs of trucks. As for baseballs, any spherical objects would do: rocks, deodorant rollers, crumpled wads of aluminum foil.

With each season, Macaco's love for coaching grew. His team won the citywide youth baseball championship in his first four seasons as coach. At the end of his fourth season, however, the Luis Vera League went broke. Macaco became a volunteer for other teams. He practiced with them during the week, and he played softball on the weekends.

In 1977, when he was twenty-eight, Macaco got married and wanted to start a family. He and his wife, however, were unable to conceive—a stinging disappointment that he still recalls with great sadness. The marriage collapsed within two years. In June 1980 Macaco, looking for a change to his life, seized a chance to immigrate to the United States. He married his cousin, who already had legal status in the United States, and divorced her shortly after his arrival.

Within six months, Macaco landed a job at Columbia Presbyterian Medical Center, just a few blocks from where Manny would later live. Built in the 1920s, along several blocks between 165th and 168th, the Medical Center sits atop the lost ruins of the former Yankees stadium, Hilltop Park. From 1903 to 1912, Hilltop was the home stadium of the New York Highlanders (in reference to the park's elevated location). That name was eventually shortened to its nickname, the Yankees.

The seating capacity at Hilltop was sixteen thousand. But as many as eight thousand additional fans typically watched from the edge of the outfield, down the foul lines, and between home plate and the backstop. From behind home plate, fans could see the Hudson River, beyond which rose the steep cliffs of the New Jersey Palisades—views that Macaco now has during his 11:00 P.M. to 7:00 A.M. shift at Presbyterian.

This shift has permitted Macaco to immerse himself in the baseball culture of Washington Heights with the same gusto that defined his life in Santiago. "I came here with a reputation," he says. "My friends told people I was coming and that I was a good outfielder and a good batter in softball. All the teams tried to recruit me."

Word of Macaco's coaching skills also preceded him. Within a year, he received a call from a community leader, Alexis Ferreira (no relation). A newly formed league had several local sponsors but lacked coaches. It was a serious league—five games a week—no easy chore for working adults. But to Macaco, it represented an opportunity to pull another generation of boys from the lure of the streets.

Serving boys aged nine to eighteen, the league had six teams, including Las Tres Marias, Rivas Travel, Pena Grocery, and Los Caciques (The Chiefs). Since Alexis Ferreira had managed to recruit only three other coaches, Macaco agreed to coach not one but *three* of the teams. On game days, if his teams were opponents, he enlisted a father or friend to manage one of the teams—or he would simply manage both. Sometimes he'd also assume the role of umpire.

When Macaco wasn't working games, he was a regular presence in Highbridge Park, where Manny and his friends played. Carlos Puello, who played in the league with Manny and who also works at Columbia Presbyterian, says, "Macaco was often one of only a few adults at the baseball field. He would hit you ground balls, pitch to you, and talk to you. Whatever you wanted. He was an approachable guy and everybody used to talk to him. And he's still like that now. He has a lot of kids that he's close to."

These days, Macaco tries to instill hope and discipline in his protégés by invoking Manny. "Right now, when I talk to the kids, I say, 'Look at Manny. When Manny was like you, ten or twelve or fourteen years old, he played for me. He listened to me when I talked. And not only in the Little League. He listens to me right now, in the major league.'"

Of course, Washington Heights is a different place today than it was in the eighties, when Macaco was first mentoring boys like Manny and Puello. The lots, schoolyards, and fields, which were once alive with baseball, are quieter these days, giving way to skateboarding, video games, television, and basketball. Factory jobs that once offered economic stability to city families have been lost to overseas manufacturing, leaving behind mostly low-paying service jobs and unemployment. Many of the immigrant families who came to Washington Heights in the 1970s and 1980s have fled to the suburbs. Respected authority figures like Macaco are in short supply.

Moreover, adults today remain wary of interacting with other people's children. It's not that adults don't recognize the importance of close, one-to-one relationships with youth. According to a Gallup poll, 75 percent of adults reported that it is "very important" to have meaningful conversations with youngsters in their communities. Yet fewer than 35 percent reported actually having such conversations.

Researchers Ron Smith and Frank Smoll have focused on interactions between coaches and young athletes, identifying practices that increase players' enjoyment, build competence, and keep them playing the sport. They observed seventy male youth baseball coaches, painstakingly coding more than eighty thousand of their actions. (The typical coach engages in more than two hundred "codeable" actions during an average game.) Not surprisingly, Smith and Smoll found that children felt better about themselves, the team, and the sport when they played for coaches who were generous in praise; responded to mistakes with encouragement and sound technical instruction; and emphasized teamwork, fun, and improvement. The researchers also found that 95 percent of children who played for coaches who had been trained in these positive acts returned to the same sports program the following seasons. That's an overwhelming number when, according to the researchers, the average annual attrition rate in youth sports programs is around 35 percent.

Admittedly, fun and self-esteem are not exactly the priorities of many professional and amateur coaches, whose job security and reputation depend mostly on winning games. But for young players who are just starting out—especially in 2008—a coach who pays attention to fun and self-esteem can determine whether the young players stick around long enough to hone their skills. Children vote with their feet in sports programs: If they don't connect with their coaches, or if their coaches are too harsh, they walk.

Of course, Macaco didn't need to review any studies to grasp the importance of blending instruction with positive reinforcement. He also knew how to use baseball to *shut out* the pressures of the outside world. "I explain to players that at practice we're going to talk about baseball, not what's happening outside this baseball field, out on the street. I tell them: I have two faces. The first is a baseball face. The second, if you want to talk about problems with your father, your family, or something that happens at home, we can do that after practice. When you are on the field, you are like a worker, my worker. Off the field we are like friends."

Here's how former player Jeffrey Ruiz, who lived in the same apartment building as Manny when they were kids, describes Macaco's coaching style: "If he sees some potential and also that you care, then he'll put more strength into you. And if I had a rip in my glove he'd sew it up. He'd bring it back the next day like brand-new. Any baseball question you have, you go to him. He's like the professor—the guy who knows about baseball. You could ask him any question. For instance, if you wanna play in the DR, you can ask him and he'll say to call this guy, or this program, or that program. He does it because of the love of the game. He could have everything. He could be living in a house in Jersey, or he could be living with Manny because I'm pretty sure Manny gave him that offer. But no, he wants to be in the projects on 178th and he wants to work in the hospital. As you can see, he's now an old man and he's still playing softball. And people do respect him where we play."

What drives men like Macaco to make such sacrifices? Macaco is quick to describe the rewards: seeing a face light up at the sight of a hastily repaired, third-hand glove; seeing a boy whose brothers have succumbed to the street discover the pleasure of hitting; feeling the hard-earned trust, respect, and dedication of forty boys in their uniforms on a Saturday afternoon. To him, all this is far more rewarding than what Ruiz figuratively describes as "a house in Jersey."

For their book *Growing Up Poor*, Terry Williams and William Kornblum spent a year with youth in poor New York City neighborhoods. The sociologists concluded that mentoring was a key difference between successful and unsuccessful teens. Similarly, sociologist Bernard Lefkowitz recognized supportive adults as a vital influence on at-risk youths: "Again and again, I found that the same pattern was repeated: the kid who managed to climb out of the morass of poverty and social pathology was the kid who found somebody, usually in school, sometimes outside, who helped them invent a promising future."

Psychologist Norman Garmezy also observed that resilient children had at least one significant adult in their lives who led them to hold a more positive attitude toward adults and authority figures in general. Garmezy reviewed the literature on children in war, looking at how boys and girls in Europe and Israel adapted. His studies pointed to nonfamily adults as prime factors in how children respond. "Such adults," Garmezy con-

cluded, "provide for the children a representation of their effi-
cacy and the demonstrable ability to exert control in the midst
of upheaval. From that standpoint, the sense of confidence in
the adult community provides a support system of enormous
importance to the well-being of children."

Psychiatrist Michael Rutter observed that vulnerable children
with "one good relationship" were less prone to delinquency
than others. And attachment theorist John Bowlby wrote that
humans seem "happiest and able to deploy their talents to best
advantage when they are confident that, standing behind them,
there are one or more trusted persons who will come to their aid
should difficulties arise."

The most ambitious of the "beating the odds" studies was a
thirty-year survey of five hundred children on the small Hawaiian
island of Kauai. Born into poverty, most were the children of
sugar plantation workers in the rapidly declining sugarcane industry. Like the youths in Washington Heights, many grew up in fear
of even greater poverty, struggling, too, through parental alco-
holism and abuse. Without exception, every child who became a
self-sufficient adult had had at least one adult—in addition to his
or her parents—who provided guidance and support.

Macaco is not the only nonparental mentor with whom Manny
has forged deep ties. None of his other mentor relationships
have matched his bond with Macaco for endurance or intimacy,
but they have served a common purpose. A successful relationship with a caring adult may, in fact, be a by-product of healthy
development. Youths who are physically attractive or intelligent,
who have engaging dispositions or intense interests, appear
primed for higher levels of involvement with adults than peers
who lack these qualities. Growing up, Manny's particular blend
of innocence, charm, talent, and drive seems to have had a gravitational pull on the hearts of the adults who entered his orbit.

These adults sensed Manny's vulnerability and wanted to protect him. On Manny's end, a close bond with his mother gave him the capacity to forge close ties, and a disappointing relationship with his father gave him the motivation to find others. And find others he did, beginning with Macaco and, as we shall see, continuing throughout his life.

CHAPTER 5

This Is Washington Heights

If the Ramirez family was united again with a new chance at prosperity, it was immediately clear that there also would be new sacrifices. For one, Manny's mother, who didn't work in Santo Domingo, had become the provider, the household's most reliable earner. In what was a daily ritual for the thousands of Washington Heights' Dominicans who commuted out of Manhattan for factory work in the city's industrial outskirts, Onelcida arose early and boarded a bus that crossed the George Washington Bridge as the first rays of sun glimmered off the Hudson River below. Her destination: a textile factory in New Jersey.

There would be less time for her to dote on her children. The girls would have to take on more responsibilities. There would be no maid to clean their apartment, as was common even in lower-middle-class households in the Dominican Republic because of the masses of poor and unskilled laborers willing to work for next to nothing. And in these new living quarters, there would be little personal space. "Things were different in New York City," Evelyn says. "Life was hectic. We didn't have as many family traditions. On Christmas, we'd eat and be together, but nothing fancy. I don't even know if we got a tree or presents."

Their new sixth-floor apartment on 168th Street was in keeping with the tenements that have served as first homes to millions of immigrant families in New York over the last century. It was dark and cramped, with two small bedrooms, one of which was nearly closet-sized. Rossy and Onelcida slept in a queen-sized bed in the larger bedroom, with a window overlooking a Dominican restaurant and storefront church on 168th, the sidewalks humming with activity; Manny and Clara slept on bunk beds in the windowless bedroom off the kitchen. Evelyn remained downstairs with Pura. Aristides slept on a sofa bed in the living room—a room that would become Manny's sleeping quarters when he got older. The family would also eat there, because the kitchen was too small for six.

But Clara and Rossy, who regularly took on cooking responsibilities, negotiated the space gracefully. The cabinet doors, made of unfinished plywood, creaked when opened. There was a small washing machine but no room for a dryer. So the girls would haul the family's wet clothes down the six flights of stairs—there was no elevator—between the apartment and the Laundromat next door. The bathroom, a sliver of a space that probably wouldn't accommodate Manny's broader-shouldered teammates, was only slightly wider than the toilet. A single-pane window in the corner of the living room provided a view—clouded by a thick layer of mineral deposits streaked on the glass—of the High Bridge Water Tower less than a quarter mile away.

An octagonal granite turret built on the bluffs overlooking the Harlem River in 1872, the High Bridge Water Tower was once a symbol of Manhattan's innovation and progress. It stored water pumped from Westchester, forty miles away, through the Croton Aqueduct, the island's first large carrier of fresh water. By 1986, the tower's timber roof, charred and sunken inward due to a fire set by vandals years earlier, had become a symbol of the neighborhood's decay and of city officials' indifference.

If the apartment was tight and dingy, there was comfort in the warmness of the building's tenants and the Dominican flavor of the neighborhood. The building was like an extended family. All the tenants were Dominican, except for the two Ecuadorians, who fit in just fine. The building's tenants shared something deep and essential: Not only were they familiar with the vagaries of immigrant life, they were well-versed in the Dominican immigrant experience, one that broke sharply with that of earlier immigrant waves.

In the early twentieth century, European migrants arrived in New York with a distinct sense of separation from their homeland. Travel was prohibitively expensive. Communication was slow. Solidly fixed in their new world, earlier immigrant waves, for the most part, were forced to cut institutional and familial ties to their native countries. But not today's Dominicans.

First-generation Dominican-Americans, like many Latin-American immigrants, have maintained strong ties to their homeland, traveling back and forth several times a year, participating in the island's political process, financially supporting core and extended family members left behind, and buying retirement homes there. This fluid movement between the United States and the Dominican Republic has challenged traditional ideas about assimilation into American society and stirred debate about first-generation Dominican-Americans' national identity and allegiance. Sociologist Peggy Levitt has dubbed Dominican immigrants who have clustered in communities in New York, New Jersey, and Massachusetts "transnational villagers." Globalization has allowed Dominicans to straddle two countries that seem worlds apart culturally and economically.

Entire communities in the island's most economically depressed areas seemed to literally relocate, through both legal and illegal immigration, to cities in the American Northeast. Thousands from the southern Dominican village of Miraflores, outside the city of Bani, settled in the Jamaica Plain neighborhood of Boston, for example. And Dominican peasants from

Tenares, a rural town on the edge of the island's central bread-basket region, laid roots in the northern Massachusetts mill city of Lawrence.

But New York City, which drew Dominicans from all parts of the island, became the most popular destination. In fact, islanders often say family members are in "Nueva York," even if they are in other northeastern cities. In the 1980s, the Dominican Republic was the largest contributor of immigrants to New York City, dramatically reshaping the city's demographics. By the end of the 1980s, there were an estimated four hundred thousand Dominicans in New York City, and nowhere was the concentration greater than in Washington Heights, home to the largest Dominican population outside the island.

The migrant pattern began in the early 1960s, after the assassination of the island's brutal dictator, Rafael Leonidas Trujillo. Trujillo had consolidated control of the country's private assets, especially the agricultural industry, and limited Dominicans' travel to and from the country. The political instability and economic distress that followed his death forced Dominicans, especially those in the economically ravaged countryside, to leave en masse, as a new era of political power struggles commenced, signaling a continuation of the island's tradition of paternalistic leaders, strong-arm politics, patronage, and corruption. Word of job opportunities in Nueva York spread through social and family networks, and Dominicans flooded into Washington Heights, which had been an Irish-American enclave with pockets of German Jews for much of the first half of the twentieth century.

By the time Manny moved to 168th Street, the neighborhood already looked like a transplanted barrio of Santo Domingo, plopped into the middle of the commercial capital of the world.

This is Washington Heights: yucca, mangoes, and plantains overflow from Dominican-owned bodegas onto the sidewalks along

Amsterdam Avenue, where they mix with the pulse of merengue and bachata music. Street vendors push carts with sliced pineapple and fried empanadas past drive-up car mechanics whose only garage is an on-street parking space. Women crowd hair salons on Friday and Saturday evenings before heading to social clubs and dance halls. Men sit on folding chairs on the sidewalk playing dominoes in the sun. Money-wiring services and international shipping companies occupy nearly every street corner, their storefront windows covered by international phone card advertisements with images of an azure Caribbean sea and cloudless skies. And everywhere, there are signs of people indulging in the commerce that is so lacking in the Dominican countryside.

Most of the tenants in Manny's building worked long hours operating machines in factories, cleaning office space in New Jersey, or driving taxis. Some were unemployed. A few partook in the lucrative drug trade so evident in the groups of boys who stood on street corners. But mostly, the building's residents were hard-working and had modest dreams: to be able to provide for their families, and perhaps, some day, when they had saved enough money, to retreat to their Caribbean homeland to enjoy retirement.

Mothers and grandmothers in the building on 168th Street cared for one another's kids. They shared gossip and, at dinnertime, they shared one another's food, a fading tradition brought from tight-knit rural towns. They watched Spanish-language soap operas in one another's living rooms. Teenagers accompanied younger children in the building to school or to relatives' homes. There was an unmistakable sense of common purpose, sacrifice, and community, one that is hard to find in America's suburbs or other urban centers. Even the building's outcasts could count on a helping hand if they found themselves in trouble.

When Manny's former next-door neighbor on the sixth floor,

Angel Grullon, a wafer-thin man whose rapidly flitting eyes and trembling hands betray years of cocaine abuse, came home from a nine-year stretch in state prison in the mid-1990s to live with his mother, Onelcida, who had already moved out of the building, bought Angel new clothes. Onelcida, a close friend of Grullon's mother, had more than enough reason to turn away from this former neighbor in need.

Grullon was a young menace, the kind of kid whose criminal antics gave the hardworking, law-abiding residents of Washington Heights an undeserved reputation. When he was younger, Grullon and his sister played in the hallways with Evelyn and other children in the building. But Angel eventually forged a different path, skipping school and learning the ways of the streets. A hard-edged criminal in his late teens and twenties, Angel once allied himself with the city's most notorious and murderous drug ring, a Washington Heights–based crew of Dominicans called the Wild Cowboys. As a teenager, he and his friends had robbed indiscriminately on the subway, once brutally beating a man who Grullon later learned was a priest—all for a few dollars.

Grullon had learned how to sell drugs from his father, who was separated from his mother. His father employed him at age seventeen as a rooftop lookout, to send signals if police came onto their block on 162nd Street. Eventually, he became his father's business partner, until police raided their apartment and found 125 grams of cocaine. A few years later, in the middle of his stint behind bars, Grullon watched his father's cancer-plagued body being lowered into the ground. Angel wore shackles and was flanked by prison guards. When he came home to his mother in 1998, she had a set of pants and shirts that she could not afford.

"[Onelcida] took my mother shopping, basically for me," said Grullon, who has left the drug trade, lives with his mother, and, at forty-one, is trying to get his life on track. "That's what kind of building this was." There were also times when tenants fought as if they were a dysfunctional family—for example, the woman on the fifth floor who constantly complained, in screams that echoed through the central stairwell, about the noise coming from the Ramirez apartment. The source of the discord was, in reality, the Ramirezes' next-door neighbors, where five small children lived. The woman's shrill complaints became so regular that one day a fed-up Evelyn found herself outside the woman's door, holding one of Manny's baseball bats, and screaming, "Why don't you come out and tell me where the noise is."

"Sometimes you have to go to extremes," Evelyn says.

Although the Ramirez family settled in one of New York City's most dangerous and drug-infested neighborhoods (between 1987 and 1991 there were 462 homicides, 58 percent of them drug-related, in Washington Heights' police precinct), residents felt they were in a sanctuary when they walked through the building's windowless wooden door, topped by a dirty green awning.

Inside, apartment doors were left open, allowing children to play on the hallway's cracked tile floors under flickering fluorescent lights. Visitors often didn't bother climbing the stairs; from the first-floor lobby they shouted an echoing call from up the open central stairwell and waited for a return shout, either from the person they were looking for, or from a neighbor telling them to come back later. *No está*, they would yell from the fourth or fifth floor. He's not here.

That sense of community was what kept Manny's grandmother from leaving the building after her grandson had become a star and the darling of the neighborhood, long after he had enough money to move his entire family out of Washington Heights. The Ramirez family finally coaxed Manny's grandmother into joining her daughter and other grandchildren in

Florida in 2000, when Manny signed a $160 million, eight-year contract with the Red Sox. But she still sends birthday cards to a few of her old neighbors.

"Manny's grandmother, she would always call when she cooked something, and I would bring something to her when I cooked," says Lissette Leonor, a Dominican émigré who moved into Manny's childhood apartment with her husband and children when the Ramirez family left for Cleveland in 1993. "The people in this building, we helped each other."

That is gradually changing, along with the ethnic makeup of the building and the demographics of Washington Heights. In the last few years, Dominicans in this neighborhood have been noticing signs of what many now say is inevitable: gentrification. Rising rents and property values in one of Manhattan's last affordable refuges are slowly pushing out working-class immigrants and replacing them with young professionals. A few Anglo residents have moved into the building, along with Peruvians, African-Americans, and Puerto Ricans. "They are different. Maybe Dominicans are more social," Leonor offers. "But still, we always say hello, and if they need something, we'll help them."

Leonor is a community worker at a New York City public school, P.S. 60. She and her husband pay $800 a month in rent, more than the $541 they paid when they moved in fourteen years ago, but far less than the building's new tenants who are snatching up the building's newly renovated apartments at rents close to $3,000 a month.

Leonor and her family came to New York City from San Pedro de Macoris, a sugarcane town in the eastern part of the Dominican Republic that is known for producing ballplayers, Sammy Sosa and Alfonso Soriano among them. In the living room—the closest thing Manny had to his own room as a teenager—Leonor's two sons, thirteen and seventeen, play a baseball video game on the living room television. It's the Red Sox versus the Yankees. The boys, well-mannered and friendly, seem as unmoved about playing the part of Manny in a video game as they do about living in his childhood home. "I've told two of my friends," the younger son, who plays in a neighborhood Little League, says with a shrug. "They think it's pretty cool."

Mostly, though, it's not a topic of conversation. The older son opens the door to the room he shares with his siblings. He points to a decorative towel hook, a four-inch wooden horse's bust, screwed into the wall next to a window. It was left by Manny's family, he says. It is the young man's only tangible sign that this space ever belonged to anyone other than *his* family. For Manny fans, this apartment would qualify as a holy site. But for these boys, the apartment is simply home. Over the years, visitors have knocked on the door, asking for a glimpse of Manny's childhood apartment. Not understanding all the fuss and unwilling to let strangers into their sanctuary, Leonor and her husband, a Red Sox fan, have always declined. She's not sure why she said yes this time—perhaps only because the boys are older now.

As the digital Manny comes to bat on the television, the boys laugh and pound the control panels. Under the spell of his teenage handler, Manny swings his virtual bat. One of the boys, the one controlling the game's pitcher, groans in disgust. Manny had hit a double.

Manny was not at ease in this new environment those first few weeks, sticking close to family members in the apartment and attending Eleanor Roosevelt I.S. 143 on 182nd Street.

One of the first boys he met was Edwin Diaz, a fourteen-year-old who lived on the fourth floor. They crossed paths when Diaz, a year older than Manny, was running down the stairs, his arms wrapped around two or three baseball gloves and a pair of aluminum bats. Diaz, an earnest, round-faced boy, was on his way to the basketball courts at 169th and Audubon Avenue, where the neighborhood kids met to play basketball and softball.

"Oh, where do you guys play?" Manny asked in Spanish.

"We play right down the block," said Diaz. "And if you don't have a glove, you can borrow mine." Manny took a glove and followed his new friend to the playground.

That was Manny's introduction to the neighborhood boys who gathered at the playground. Manny became one the regulars, hitting softballs onto the roof of the tenements that line Audubon Avenue and avoiding fights with the older basketball players who ran games on the adjacent courts. "And he was just average," says Diaz, who later played with Manny on All-Star Little League teams and against him in high school.

Some of the boys Manny met that first summer would become his closest friends well into his professional baseball career—boys like Nestor Cruz, who was introduced to the then-unremarkable Manny during a basketball game. "He was just a regular kid," said Cruz, a former high school teammate who now works as an X-ray technician at Columbia Presbyterian (where Puello and Macaco also work). "I don't think there was anything special about him, nothing wrong either. Just another kid in the neighborhood."

But as Manny began playing on the sandlots in Washington Heights and joined the neighborhood's Pablo Morales and Alexis Ferreira Little Leagues a year later, something changed. Natural talent emerged. To hear childhood friends tell it, it happened all of a sudden, like a freight train bursting from behind a wall of fog. Manny began hitting "bombs," as the boys in Washington Heights say.

The Little Leagues in Washington Heights were stocked with young talent. "One of the best leagues around," Cruz said. "All the kids who were good at baseball were in the Alexis Ferreira

League." That became obvious when the All-Stars from the league, coached by Macaco, played other city All-Star teams. "We were very tough to beat," Cruz said. And their most consistent slugger was Manny, a strong-armed center fielder who seemed to live at the baseball field.

"You'd show up to the game, and there would be Manny," Cruz says. "Just like he does in the majors. He was the first one to the field and he used to be the last one to leave the field. And this was when we were kids. It was just incredible that he had that drive. He knew what he wanted to be and he knew he had a shot and he didn't just lie down and let it come to him. He was gifted, he was born with it, but he really worked at it."

Within a year of arriving in the United States, the gangly boy was inspiring fear and awe. That was around the time Puello, who had arrived from the Dominican Republic at age thirteen, first met Manny. Puello was standing forty-six feet away on the pitcher's mound. Manny, wearing a uniform for the Little League team Las Tres Marias, the team's sponsor and Washington Heights' most popular Dominican eatery, was at the plate. Puello was a standout athlete who would go on to play high school ball with Manny and win a baseball scholarship to a small college in Oklahoma. He had enough talent to play any position on the field. On this particular Saturday, he tried pitching in a game for the first time.

"My coach asked me to try it out," Puello says. "I pitched to Manny and the guy hit a fucking bomb. He hit it into the trees. Not once. Twice." Puello never pitched in a game again. To this day, he wonders whether his baseball fortunes might have been different had he started out pitching to a more modest opponent.

Increasingly, as Manny recognized his ability, his life became baseball. After school. In the summer. In the winter. School became an afterthought, if a thought at all. Friends say that in junior high Manny was bright—he attended Eleanor Roosevelt

I.S. 143 in the eighth grade—but his interest was elsewhere. "This guy was smart, and he has beautiful handwriting," says Trovin "Kiki" Valdez, another immigrant student who attended junior high with Manny and went on to play professional baseball. "I'd have him write out some of my homework. But I think he eventually figured that his talent [in baseball] was going to take over everything else. He didn't understand that here in the States school comes first, then baseball. But he's smart."

"He dedicated himself more to baseball than to school," Diaz said. That was despite the help he got from his older sisters.

"After dinner, we always ended up helping my brother with homework," Evelyn says. "Because that was not his favorite cup of tea. It was almost always social studies. He just didn't grasp all of the concepts and questions. But other than that, Manny was never around because he was outside with his friends."

Work was a no-go, too. Manny tried a job, but it didn't last, to his father's frustration. Only a year after he arrived, Manny began bagging groceries at a supermarket in Fort Lee, New Jersey, just a short bus ride across the George Washington Bridge. He lasted only about one month. Unlike his older sisters, who worked throughout their teens, Manny was free to play.

"I was always in the street playing," Manny recalls. "My sisters, being older than me, they always worked. They would buy me clothes and other things." It is this carefree street play, devoid of the pressure and tension of suburban Little Leagues, with their wound-up, competitive parents—and perhaps also without discipline and organization—that shaped Manny's boyish approach to professional baseball. That approach at once angers, endears, and confuses fans and baseball managers. It is Manny being a boy, shirking responsibility but reveling in a pure love of the sport.

In the summer, Manny and the other boys floated from field to field, playing pickup games when their Little League teams weren't competing. In the winter after school, they gathered in the basement of an apartment building on 170th, between Amsterdam and Audubon, owned by the president of the Little League. They took turns swinging broomsticks at swerving, dipping bottle caps when they weren't talking to girls.

With time, Manny's reputation spread, aided by Dominican fathers and spectators who argued about the best young talents on each block, in each neighborhood, in each borough. By age fifteen, Manny had become so dominant with a bat that Little League coaches from other boroughs began showing up unannounced at his house in taxicabs. "They used to go pick him up to take him to play with bigger guys, guys two or three years older," Puello said. "They'd give him a sandwich and say, 'Let's go.' He used to go and hit bombs."

Men in their twenties and thirties, some of them drug dealers, most of them former ballplayers, also began looking for Manny to play in the pickup games held on the grass field behind George Washington High School on Audubon Avenue. These games were not just for fun; they involved money. Dominicans call it *desafío*, or challenge. The rules were simple: Two men took turns picking players out of a lineup, as if choosing for a schoolyard game. Each player put money in the pot, which sometimes grew into the thousands of dollars. And the winning team split the money however they saw fit.

Manny, often the youngest but usually one of the first picked, was not expected to put in money. His reward was limited to playing with bigger, stronger, and faster players—men he could compete with and impress. Even when his team won, Manny rarely left with more than enough money to buy a snack: a piece of bread and a carton of orange juice at a corner bodega. But when a team lost, things could get dicey.

Mandl, Manny's future high school coach, says the first time he saw Manny, men wielding a baseball bat where chasing him from the George Washington High School field. Manny doesn't remember the occasion. Mandl, who still coaches at George Washington, assumes Manny had made a mistake. "If you made the last out or if you made an error, there was a lot of money on the line, and they'd chase you and beat the crap out of you."

When Manny wasn't at the ballfields, he was often at Las Tres Marias, a Dominican restaurant on Amsterdam Avenue, just across the street from Highbridge Park. The boys, usually dressed in baseball gear, gathered at the eatery before and after weekend games. They sat on the eleven swiveling diner stools oriented toward the park, where they could watch baseball games while sipping sodas through long straws, listen to Dominican jukebox tunes (four for a dollar), and watch big league games on the mounted televisions.

Standing behind the counter—or more likely presiding over the basement kitchen—was Maria Balbuena, one of the more than three Marias who ran the restaurant. (Her mother is also named Maria; so are her three sisters, who luckily all have different middle names.) Inside Las Tres Marias, Balbuena went by her middle name, Miguelina, to prevent confusion. But inevitably, a patron would call out "Maria," turning more than one head.

The restaurant is significant not only because it was Manny's teenage hangout. In its story is also the randomness with which tragedy can strike even the most well-intentioned in Washington Heights.

Miguelina's mother opened the small eatery in 1972, a few years after arriving from the Dominican Republic. Miguelina initially worked at a sewing factory. She dropped out of school almost a year later, before she reached ninth grade. Her mom was resolved not to take public assistance, which meant everyone in the household had to pitch in. So Miguelina began working at the restaurant full-time. She poured her soul into the place, and in 1976, when she was twenty-one, she took over as owner. The most popular Dominican restaurant in Washington Heights by the mid-1980s, Las Tres Marias drew customers from all the boroughs and beyond. Their specialties became neighborhood staples: *sancocho* (a meat stew with plantains, yucca, and potato) and *mudongo* (a soup with slow-cooked tripe and vegetables).

In 1987, Miguelina took out $225,000 in loans, enough to expand and renovate, nearly doubling the restaurant's size and giving its decor a more Dominican flair. On one of the restaurant's walls, she commissioned a mural of the El Monumento a los Héroes de la Restauración, a large column monument built by Trujillo in the center of Santiago, her mother's hometown. Unlike some other Dominican eateries, which tried to lure male clients by employing scantily clad, curvaceous women, Las Tres Marias had a male-only wait staff during daytime hours. The emphasis would remain on the food, Miguelina insisted. In a nod to her mother, the eldest Maria, she reopened the renovated restaurant on Mother's Day in 1988.

On Saturdays, the restaurant was packed with patrons, and the pace picked up in the evening hours when the music got louder, the alcohol flowed more freely, and the restaurant turned into a sort of dance hall. But during the day, Miguelina, then in her early thirties, made it clear that the young baseball players were priority customers: She sponsored one of the teams in the Alexis Ferreira League every year, paying for their uniforms; she showed up at games at Highbridge with Dominican delicacies, such as *quipes*, deep fried bulgur rolls; and she congratulated winning teams with encouragement and free sodas when they came to the restaurant after their games, usually accompanied by Macaco.

Manny sat on the swiveling chairs with the other boys. He always held an aluminum bat. But he never seemed to talk much, while others teased and told stories. "I think he had problems communicating, socializing with people," Miguelina says. "He wasn't like the other boys, running around. He was quiet." He loved Miguelina's *arroz, con-con, y habichuelas*, the crunchy, almost burned, rice that stuck to the bottom of the pot, scraped up and then soaked in beans. Years later, after signing his contract with the Indians, Manny would come back for his favorite dish one last time.

But by then sitting in silence was no longer an option.

"When people are famous, especially in Washington Heights, when Manny is in the restaurant, everybody crowds in and they don't let him eat. The same with the Yankees players that used to come in. They weren't allowed to eat in peace. People crowded them and asked for autographs," says Miguelina.

What had become a neighborhood institution began crumbling with a single gun shot one early morning in September 1995. It was around 4:30 A.M. The restaurant was crowded, as usual, probably close to its legal capacity of 111 people, if not exceeding it. The lights were low, the music was loud. At least two people were celebrating their birthdays: twenty-five-year-old Maria Rivas and twenty-eight-year-old police officer Frank Speringo. Speringo, off-duty, appeared drunk to anyone who bothered to notice him: He was kissing the hands of waitresses, flinging ice around the restaurant, and stumbling when he walked. And he seemed belligerent.

When another man, Enrique Paulino, tripped over Speringo's legs, the off-duty officer took exception. They talked it out. But after Paulino returned to his table, a piece of ice hurled from Speringo's direction hit him, igniting a confrontation that ended tragically. The two exchanged words, and then blows. One of Speringo's friends yelled out, "He's a cop." Paulino drew back, and as he retreated, patrons said, Speringo pulled a gun from his waist and pointed it at Paulino's head. People scurried under tables. Paulino lunged at Speringo, grabbing his arm. A struggle ensued, and in a matter of seconds, a shot was fired. The bullet pierced the wrist of another patron, and then exited, hitting twenty-five-year-old Maria Rivas in the head as she fled and killing her instantly. Screams turned to gasps and cries of sorrow.

Speringo was convicted of second-degree manslaughter a year later, escaping a more serious charge of second-degree murder. "It really wasn't enough, and it did not live up to my expectations," Rivas's mother told a reporter after the trial. "But at least I have some justice."

Before the verdict was announced, Speringo paced the court's hallway, insisting that he had only been trying to hold on to his gun, that he didn't pull the trigger, that he had been attacked. "Why am I here?" he was quoted as saying. "Because this is the Dominican community and I'm a white cop."

In the five years after the shooting, Miguelina says, business slowed, an increased police presence outside the restaurant drove some customers away. The landlord raised the rent 20 percent. Miguelina gave up. The restaurant closed in 2000.

Now, Miguelina cooks at a nursing home close to her own home in a quiet New Jersey suburb. But she still holds on to the past. Twenty Little League trophies from the teams she sponsored, some of them Manny's, sit covered in dust on her living room mantel. Sitting at her dining room table, telling the story, photos of the restaurant spread out before her, she sobs. "There's so much sentiment because I put my life in there, in that building. I woke up at four-thirty in the morning and sometimes I'd come home at midnight. Sometimes I'd have to sleep in the restaurant's basement. I can't believe it's gone."

Only a few doors down from Las Tres Marias, another Dominican-owned store prospered, with some help from Manny. But Jose Mateo's business idea was not nearly as focused as Miguelina's. In

1992, three years after arriving from the Dominican Republic and two years out of high school, Mateo rented a run-down retail office on Amsterdam Avenue with $500 he borrowed from a friend. He installed a pool table and a sandwich press to sell two-dollar ham-and-cheeses, and opened for business.

To his surprise, the store became a social epicenter. The grilled sandwiches were simple—ham, cheese, lettuce, tomato, ketchup, and mayo—but the draw was the price. Soon, Mateo put in a refrigerator stocked with bottled coconut soda. Then a pinball machine. An extra pool table. Then he began selling comic books. Then CDs. Then baseball cards. Then baseball hats. The store was still called Peligro Sandwich, but it was, in fact, a community recreation room that also sold miscellany. Mateo's brother, Henry, even began cutting hair in the basement, a makeshift barbershop.

Manny, in the minor leagues by the time the store opened, would come in during the off-season, eat sandwiches, play pinball, and look at baseball cards. "He would call looking for his own baseball cards," said Mateo, who earned his nickname, Peligro—which means danger in Spanish—for his aggressive style on the basketball court. Despite that name, the tall, smiling, muscular Mateo is a soft talker who quickly relents when young baseball players haggle for a good deal.

Today, what was once a small sandwich shop is Washington Heights' premiere baseball apparel shop, and the place where the baseball cognoscenti meet to talk about all things baseball. Manny's old teammates still meet here to watch his games on the television, as they did when he was making a name for himself in Cleveland. It's also where Macaco can be found on any given afternoon, before his nighttime hospital shift, folding jerseys, acting as a salesman or holding court on the latest story-behind-the-story about Manny. Macaco is not a paid employee, but any visitor would think otherwise.

On Mateo's second day in the United States, his second cousin, Wellington Cepeda, introduced him to Manny. Cepeda himself was a standout player from the neighborhood who played with and against Manny, and was drafted in 1997 by the Arizona Diamondbacks. Mateo and Manny became close friends. Their connection is apparent in the store. A baseball card from Manny's days with the Indians adorns the store's blue awning. Days after Manny was traded from the Red Sox to the Dodgers, Mateo had the bestselling number 99 blue-and-white jersey hanging on the walls.

Manny also has a less-well-known connection to the store: Manny loaned Mateo money to expand while he was with the Indians. It's a loan that neither Manny nor Mateo likes to talk about—an example of Manny's privacy when it comes to any acts of generosity—but one that Mateo undoubtedly appreciates. "He's a very gentle, gentle man," Mateo says. "Very shy." Then Mateo's competitive but playful streak appears, as he adds with a laugh: "Manny likes to play basketball, but he's not very good."

For the boys who grew up with Manny, baseball was a guiding force.

These boys look back on their Little League days with both pride and disappointment. They are proud they dedicated themselves to the sport. Proud they played with one of the best right-handed hitters to ever play the game. Proud their devotion kept them from the insidious drug trade that swept up some of their classmates and friends. But they are disappointed they didn't make it themselves, that they didn't put more effort into alternative career pursuits. As the boys approached adulthood, and the exigencies of real life loomed larger, the boys began to see baseball as the *only* ticket out of Washington Heights. And making it out meant getting signed to a pro contract.

That view has its roots in the Dominican Republic, although on the island, it takes on a much more desperate form. Dominican fathers, it is said, often buy their sons baseball gloves or a bat before they can even walk, with the hope that their gift will bring the entire family good fortune.

On the island, baseball has become the elusive ladder out of entrenched poverty. With the island's high unemployment rates and neglected public education system, the paths to economic freedom seem limited. But everyone is familiar with the rags-to-riches stories of Dominican stars like Ortiz, Sosa, Pedro Martinez, and, of course, Manny.

Major league teams have capitalized on the idea of baseball as a ticket off the island. Every professional club has established a so-called "baseball academy" there in the last twenty years, since the Dodgers first hatched the idea in the late 1970s and found that the Dominican sugar mills and slums were veritable quarries of big league talent. The gleaming, state-of-the-art academies or recruitment hubs are often the prize attractions of Dominican towns so impoverished that their public schools lack electricity, textbooks, and desks.

These academies attract thousands of teenage boys from the island's countryside and shantytowns, boys who often drop out of school early. Accompanied by Dominican street agents, called *buscones,* who will take a cut of a player's meager signing bonus if he is accepted into an academy, the boys rove from one team's camp to another for tryouts in front of major league scouts. Most of the boys have never used indoor plumbing. Many don't know how to read in Spanish. If they fail to make it into an academy, their chances of living on the streets grow.

"Twenty-five years ago, if you asked Dominican parents, 'What do you want from your sons?' they would say, 'First a career, then baseball,'" says Richard Paulino, general manager for the Atlanta Braves' academy in San Francisco de Macoris.

"Now, it's, 'Try to be a baseball player first and if you don't finish school, don't worry about it.'

"Baseball is a big factory," he adds. "In so many ways it brings people from the bad to the good, to education, to discipline. But a big percentage that don't make it end up living on the street."

If a boy is signed to join the academy, he might get a $20,000 contract. That's a fortune in the Dominican Republic but a fraction of what American prospects receive. He will live and play at the academy for a year, maybe two, before scouts decide whether he has the potential to play in the U.S. minor leagues. Those who don't make it often return to the poverty they sought to escape, having forgone educational pursuits.

For major league teams, the academies are a boon. Talent is cheap and plentiful. Boys are eager. And major league teams have contractual rights to a player without having to expend their limited number of temporary U.S. work visas. But for the players, the academies are a gamble. Only a few hundred—a fraction of the estimated ten thousand boys auditioning each year—make it into the academy. About 130, on average, will make it off the island and onto a minor league team. And only a handful signed each year will someday appear on a big league roster. Many of the boys are too old, even in their late teens, and are therefore "not projectable," in baseball parlance.

Scouts on the island value youth as much as talent. Because many of the boys exhibit raw, undeveloped skills that will require years of refinement, they are waved off if they are eighteen or older. Knowing this, many boys lie about their age. Major league scouts in the Dominican Republic have become adept at estimating age from the boys' physical appearance. A boy's face, they say, is more indicative of age than a document is.

For the boys in Washington Heights, the stakes were not so high. Only a handful of Manny's contemporaries played profes-

sional baseball. Although Trovin "Kiki" Valdez, Cepeda, Dio-
genes Baez, and Frankie Rodriguez never became fixtures on
major league clubs, they also did not fall victim to the streets.
Neither did the vast majority of Manny's childhood teammates.
They have children and mortgages and steady jobs. They are
water boiler mechanics, X-ray technicians, and early-morning
bread deliverymen.

Richard Lopez, for example, calls himself "the muffin man."
He is diminutive but muscular, with a sharp jawline and an
ebullient smile. A speedy second baseman and a solid contact
hitter for George Washington High, he was the first of Manny's
teammates to get a job delivering Thomas' English Muffins to
grocery stores and restaurants. Now, he is one of at least five former teammates who work at a large bread depot in Greenwich,
Connecticut. They rise at 4:00 A.M., carpool forty miles, and
drive their delivery routes.

The group is less cohesive these days than it was when they
were just out of high school and college, regularly gathering at
Peligro Sports to watch Manny play. Until a few years ago, they
all played on the same weekend softball team, the Trojans,
named after George Washington High's mascot. The team has
disbanded, their new commitments—marriage, children,
work—overriding bachelor routines. But the men—Puello,
Cruz, and Lopez among them—still run into one another, and
Macaco, at Peligro Sports. These men are mindful of what baseball did for them, even if they fell short of their dreams.

"The neighborhood back then was really bad," Puello says.
"There was a lot of drugs. All these corners had drug dealers on
them. When we'd go work out," he says, pointing south while
standing on Audubon Avenue, "we'd pass that intersection, 163rd
and Amsterdam, which was really bad. But baseball, it keeps you
straight because all you want to do is get better. You keep taking
ground balls. You want to improve this, you want to improve that.

You know, by the time you're twenty, twenty-one, at least you're out of trouble. Maybe you can do something with your life."

Puello, a married father, only regrets not taking school more seriously. He came to George Washington, known in the neighborhood as "G-Dubs," for baseball, nothing more. In fact, he lived in Queens but reported that he lived in Manhattan so he could play on the baseball team. G-Dubs, after all, was a perennial juggernaut whose roster was predominantly Dominican.

Puello partly blames George Washington High School for letting him slide, for letting him stake his future on baseball alone.

George Washington High School is a neoclassical four-story brick building with a columned facade. It occupies almost the entire block between 192nd and 193rd streets. It sits on the bluffs of Washington Heights, high above the Harlem River to the east and the Hudson River to the west. The school has educated thousands of immigrant Americans, and boasts distinguished alumni such as the late New York senator Jacob Javits ('20), former secretary of state Henry Kissinger ('41), former Federal Reserve Board chairman Alan Greenspan ('43), and entertainer Harry Belafonte ('43). Baseball Hall of Famer Rod Carew ('62) is also an alum.

Sunlight pours into the spacious second-story atrium. But security is tight. A red rope stretches across the atrium, linking symmetrical twisting staircases and corralling students toward a metal detector in the center of the room. Uniformed security guards watch as students pull key chains and coins from their pockets before passing through.

When Manny and Puello attended from 1988 to 1991, it was overcrowded and violent. During those years, students got stabbed, beaten, and shot in front of the building. Mandl called the school a "war zone." Back then, nearly five thousand students were enrolled—twice the number attending today. Fewer than 40 percent of that five thousand graduated.

Puello realized how poorly prepared he was for college when he arrived at Connors State, a junior college baseball power-house in Oklahoma. "When I went to high school, we didn't have to work or study. I used to pass my classes with low grades," says Puello. "In Oklahoma, everybody used to study. I didn't. I didn't know how to study. So I used to read this book, that book. Then, I'd just fail the test."

Like several of the boys who got baseball scholarships to junior colleges but then felt unprepared for life outside their Dominican neighborhood, Puello did not finish college. He dropped out after one year and started looking for a job. "If I could have finished Connors State and gone to play at a Division I school," he says, trailing off. "If I did it again, I'd really hit the books more."

Roberto Ceballos was a winner. That much was clear to anyone who knew him. The young pitcher had charisma, street smarts, and an air of self-confidence. And when a game was on the line, when the pressure was the greatest, he wanted the ball in his hands. Ceballos, his high school coaches would say, loved the big stage. He was fearless.

In June 1988, Ceballos got what he wanted. G-Dubs, loaded with talent, had made it to the city championship. And the lean six-footer with a diabolical curveball had proven himself as the ace of the team.

He stood on the pitcher's mound in Yankee Stadium in what would be the biggest moment of his short career. George Washington led 3–2 in the fifth. Bases loaded, one out. And Ceballos was fatigued. He'd been cruising until two fielding errors loaded the bases with runners from rival Cardozo High School in Queens. "Give me the ball," is what Ceballos typically told his coaches in those situations, says Luis Valdez, the junior varsity coach and a dean at the school, who was sitting in the dugout as an assistant coach that day. And judging by the determined look on Ceballos's face, he was thinking the same thing as he waited for a signal from the dugout.

But Coach Mandl had doubts. Was Ceballos, only a junior, trying to do too much? Was he too tired? Was he too proud to back down? With the Cardozo fans in a frenzy, Mandl turned to Valdez, who advised him to ask Ceballos how he was feeling. But in those few seconds, Mandl made a decision that came from the gut.

Years later, he would describe Ceballos as the best pitcher he had ever coached, but something told him that this time, his intrepid hurler was in over his head. With a right-handed batter coming up, Mandl brought in a reliable reliever, Fernando Castillo, who had been impressive in the city's All-Star game only days earlier. Ceballos walked off the field visibly dejected. Before he had time to untie his cleats, the ping of the aluminum bat echoed in the stadium. A double scored two runs. Cardozo wound up winning the championship by a single run.

Manny and Ceballos connected from the start. Ceballos, two years older, had met Manny on the ballfields of Washington Heights. Ceballos was the kind of kid younger boys were drawn to. He had a wild streak, a dash of daring. But if he liked you, he was like an older brother: inclusive and encouraging.

When Ceballos, then a sophomore, recognized Manny's talent, he brought him to high school practice. Manny wasn't in high school yet. It was as if Ceballos was giving Mandl a preview of incoming talent. That is, if Manny came to George Washington. G-Dubs was one of the strongest programs in the city. In 1987, they had gone to the city's quarterfinals with a 28–5 record. In 1988, the year they lost in the championship, they finished 33–4. But for talented baseball players, high school registration could take on the feel of a draft. Coaches from the top baseball schools,

Kennedy High and Chelsea High, paid visits to students' homes, trying to win families' ears. Players weighed which high school teams lured major league scouts, and on which teams they could win starting spots. About 175 students tried out for the Trojans each fall, making it an internally competitive program.

Of course, older friends played critical roles in recruiting the best young players to their school. "Roberto had a good grip on him," said Valdez. "Manny would listen to him."

Getting Manny to choose George Washington High was one thing. But getting Manny to actually come to the school was a challenge of a different scale. In 1987, the year Ceballos pitched in Yankee Stadium, Manny, then a freshman, scarcely appeared at George Washington High.

"His first year, it was bad. I think he thought school was like Little League," Mandl says. "You just show up when you want. He just saved all his energy for baseball."

"The team was too good," explained Puello. "He knew he wasn't going to play, so he didn't even bother coming to school that year."

His sophomore year didn't start much better. G-Dubs, a preseason roundup in *Newsday* said, "again figures to be the class of Manhattan." The story mentioned Ceballos as a player to watch, along with the Trojans' catcher, shortstop, and second baseman. But a veil still hung over George Washington's surprise slugger. Manny did not yet exist in the world of high school baseball. And when he finally did, in the first game of the season, his departure would be as abrupt and stirring and Manny-esque as his arrival.

"Before baseball season started, he never went to school," Puello said. "And when we started playing, all of a sudden there was Manny, on the field playing with us. We were playing against Kennedy High School. I can remember the day. [Manny] went 4 for 4. Then [the other coaches in the league] came out and said there was a rule: You have to be in school for 80 percent of the time. And he couldn't play until the next report card."

But Manny's nonchalance about school did not carry over to his baseball regimen. Sister Evelyn remembers that in high school, the Ramirez family would pass Manny asleep on the couch as they left the apartment in the early morning hours. Manny had already gotten up to run in the streets of Washington Heights and had returned to his spot on the couch, where he would spend much of the rest of the day, or he would take refuge on Macaco's couch during his hospital shift, then during the daytime.

"When we left in the morning, Manny always stayed behind because he had been up running and sometimes, when we got home, we'd discover that he didn't go to school. We tried to watch him, but it was hard at the end."

With Mandl's encouragement, Valdez, the junior varsity coach and a dean at the school, turned Manny into his special project. Valdez approached another young male Dominican teacher—a fan of the baseball team—who ran a pilot program aimed at keeping truant students in school. Would he be interested in bringing Manny into the program? Valdez asked. The response, according to Valdez, was: "Hell yeah."

To be sure, not all teachers at George Washington High were crazy about the baseball team. Some disdained the favoritism and leniency teachers showed to players. Years later, when Manny visited the high school after having signed with the Indians, a teacher, the school's representative to the teachers' union, would bristle at the sight of Manny entering the teachers' lounge to sign autographs. "Why are you bringing him in here?" she seethed. If the throng of teachers-turned-Manny-admirers was irksome, the irony of the huge banner hanging in the school's atrium must have been grating. It showed a larger-than-life Manny at the plate in an Indians uniform and was signed: "Stay in school. Manny."

But Valdez fell into the camp of educators who relished the opportunity to watch and teach the city's most talented baseball players. Years later, Valdez would follow Manny into the business of baseball; he was, in fact, hired by Manny's agent, Jaime Torres, to attend to every need of Manny and his family, from buying equipment to paying speeding tickets to driving Onelcida to the airport. But when Manny was a sophomore, Valdez had no inkling of his potential, no idea of his future fame. Valdez took an interest in Manny simply because he loved to watch him play baseball and he loved to watch the Trojans win.

And the Trojans needed Manny's help. Ceballos, a good student and once considered a possible draftee, had begun running with a new crowd. He was using his fearlessness in a different kind of game, a dangerous one. The scam was simple—"easy money," he would say. A group of boys would go to one of the corner bodegas in Washington Heights that had illegal slot machines. In Ceballos's pocket would be a quarter taped to a long, thin sock thread. Two boys, preferably large boys, would crowd around Ceballos while he dipped the quarter into the slot machine, pulling it up by the thread each time a credit was registered, until he hit the jackpot. Making rounds from bodega to bodega, the boys cashed out day after day, alternating bodegas so owners would not grow suspicious.

The money was intoxicating. Ceballos stopped coming to school. Mandl went to his house to convince him to return to the classroom. Otherwise, he wouldn't be able to play baseball, Mandl told him. "I guess in his heart he thought he was smart enough to get by and pass his classes [without going to school] and play baseball and make all this money," Mandl said. "But unfortunately he couldn't play on the baseball team that way."

Ceballos returned, but only temporarily. He played in George Washington's third game of the season in mid-April, besting rival Brandeis with a three-hitter and ten strikeouts, the last notable performance of his career. Soon after, Ceballos returned to the streets and left school for good. He would remain good friends with Manny, though, coming to the high school field to watch him play. After he bought a brand-new Nissan 300ZX, he taught Manny how to drive it and loaned it to Manny when Manny wanted to impress girls. When Manny got into a minor accident with the car, Ceballos laughed and told him not to worry about it. It was just a car, he said. Besides, he said, Manny would make enough money one day to buy Ceballos a new one. The first car Manny bought after signing a professional contract in 1991 was a Nissan 300ZX.

By that time, Ceballos's good luck had come to an end. During Manny's junior year, Ceballos was hit by a car while crossing the street during a trip in Florida. Suffering severe trauma, he slipped into a coma but later regained consciousness. Lying in a hospital bed, talking to his high school coach, he reflected, for a moment, on his decision to leave school. "He put his hand on my shoulder and he started to cry," Mandl says. "He told me, 'Coach, you are the only one who ever cared. And I screwed up.'"

Ceballos's remorse lasted only so long. Years later—after Mandl had unsuccessfully tried to get him back into school, after Manny had signed with the Indians—Ceballos returned to the crime game he thought he had no chance of losing.

Just after midnight on October 7, 1993, Ceballos was pronounced dead at Columbia Presbyterian Hospital with shotgun wounds that tore into his lungs and his head. He had been found bleeding on a sidewalk on 161st Street, not far from a bodega whose slot machine he had emptied a few days earlier, friends said.

His death was not mentioned in the newspapers. And no arrest was ever made. But Ceballos's old friends say they've heard, through whispers, what happened. Valdez rattles off the grim specifics matter-of-factly. "They went to this particular place, a bodega with a machine in the back. The guy who owned the bodega knew they were doing something fishy and he told Ceballos, 'I'm not gonna pay you.' So they got into a confrontation. Ceballos said 'If you don't pay me, I'm gonna call the cops right now. You're not supposed to have that machine in the back.' So the guy, of course, paid him. And the guy told Ceballos, 'I'm gonna pay you, but don't you ever come back here. Never.'"

Ceballos reappeared at the bodega a few days later. Within hours, a coroner was drawing up Ceballos's death certificate. Valdez heard about the shooting the next morning while at George Washington. He immediately called Manny, who was back in Washington Heights between minor league seasons. "I got bad news for you," Valdez said into the receiver. "They killed Ceballos."

Manny, still half-asleep, said, "What?"

Then silence. "They killed Ceballos."

In many ways, Ceballos's early high school career, on and off the field, had the same contours as Manny's: Both were considered rising baseball stars by their junior years; both were drawing attention from professional scouts; and both were repelled by the classroom. But Valdez helped to make sure that Manny's path would be different. During Manny's junior year, Valdez paid a visit to a receptive Onelcida at the apartment. He told her about Manny's attendance problem and asked for her help. "What should I do?" she asked Valdez. "Come down to the school and sign papers," he said, explaining that the school's truancy-prevention program would mean smaller class sizes, more attention, and bilingual instruction. An extremely over-crowded school, George Washington had class sizes averaging nearly thirty-five students.

Onelcida didn't hesitate. The next day, she called her

employer to say she would be late—something she rarely did— and she walked twenty blocks to George Washington with Evelyn to sign the consent papers.

"They told him if he didn't fix up his grades, he wouldn't play baseball," says Evelyn, who served as translator for her mother and school administrators.

Valdez also went to Macaco's apartment. The haven Macaco was providing was, in fact, imperiling Manny's future. Macaco took a tough-love stance. "I told him one day, 'If you don't go to school, if you choose the streets, I close my door, and you can no longer play in my league. If you go to school, my door is always open to you—every hour, every day, every night, whenever you need,'" Macaco says.

One month later, Manny was back in school—and back in action. But instead of going to class, he gravitated to the lunchroom, the school's social epicenter. He sat at cafeteria tables, talking to his girlfriend, Kathy Guzman, or to baseball fans, even the cafeteria workers. He ingratiated himself with the security guards who stood at the cafeteria doors, restricting access only to students who were on their lunch breaks, and he befriended the women who worked behind the lunch counter, much as he has done with clubhouse attendants and other service workers in Cleveland and Boston.

"You gotta go to class, you gotta pass your classes," Valdez would tell him when he found him lunching during class. "Baseball's your ticket."

Kathy would point to the dozens of other kids who skipped class and socialized in the cafeteria and plead, "Hey, there are a hundred others cutting class. Why do you take him?"

"Because he has a future," Valdez would say. "Get him out of here. This is his ticket."

He made his presence felt on the baseball field in mid-May, leading G-Dubs with 4 hits and 3 RBIs in a 17–1 victory over

King that clinched their division. One day later, he homered in a 5–0 victory. In his shortened season, Manny would announce his arrival with a .592 average.

But the G-Dubs was not the only team on which he showcased his talent during high school.

CHAPTER 6

Brooklyn Ball

"You awake, Billy?"

Above the bat-cracking, leather-snapping acoustics of weekend practices, Billy Blitzer, a Brooklyn-based scout for the Chicago Cubs, could hear the excitement in the voice of Melvin Zitter, director of a Brooklyn-based sandlot program called the Youth Service League.

To call Zitter's YSL squads "sandlot" is to minimize the talent that has come and gone through the years. Zitter's alumni include Shawon Dunston, Julio and Ruddy Lugo, John Rodriguez, Alex Arias, and Frankie Rodriguez. All told, sixty-five YSL grads have gone on to play professional ball.

"Billy, you gotta get down here. Come now," Zitter commanded. "There's a kid, around fourteen years old. Somebody just brought him out here. He doesn't speak a word of English. But I swear to God, he's the best hitter I've ever seen."

Then Zitter added the kicker. "I've never said this to you before, but I think he might even be better than Shawon."

Blitzer—who was still sleeping when Zitter phoned him on this January morning—shot up in bed. "Mel, you gotta be pulling my leg," he said groggily. Blitzer had signed cannon-armed shortstop Shawon Dunston to the Cubs five years earlier as the first overall pick of the 1982 amateur draft.

Dunston was the benchmark against whom all New York

prospects were measured. He had batted .790 during his senior year at Brooklyn's Thomas Jefferson High School. A standout in the Cubs' minor league system, he had made the majors in just three years—a remarkable feat in the 1980s.

As Blitzer drove his blue Chevy from his home in Sea Gate up the Ocean Parkway, he entertained the possibility that Zitter, who never exaggerated, was on to something. Still Blitzer was skeptical, mainly because of Dunston's nonpareil talents. "As I'm driving, I'm thinking, naw, there's only one Shawon," he recalls.

He trudged through the snow-covered parking lot toward the crowded gym at Ditmas Junior High School. A burst of hot air engulfed him as he opened the heavy doors and heard the squeak of rubber on the polished hardwood. Blitzer scanned the crowd and identified the new boy almost immediately.

"There he was, this skinny kid, hitting balls off a tee. Right away, I could see the quickness and fluidity of his swing. He wasn't holding the bat quite right, so I went over and showed him. But that swing! I immediately knew what Mel was talking about. I can't say exactly what it was, just scout's instincts."

Over the next few months, Blitzer kept careful notes of Manny's progress. "It's amazing, but the very same things I noted those first few days and months still apply today," he recalls. "During practice games, he'd get picked off first or something, you know, the same sort of boneheaded stuff he does today. Mel would get so mad; he'd make Manny sprint. He was always sprinting. But what Manny did was hit. Better than any-one I've ever seen."

Manny showed up every weekend to practice fielding and hit-ting and run sprints. And more sprints. Sometimes for up to three hours at a stretch. By spring, Zitter was holding tryouts, whittling the eighty or so interested boys down to a mere fifteen-player roster.

To this day, Zitter runs a very tight ship on tryout day, with no margin for tardiness, silliness, or anything less than serious effort. So he was surprised when his fourteen-year-old prodigy was late. As the minutes ticked by, it slowly dawned on Zitter: Manny was going to be a no-show.

That evening, Zitter answered his phone to the sound of quiet sobbing on the other end. Eventually, Manny's voice broke through. It searched for the right English words to express the complex mix of emotions he was feeling. "I'm not good enough. I'm too slow."

But Manny also conveyed that there was nothing he wanted more than to play in the YSL. Mel managed to coax a shy Manny down from the tree. Vulnerability met reassurance: a bond was forming. "Most kids think they've got more talent than they actually do," says Zitter. "With Manny it's always been the exact opposite. That's one of the things I've always loved about him."

"Kiki" Valdez believes that the seeds for Ramirez's work ethic were planted when he decided, at age fourteen, to try out for YSL. "You got yourself in shape before you go over there or you wouldn't make it," Valdez said. "The first workout we had over there, we were throwing up. So we'd get ourselves in shape, get ready for his workout."

In the YSL, the effort required was not limited to the field. In the late winter and early spring, before the season began, it was first-come, first-served at Brooklyn's Parade Grounds. So players took turns arriving early enough to secure fields for practice. For Manny and the handful of players from Washington Heights, that meant waking up at 4:30 A.M. for the subway ride to Brooklyn.

There are no boundaries between the YSL and Zitter. As director for thirty-three years, his devotion to the program and its players has eclipsed the ordinary milestones of life. His longest marriage has been to the program, and his children are the young players on whose lives he's left an indelible mark. Although his graying hairline has receded a bit, and his body amply fills a grease-stained team jacket, he still carries the tall frame and wide shoulders of his days as a starting pitcher for Sheepshead Bay High School.

Melvin Zitter was born in Brooklyn on March 3, 1951, the second son of Herb and Frances Zitter. Herb, a building inspector, enrolled Mel's older brother Donald in what was then a newly established Little League in Lincoln Terrace Park. By 1957, Herb was coaching both of his young sons while expanding the reach and mission of the Youth Service League. Over the next forty-four years, as Frances quietly kept the books, Herb moved the league into a competitive sandlot program that included both young novices and elite collegians.

In doing so, the YSL joined a larger network of sandlot programs springing up across Brooklyn. Although only a handful of today's MLB players trace their roots to Brooklyn, these programs produced twenty-six major league players in the 1950s. And if Brooklyn was the capital of sandlot ball, Zitter lived in the White House. When he wasn't on the pitcher's mound, he was in the cages, on the third-base line, or discussing players over the dinner table. By the time Zitter enrolled at Brooklyn College, he was volunteering most of his free time to the YSL. He coached the YSL's high school age team, managed the books, and spearheaded fund-raising.

It was at Brooklyn College, in accounting class, that he met Blitzer. Blitzer is still impressed by Zitter's brainpower. Mel was "one of those people who went through school without ever having to crack a book," says Blitzer. After completing his MBA at Baruch College, Zitter took a job in the Defense Logistics Agency, a procurement wing of the Department of Defense.

Surrounded by uniformed military officers, Zitter had to give up his baggy sweats and track shoes.

Zitter liked the job—he held it for twenty-eight years—but what he liked best was that there was always time for the YSL.

By the time Manny was playing for Zitter, the YSL had twenty-five volunteer coaches and averaged $100,000 in annual contributions. Over the years, Zitter cultivated a network of college coaches to whom he sends nearly all of his players.

Until their deaths in 2001—separated by fewer than three weeks—Fran and Herb Zitter were the YSL's most loyal fans, following players' statistics the way other New Yorkers follow the Yankees and Mets. Herb coached well into his eighties. "He'd stand there coaching third base with a scorebook in one hand, a cigar in the other, and still trying to give signs," says Zitter. "And he loved to second-guess my coaching.

"I grew up playing for my father. When I was fourteen, I was probably the best pitcher in New York. By eighteen, other pitchers had reached and passed me. The biggest reason for this, I think, was that I was a spoiled and lazy middle-class kid. I was not spoiled by my parents' being rich, because they were not. I was spoiled in that I played for my father, so I never practiced on my own. I simply did not work hard."

Zitter's style of coaching ensures that his players will not make the same mistakes he did. He runs the program like a drill sergeant, imposing grueling sanctions for tardiness or speaking Spanish on the field. Manny's goofiness sometimes tested Zitter's patience. "I never knew whether to hug him or knock him on his ass," says Zitter. "But he was a good boy, he had a good heart."

Most young players couldn't hit sliders; Manny could. Most right-handed batters pull the ball to left field; Manny had the bat speed and power to distribute the ball to all fields. And Manny always worked as long and as hard as Zitter wanted.

Soon, other scouts took notice. Buddy Paine, a tall, droopy-eyed, now sixty-two-year-old employed by the Pittsburgh Pirates, came out to see the young Dominican. Like Zitter and Blitzer, Paine grew up in Brooklyn and had spent his life around ballparks, coaching sandlot teams and scouting. Also like Zitter and Blitzer, Paine had the occasional girlfriend but never married. These men are like dinosaurs, unlikely to be replaced as Brooklyn's baseball culture evolves. But their memories of Manny's early talents are as vivid as ever.

Paine speaks in a deep, slow drawl, and his initial impression of Manny's swing emphasizes the acoustics of bat on ball: "This is gonna sound funny, but Manny's hits just sounded different. If you hang around ballparks long enough, you learn that the best-hit balls just come off the bat differently. Kids take batting practice and we hear it. Billy and I can tell who's at bat with our eyes closed. Manny's hits always sounded better. They sounded like a fly ball, but had also something extra that let you know that the ball was going to sprout legs and just keep running. Right from the start, Manny had this unbelievable ability to relax and lock in on the ball, to somehow, in his mind, slow it down, see its spin, figure it out."

Major league pitchers still marvel at this. Red Sox pitcher Paul Byrd used to play for the Cleveland Indians. In the 2007 American League Championship Series, he faced Manny numerous times, and observed: "He just has such an eye. He sees it better than anyone else I pitch to. I can give him my best and it's no use. He'll give up on a ball way before anyone else."

These days, the YSL plays at the American Legion baseball field in Canarsie. In the eighties, Manny played at the forty-acre Prospect Park Parade Ground in East Flatbush. It took him ninety minutes on the D train to reach the field by 7:00 A.M. Players who showed up even a few minutes late were consigned to a day of running.

At the Parade Grounds, where all eight diamonds were sometimes filled, the young players mingled with the city's other top players, passed summer days in scrimmages, and bought knishes and mustard-drizzled pretzels between doubleheaders.

Playing at the Parade Grounds was no small honor. Several legends had played there as boys: Sandy Koufax, Willie Randolph, John Franco, Joe Torre, Frank Torre, Omar Minaya, Lee Mazzilli, and, of course, Shawon Dunston.

In the early twentieth century, the Parade Grounds served as marching grounds for National Guard battalions. By 1940, the only marching orders that could be heard came from sandlot baseball coaches. Today, the Grounds have ceded turf to soccer, football, basketball, and, with the influx of Pakistani and Indian immigrants, cricket. But in the 1980s, it was all baseball—all the time. And it was not exactly a field of dreams. "It was one of those rock-hard, all-dirt infields," recalls Mickey White, a scout for the Cleveland Indians. "The outfield was weeds. The backstop wasn't much better than chicken wire. It was not the kind of place where you wanted to go alone at night." In fact, neighborhood junkies habitually cut down the fence and light poles so that they could melt them down and sell the lead.

Zitter's current field in Canarsie sits beside a dirt parking lot. It is litter-strewn, but that doesn't stop New York City's finest amateurs from honing skills there. A foul cracks off the hitter's bat with a force that sends it sailing across the field. The next hit bullets up the middle, where it is greeted by the shortstop, who drills it, smack, into the first baseman's glove. This is not your son's Little League. But speaking of sons, where are the parents? As Mel explains, they are mostly single moms, holding down weekend jobs, caring for young children, attending masses, and living their lives. Certainly this was also the case in the 1980s for the young Manny, whose parents never made it to the Parade Grounds.

• • •

Zitter has played father to many boys, which is to say he has also played financial aid officer, agent, accountant, cook, guidance counselor, tutor, and friend. His mission, as he sees it, is to use baseball as the carrot to get players to finish school. His formula is simple. First, identify talented boys who want nothing more in life than to play baseball. Second, harness that desire with tough discipline and hard work, and make them speak English at all times, so that even if they don't succeed in baseball, they'll find success in other pursuits.

Zitter's mantra is, "Don't let baseball use you; use baseball." He has so thoroughly devoted himself to this cause that his name is synonymous with amateur baseball in New York. Players compete to play for him. College coaches try to ingratiate themselves to him. Major league scouts and managers find themselves calling his Brooklyn home. Baseball, Zitter believes, can help stem the tide of dropout from urban schools.

Zitter believes kids drop out of high school for a variety of reasons. They begin slipping and there are no safety nets to catch them. Their parents, many of whom are first-generation immigrants, do not have the wherewithal to negotiate the Byzantine administrative world of public high schools in New York City. And that's where Zitter steps in, playing the role of the nudging, middle-class parent. He talks to teachers, meets with guidance counselors, and insists on seeing report cards before filling out his roster.

If a student is skipping classes, Zitter insists that he sign in with the main office every day. No signature on the sheet? No baseball. It's as simple as that. "Most of our kids don't become major leaguers," he explains. "But what you want to happen is to take kids whose only dream is baseball and, in a sense, *take advantage* of that dream. Use it to teach them self-discipline and how to dedicate themselves to an objective. My hope is that by the time they realize they don't have the goods to be a major league player, they've found other goals."

Zitter's carrot and stick approach worked with Manny. When Manny's grades began to slip as a senior, Zitter offered a choice carrot. "I'd get him whatever glove he wanted if he passed all his classes. So, a couple of afternoons a week he'd come over with a couple of friends and we'd go to a batting cage, or we'd go down to the schoolyard and hit. After a while we'd get to the tutoring. The kids all called Manny my son."

Another of Zitter's protégés, Jason Miranda, a recent graduate of Texas State University, describes Zitter's approach: "I'd show him something I was writing, and he'd say, 'Jason, this is terrible, the ideas are good, but it's all over the place.'" The two of them would work together to organize Miranda's thoughts. Miranda adds that Zitter's role in players' lives extended far and wide. "I remember a player coming in and saying, 'Oh, man, I got a girl pregnant.' Mel just laid out all the options, helped him figure out what to do. There were a lot of things like that for us growing up. Not everyone can talk to their mother or father. But Mel was always there."

Zitter recalls how, over time, Manny began to open up. "Manny is the same person he was as a kid, terribly shy and timid, but also goofy. I mean, have you ever heard of a teammate who didn't love Manny to death? He may be thirty-five, but look at his baby face. Look at his attitude. He's a kid! Compare that to Jeter. He's a frickin' robot! The same blank expression whether he just bombed it or struck out. When Manny's happy, you *see* happy."

And Zitter saw the whole range. Through years of practices and games, tutoring and tournaments, traveling and simply hanging out, Zitter learned how to manage Manny's ups and downs. And there were downs, including a violent incident that took place in 1989, during the Connie Mack North Atlantic

Regional Tournament in Waltham, Massachusetts. In the first game of the series, Manny went 0 for 4 and the team lost.

Lying in his hotel bed, brooding, Manny blamed himself for the team's defeat. He typically went to sleep after a game and woke up around 2:00 A.M. to watch television. On this particular evening, Manny's roommate wouldn't leave him alone when he was trying to zone out in front of the TV. He kept antagonizing Manny, who got madder and madder. In a move foreshadowing his later skirmishes with teammates and team personnel, Manny flew off the handle. He stood up, ripped the phone out of the wall, and hurled it at the antagonizing roommate.

Terrified, the roommate ran down the hall to Zitter's room. "Coach, Manny is trying to kill me." Zitter made a deal with Manny: Hit well in tomorrow's game, and he wouldn't make Manny pay for the damage. Manny went 3 for 4 in game two, with one hit clearing the 410-foot center-field fence by forty feet. "Manny wanted to do well for the team. All those impressions that Manny is only out for himself are so wrong. He'd be much happier to go 0 for 4 but see the team win, than to go 4 for 4 and they lose. Manny looks out for the team. People who know him really do love him."

One of those people is Sherry Magee. He met her in 1989 when YSL played in the Connie Mack World Series (CMWS) in Farmington, New Mexico. Every August, for the past twenty-five years, Magee and her network in nearby Aztec have opened their homes to transplanted teen boys from the North Atlantic region.

As it happens, Aztec also hosts an annual UFO symposium, to commemorate the alleged 1948 crash of a UFO in the town's foothills. But to some of the residents in this rural town of seven thousand, situated near the Colorado border, the real aliens are the busloads of city kids who have arrived each year since 1964. In 1975, Magee, a friendly blond elementary school teacher with an easy laugh, helped to develop what she called the "foster parent plan." This not only ensured the long-term financial viability of the CMWS in the region, but also provided players with a taste of traditional white American family life.

In 1989, Manny's view of the United States corresponded to the famous Saul Steinberg *New Yorker* cover from 1976, in which the area between Ninth Avenue and the Hudson is roughly the same size as the rest of the world. On the map, some rocks and a single bush form the only distinguishing features of the American Southwest. As if New Mexico wasn't mysterious enough, Manny and his teammates were to stay in foster homes. This term carried ominous connotations for children born into urban poverty. Manny and his teammates left Washington Heights at 1:40 A.M. and boarded subway trains, sitting beside crack dealers, drunks, and other late-night revelers to reach Brooklyn in time for a 4:00 A.M. bus departure. The crowded bus rolled through the Holland Tunnel and on to the Midwest, the Texas panhandle, and up through Albuquerque, before pulling into the dimly lit parking lot of Aztec's Safeway at 1:00 A.M. (CST) a couple of days later.

Mingling among the so-called foster parents, Magee saw the approaching headlights of the bus along U.S. 64. Its motor was the only noise for miles. "As we watched the boys get off the bus, they had this look of puzzlement in their faces seeing all these white people standing there waiting to pick them up," she recalls.

The boys gathered their team coats and descended the bus stairs to the pavement. But the quiet trance was soon broken, Magee recalls: "One boy comes off the bus with this huge smile and his arms outstretched yelling, 'Where's my mama? Where's my mama?' We all looked at each other, thinking, 'Who gets this guy?' I was lucky enough to take him home with me and he became my son for the week. His name was Unique Rencher and, needless to say, he was and is very unique, and a very good friend to Manny. Since Manny didn't speak very good English, and Unique spoke Spanish, he really looked out for [Manny]."

Exhausted and overwrought, Manny climbed into the backseat of his "foster parents'" car. During the long, awkward ride, the shy boy drew into himself further, barely able to converse with his hosts. He kept them at arm's length for the week but, through Unique, Manny eventually found his way to Magee. He watched the way she interacted with Unique and sensed something different—something *trustworthy*.

The following year, when the team made it to the CMWS again, Magee arranged for Manny to stay with a Spanish-speaking family. But that wasn't quite good enough for Manny, Magee recalls: "Manny gets off the bus, walks over to me, gives me this big hug, and starts marching toward my car. I was like, 'Manny, I've got a different family for you.' Well, you should have seen his face. He was just crushed. And he says to me, 'No, Mom, I'm staying with you.' Apparently he had even talked about it with Unique on the bus ride out to Aztec. And that was when Unique told me that Manny had been practicing his English so he could talk to me more. How could I resist? Then and there, I went and made a change and Manny stayed with us. He became my 'son.'"

As for Manny, he remembers Magee fondly, though he doesn't go on at length about her. "I stayed there when I was a kid, you know. She was real nice, treated us like family," he recalls from the poolside patio of his Florida mansion.

Zitter wasn't surprised to see Magee waving during the opening ceremonies that second year; what surprised him was her shirt. "I look over at her and she's wearing a YSL jersey," he explains. "And I'm thinking: Wait a second. Manny told me he lost his uniform. I'd made him run countless sprints. I made him play games with no spikes or gloves. And it was all a big lie. He gave it all to Magee. He saw me looking in the stands—he's looking at me, looking at Magee—and he's just laughing. That woman loved him so much, and he wanted to show his appreciation."

Magee also recalls this incident. "Manny handed me this bag. I look inside and there's his entire uniform. I mean, we're talking everything. His shirt, his pants, his cleats, and gloves. I was so touched; it was all he had to give. I tried to give it back to him but he simply refused."

In Magee and Zitter, Manny had found people he could trust. He showed his loyalty in whatever way he could, even if it was overkill—and even if it created problems for others.

Zitter—though he is not affiliated with any high schools—has enlisted a cadre of volunteers to help steer his players toward college. He and this team of YSL volunteers track grades and test scores, guide preparation for college entrance exams, help complete applications, and sometimes, at the end of the process, drive players to their freshman dorms.

YSL claims that it places over 95 percent of its seniors into four-year or junior colleges each year, generally on a combination of need-based financial aid and academic or athletic scholarships. Ivy League colleges they are not, but for many, these small colleges, situated in one-horse towns across the Midwest, represent a different world and the promise of a better life. "Most of these boys will never sign or, if they do, they'll never break into the majors. But in the end, if they finish high school, and I can help get them into college, they'll move up the ladder." Zitter identifies colleges that he thinks are a good fit, often pairing two of his players for one school, and negotiates a financial aid package. When parent weekend rolls around, he packs his car with his players and drives as far as Texas, to catch a game and take them out to dinner.

Over the years, Zitter has sent his students to both prestigious schools (Cornell, NYU, Duke, Lehigh, Rice, Yale) and obscure ones (Tarleton State University, Dowling College, Dundalk Junior College). He has sent the most (sixteen) to Connors State College in Oklahoma, including Puello.

Connors State has campuses in two Oklahoma towns: Muskogee and Warner. Blacks and Hispanics constitute less than 5 percent of Warner's population of twenty-five hundred. "The closest decent hotel to Warner was fifty miles away," says Zitter. For a time, two of Zitter's players contributed to the minority population: John Rodriguez, who signed with the Yankees in 2005, and Julio Lugo, now a shortstop for the Red Sox.

As Zitter recalls, Lugo was just a little skinny kid in high school, not even a starter. "I would never have pegged him for a major league career when he first showed up in 1990." Yet Lugo was, in fact, drafted out of high school by the Houston Astros in the forty-second round of the 1994 amateur draft. Zitter advised him to attend Connors instead. Lugo believes he improved drastically as a player because he went to college, and he credits Zitter with advising him to head to Connors. "Zitter was like a father to everyone," said Lugo. "I've never known anyone in my life that did more for kids. He's the reason I went to college. He's given his whole life to helping kids."

Lugo's agent Juan Nunez, who had two brothers come through YSL, arranged for Zitter to meet with Manny after a 2007 game at Yankee Stadium. Manny was boarding the team bus when Lugo pointed to Zitter. Manny and Zitter hugged and talked for a few minutes. As Manny went back toward the bus, Zitter overheard him say something in Spanish to another player. He later learned the translation: "That's my real father."

Zitter tells and retells that story, as if hoping to wring a little more from it each time. There's sadness to his claims on former players. He knows that if he's helped launch a young man into the world, the consequence is his own importance fading into their past.

After a particularly painful season, feeling abandoned by players to whom he had grown attached, Zitter decided it was finally time to meet a woman and have a life apart from the YSL. He recently married a much younger, rural Filipino woman whom he met online. Still, he couldn't resist the urge to coach. During his first trip overseas to visit his wife's family, he organized her younger brothers and their friends into a baseball team and began coaching them on the basics of hitting and pitching. On his second trip he arrived with uniforms and, with each visit, he brought more equipment for the team. He later received team photos and noticed that their uniforms bore a new team name: The Zitters.

CHAPTER 7

High School Hero

If Manny's sophomore year at George Washington High
School was a brief showcase of his talent, his junior year was
proof that it was no fluke. At the start of the season, G-Dubs and
Manny drew national attention. *USA Today* ranked the team
twenty-fourth in the country—an unusual token of respect to an
urban team in the Northeast. As *Newsday* reported: "Those who
chronicle high school sports on a national basis normally act as if
New York's scholastic sports season begins with the opening tip-
off of the basketball season and ends with the final buzzer at the
state tournament in Glens Falls. So the presence of the George
Washington baseball team in *USA Today*'s preseason national
rankings—even if it is at No. 24 on a 25-team list—qualifies as
something of a pleasant surprise for the city's overlooked baseball community. Still, the important question remains: Are the
Trojans that good?"

Another question in the minds of the team's biggest fans,
those who knew the players, was: Is Manny really that good?

The answer to both questions was: Yes.

In the eight days after the *Newsday* story, Manny went 13 for
21 with 2 doubles, 2 triples, 1 home run, 9 RBIs, and 8 steals,
leading George Washington to a victory in the Bronx Monroe
Easter Tournament. He was named the tournament's most valuable player.

"He had a great sophomore year," Mandl said. "But his junior year was off the charts. That's when he really started believing in himself. And the kids on the team started looking up to him, and people started talking about him. He picked up his work ethic. I have had kids who you have to watch them to believe how hard they work. You would throw up if you watched them. But Manny was a step above. A lot of people criticize him a lot. But that kid, if you have to be at the ballpark at five o'clock like everyone else, and you have to be in uniform, he's there at ten in the morning. He was always like that. There was nothing like it.

"He'd say, 'Coach, will you work with me on this or that?' It was pitch black and sometimes I'd have to take my car and point it toward the field and put the lights on. It started at the end of his sophomore year, when he began believing how good he could be. I'd tell him all the time, but I don't think he believed it. But when he started playing with the older kids on the field and he started getting hits on the field, he started realizing, 'Hey, if I practice a little more, I'll get there.'"

In Mandl, Manny found a high school coach willing to put in the extra time, and money, to help his players reach their goals. "Mandl was a tremendous person," Manny says. "He always helped the Latino boys. He always helped us because he knew we came from poor families. He gave us spikes and gloves. In that time, we couldn't buy shoes or gloves." And Mandl also worked with Manny countless hours on weekday evenings during the school year. Manny would sometimes begin warming up while his classmates were still in school. The team practice would include running, weight lifting, and countless drills. "Mandl used to work us like dogs, man," recalls Puello. Even so, Manny would beg Mandl to work with him for an extra hour after practice. When all else failed, Manny would head to Highbridge Park, where he'd drill baseballs against the fence in the dark. Mandl still uses Manny's work ethic to inspire his players.

And nothing illustrates Manny's work ethic more dramatically than his early morning runs up Snake Hill, dragging a tire from his waist.

Manny was working on his biggest weakness. Puello recalls: "That motherfucker used to run up [the same hill] over and over again because the players told him he was too slow. And he *was* slow. But then he worked at it. He ran a 7.2 [second] sixty-yard sprint and then he went down to like a 6.5 or a 6.6. That's why he's got big legs. That hill he used to run up." Indeed, Manny ran the 60-yard dash in 6.5 seconds as a senior, not bad when you consider 6.9 seconds is the major league average.

Snake Hill rose more than two hundred feet from the western edge of Washington Heights, near sea level, to one of the highest points in Manhattan. As reported in the *New York Times,* a lady who worked in the high school lunchroom often passed Manny on her way to work. "Keep on! Or I'm not going to give you lunch," she yelled. Manny kept on when it rained, even with snow on the ground. When he wasn't sprinting up Snake Hill, he was scaling a slope behind Highbridge Park. Or doing a flat run over long distance. Early scouting reports, after all, had raised questions about his speed.

Manny's friends took turns joining him. No one had the energy to do it every day, but Richard Lopez ran with him most often. Old teammates still rib Lopez about the time he and Manny woke up one early winter morning for a long, snowy jog to Midtown Manhattan. Feeling ambitious, they resolved to run from 170th Street to Fiftieth Street—more than six miles each way. By the time they reached Fiftieth Street and Fifth Avenue they found themselves in what felt like a souvenir snow globe, with an imposing Rockefeller Center, Saks Fifth Avenue, and St. Patrick's Cathedral sitting beneath a mounting blizzard. "They had to take a cab back because they got too tired," Puello recalls. "We were making fun of them for a while."

Then there was the time Manny and Lopez were mistaken for fleeing criminals. When police saw the boys in dark sweatsuits running down the empty streets of Washington Heights in the early morning hours, they flashed their patrol car lights and ordered the boys to stand facing a nearby building with their hands on the wall. They frisked Manny and Lopez.

"What are you two doing?" the officer asked, Lopez recalls.

"We're running," the boys answered.

"From who?" the officer responded.

Manny and Lopez burst into a fit of laughter at the officer's question. The police let them go, and they continued on their jog.

By late April, less than a month into the season, Manny's performances at the plate were mentioned in *USA Today* rankings, as George Washington climbed the weekly chart and posted impressive wins. His photo appeared April 25, along with a feature focusing on the nearly all-Dominican roster. One player was from Cuba, another from Puerto Rico, the rest from the Dominican Republic.

"They've been playing since they were three, but nobody ever told them what was wrong or right on the field," Mandl told the paper. "Just because you're Dominican doesn't mean you're a great player." In Mandl's eight seasons at G-Dubs, he had amassed a record of 189–30. But this, he thought, might be his best team ever. "It seems like everyone's pitching in at the right time. They know they have to work hard; I won't let this team get overconfident." At that point, Manny was batting .626, with 8 home runs, 38 RBIs, and 39 runs. "I foresee this kid, when he makes it to the major leagues, really blossoming into a superstar," Mandl told the reporter.

"Manny used to do incredible things every day; he hit bombs," Puello says. "In Central Park, they'd play him deep and he'd still hit it over their heads (there was no fence). They used to walk this guy with the bases loaded. They'd walk him."

Popularity and an adoring girlfriend were prerequisites that came with Manny's glory on the Washington Heights baseball field. But Manny never quite felt comfortable with his newfound status. "He was popular because he was on the baseball team. People on the baseball team here are like icons," Mandl says. "But he was never a leader. Never. Never. Never. Never. Never. Never. He was a follower. But the players loved him. He was like he is now. He was a clown. The kind of guy that would tap you on the back and then pretend he didn't do it. He was shy, unless he was around close friends. Then he'd laugh and open up. But otherwise, you'd never hear a sound out of him."

Nestor Payano, who played on G-Dubs, said Manny's modesty is what endeared him to so many people in Washington Heights. "He was so humble," Payano says. "He was so good, but you'd never hear him bragging. Never."

Mandl and Luis Valdez believe Manny had low self-esteem on and off the field, partly because of his struggles with English. "He didn't speak a word of English his freshman year, not one word," Mandl says. "The next year, he got a little better, but he didn't want to speak English. A lot of them do that. They pretend they can't speak English because they are ashamed, embarrassed, or not confident in it. By his junior year, he started speaking a lot more. But a lot of times he'd talk to me and he'd say, 'You know, Coach, yesterday I was sitting uh, uh, uh.' Then he'd turn and say, 'Can you translate?' I'd say, 'No, you say it. Try.'

"When you talk to him, you don't think he's genuine because he has very low self-esteem. Sometimes people think it's put on, that he's trying to be humble or aloof or something, which is very contradictory to what I know of Manny. He always wanted to be the best. He really, really wanted to be. But he always thought he wasn't good enough no matter what you said to him.

He'd hit three home runs and a pop-up to left field and you'd say, 'How'd you do yesterday?' And he'd say, 'Okay.' And you'd say, 'What'd you do?' and he'd say, 'A pop-up to left field.'"

By the end of his junior year, Manny had done better than okay. So well that teammates and fans had nicknamed him "Hit Man." And hit, he did: .630 with 16 homers and 56 RBIs. He was named to the All-City team. The personal accolades didn't translate into team success, however, with Washington sputtering in the playoffs.

That summer, Manny and Zitter returned to the Connie Mack World Series but fell to Puerto Rico 7–3 in the semifinals in Farmington, New Mexico. But the team was the first from the North Atlantic region to win more than one game in the World Series. And Manny continued to impress against better pitching, going 11 for 20 with 2 homers and 10 RBIs in five games.

One of the two home runs was crushed over the right-center fence and deep into a trailer park outside the ballpark. It was as far as the most loyal tournament attendees could remember seeing the ball hit. And it came on a swing that was so smooth, it looked effortless. Manny's performance was confirmation that he could hit at the highest levels of the game in his age group. And it sent the dozens of college coaches in the stands into a frenzy. They clamored around Manny with offers to take him to lunch to sell their programs. When Manny declined, the coaches tried to get his promise to play for their college, in the form of a signature. "Coaches were getting his signature on napkins, anything they could find," said Ray Birmingham, then coach of New Mexico Junior College, who has recruited many YSL players. "We'd never seen a young man hit a ball like that. There's not a purer swing that I've seen in a young man that age."

Manny's home life presented a stark contrast to his new renown. All his success on the baseball field went virtually unnoticed by his family, partly because it didn't occur to him that anyone would be interested. And baseball seemed insignificant next to his family's struggles. Money was tight. His mother was putting in long hours at the factory to support the household. His father was in and out of work. And his parents were unhappy with each other—the entire building could see that.

Edwin Diaz, Manny's neighbor on the fourth floor, had no doubt that the tensions at home contributed to what was nearly a breaking point for Manny, just as he was showing promise of a successful professional career. During his junior year, Manny came into the building with a dilemma—he had been offered easy money to serve as a lookout for drug dealers.

"They offered me a job," Manny said, sitting on the fourth-floor landing of his building. "What should I do?"

Manny told Edwin he thought his girlfriend might be pregnant. He wanted to buy her nice things, to provide.

"He was crushed . . . If he had gone to that side, it would have been because of poverty," Edwin says, "and because of what was going on in his house. He was going through a hard time."

Edwin says Manny's teammates steered him clear of the temptation.

"He was saved by his friends, I can say that," Edwin said. "They told him, 'What are you going to do with your career like that?' Because we were all trying for the same thing. We were all trying to get signed. But not all of us can. I said, 'You got something special.'"

Manny's senior year baseball season started with a coaching feud over the star slugger.

In the preseason, George Washington players got what coach Steve Mandl considered a rare treat, a chance to escape the city's dirt baseball diamonds, a chance to get out of Washington Heights. They boarded a bus—instead of their common mode of transportation, the subway—in their white uniforms with black and orange trim. They were excited about their two-hour trip north to the quiet upstate New York town of Wappinger. Nearly every year, G-Dubs took the preseason trip to play an exhibition against Ketcham High School.

This year, Ketcham had reason to look forward to the game also: Manny had become the most talked-about player out of New York City since Shawon Dunston. But would Manny show up? It was 8:00 A.M., the time that Mandl had told everyone to be ready to pull out of the George Washington parking lot, but Manny had not arrived.

"We better just go," Valdez told Mandl. "I don't think he's coming."

"No, he's coming," Mandl said. "He told me he'd be here."

Fifteen minutes passed. Thirty minutes passed. And Valdez shook his head, knowing that Manny would be a no-show.

This was Manny's way of dealing with the power struggle between Mandl and Zitter. The feud had begun years before, when Mandl and Zitter competed for the loyalty of Alex Arias, another Washington Heights kid who went on to play in the major leagues. In the typical custody arrangement for outstanding New York City prospects, players report to their high school coaches on weekday afternoons during the fourteen-game season, preserving weekends and off-seasons for their sandlot coaches. Nevertheless, Mandl did not like divided loyalties— from Manny or anyone. In fact, Mandl's tension with Zitter boiled into an all-out battle *before* Manny even entered high school—in 1986, when Mandl banned his players from joining the YSL.

Arias, who went on to play eleven seasons in the majors, called Mandl's bluff. He quit the Trojans and played exclusively for Zitter. Baseball-wise, everything worked out for Arias: He was drafted by the Cubs in the third round of the 1987 draft.

So Mandl tried other tactics. He told players not to sit at cafeteria lunch tables with Manny and the other YSL players. He began scheduling games and practices on weekends. Things came to a head when Mandl scheduled the Ketcham game during Manny's senior year.

In Zitter's mind, Mandl's time with the kids was weekdays. So when Manny and two other G-Dubs players had approached Zitter two days before the Ketcham trip and asked him if they could go with the high school team, Zitter told them he expected them in Brooklyn, as usual. Zitter had arranged for professional scouts to be at the YSL game that weekend, after all.

The conflict was settled in Manny's mind as soon as Zitter spoke. When Valdez asked Manny on Friday night if he was coming to the Ketcham game, Manny remained silent, a sign that Valdez knew how to interpret. "He's expecting you to go, Manny," Valdez said, referring to Mandl.

"Please don't tell him I'm not coming," Manny pleaded, in an early example of his aversion to confrontation and his puzzling and often self-defeating approach to avoiding it. Valdez honored his request, and the next morning, Mandl fumed on the two-hour bus ride, which was delayed an hour while he waited in vain.

Mandl called the absence by Manny and two other players a betrayal, but there was little consequence. How could Mandl discipline the only player in the Northeast named that month to USA *Today*'s list of the top twenty-five players in the country, especially when Manny was put in the position of having to choose between rival mentors?

The two coaches took their fight to the press. "Mel is obliterating my program," Mandl complained to the *New York Times* in May 1991. Zitter countered, "I look at Mandl as being an immature, threatened person. Mandl will tell a kid to do the one thing he knows is the opposite of what I told him."

"That's when I said, 'Steve, don't do this to the kids,'" Valdez said. "If they want to play, let them play." Valdez knew that Manny didn't want to be in the middle of the power struggle; his sole motivation was to play pro ball. That was clear months earlier, when Valdez, who patrolled the school's halls every morning for stragglers and late arrivals, came across a surprising sight. Walking down the hallway, he looked through the window of a classroom door. There was Manny, hunched over his desk, writing intently, concentrating on the task before him. Valdez entered the classroom and snuck up behind Manny to see what assignment he was working on. On the piece of paper, Valdez saw "Manny Ramirez" scribbled hundreds of times. "He was practicing his autograph." Valdez laughs. "He knew exactly what he wanted, and he knew that's where he was going."

Although Manny started out the season missing five games over the span of two weeks due to the flu, he wasted no time rewarding the hundreds of people who packed the stands at George Washington High each game. Home runs, triples, and doubles were commonplace when he was in the batter's box. Scouts began to haunt George Washington games. ESPN even showed up at G-Dubs to do a piece on Washington Heights' rising star. But one at-bat from that senior year stands out to the people who followed Manny. It's still talked about in Washington Heights, and often embellished.

George Washington was playing Brandeis in their second match-up of the season. Brandeis was considered the team to beat in Manhattan that year, largely because of Trovin "Kiki" Valdez. As a young boy in the Dominican Republic, Valdez was nicknamed Kiki, as in the sound made by chickens that seem always to be strutting along dirt roads and in and out of farmhouses in the Dominican countryside. Kiki was a small child, a late bloomer, who seemed to have a will to wander. But as a teenager, he was a specimen of speed and strength—nothing like a chicken. He could run a 60-yard dash in 6.1 seconds. And he could throw his fastball at close to 90 mph. Manny had missed the first game with Brandeis, one of two losses G-Dubs had suffered while he was out sick.

Now, Manny and Kiki would face off. Before the game, Manny joked with Valdez that he needed only three hits to break Dunston's record for hits in a single season. Couldn't Kiki take a little off that fastball? "If the game gets close," Kiki warned him, "I gotta get my out."

Behind the lighthearted jokes were two boys who knew they needed to impress—and win. Scouts were watching both of them. They were two of the best players in the city on two of the best teams. So Kiki laughed to himself when, in the bottom of the sixth, Manny came up with two men on and G-Dubs down a few runs. Kiki knew he was going to have to bring something extra.

Manny had already hit one home run—a blast to dead center. A scout standing near first base was overheard—by G-Dubs' first-base coach—asking another scout, "Okay, but can he hit a curveball?" Soon enough, that scout got his answer. Kiki's first pitch was a fastball that Manny fouled off. The second was the same, a foul ball. Sensing Manny was expecting the fastball, and not wanting to give him time to collect himself, Kiki decided to finish him with a curve. He set quickly, then moved into his windup.

What he hadn't noticed, what the umpire hadn't noticed, but what everybody in the stands had noticed, was that Manny had lifted his right hand, asking the umpire for time. By the time Kiki saw Manny's uplifted hand, it was too late: He had already released the ball. And Manny was unprepared: One hand on the bat, a tight curving baseball heading for the catcher's mitt. A surefire strike.

"He hit the thing 550 feet," Kiki says, with a laugh. The real distance is impossible to know, but the ball soared over the left-field wall, which stretches to 396 feet. Some, including Puello and Mandl, say that Manny didn't have time to grab the bat with his right hand. It was a one-handed swing, they say. Puello adds, "I never hit it to that fence swinging the bat with two hands." Others, no less amazed, say Manny had the quickness of hand and mind to grip the bat and perfectly time his swing, all in a blink. The crowd erupted. Manny trotted around the bases. And Kiki looked back at the scouts who had gathered behind first base.

"They were all packing up to leave," he says. "They had seen all they needed to see."

After the game, Kiki, Manny, and three other Washington Heights boys who played for Brandeis walked back down Amsterdam Avenue toward Las Tres Marias. What did Manny say to him, after delivering the hit that sealed George Washington's victory? "He just said, 'Good game,'" recalls Kiki, who would be drafted by the Orioles after a junior college career. "Everybody was laughing at me. They were teasing me about it. But I said, 'I know this guy, he's one of my best friends, and he'll probably be one of the top draft picks, so I don't mind so much.'"

Manny is now the godfather to Kiki's son.

Despite Manny's success—in only twenty-two games his senior year, he batted .650 with 14 home runs, 40 RBIs, and 31 stolen bases, and he was named New York City's Player of the Year—the Trojans failed to win the Manhattan championship for the first time in seven years, losing to rival Kennedy in the first round of the playoffs. But Manny would give Washington Heights plenty to be proud of in the years to come.

CHAPTER 8

Scouting Manny

Despite all of baseball's sacred traditions, its resistance to change is no match for the gentle, persistent tug of time. Time changes people and places, and people and places, by their altered presence, change how we experience the game. Consider Pittsburgh in the late 1950s, when a young boy named Mickey White and the rest of the blue-collar steel city fell in love with the magical swing of a Latin-American legend. Back then, a working single mother like Imelda White could still afford to take her son to a Pirates game every few nights—if he behaved. Imelda took a stern approach to discipline, even instructing the neighborhood Little League coach to "belt him" if Mickey acted out on the field. It was not an unreasonable request in 1950s Pittsburgh.

On days when the Pirates played at home, the city seemed as alive and clamorous as its booming steel mills. Children as young as nine boarded trolleys to Forbes Field and, in exchange for pushing a broom, watched Roberto Clemente hammer the ball all over the park.

White sat in the bleachers with his scorecard, among a virtual sea of middle-class families, closely studying Clemente's graceful twitches in the batter's box. White estimates that he attended no fewer than five hundred Pirates games as a child, and he has dozens of Clemente autographs to show for it.

Decades later, as a scout, he promised himself that if he ever witnessed anyone swing the bat with that same elegant fury, he'd do everything he could to sign him. And if he failed, he told himself, he would leave the profession.

White would stumble upon his chance in 1990, while he was the East Coast scouting supervisor for the Seattle Mariners. That's when he first saw Manny at the plate; that's when he saw that swing: sublime, pure, and timeless. It reawakened memories of a different era, a different game, as only the most transcendent sports figures and events can.

A year later, after taking the top scouting job in Cleveland, White fulfilled his promise to himself, signing Manny to a big league contract after drafting him in the first round.

At the time, the decision was as groundbreaking as it was fraught with risk: Although baseball was on the cusp of another Latin-American wave, few teams in recent years had put first-round money on a rough-around-the-edges immigrant lacking English skills and a high school diploma.

White also had to overcome his own private doubts, betting his young career on a kid who most scouts and executives projected as a fifth-round pick.

An avid reader and accomplished musician, as well as a former minor league catcher and standup comedian, White was well suited to the blend of empiricism and artistry that scouting demands. Scouting is a high-uncertainty, high-stakes game where winnings depend on the alchemy of calculations, bluffs, persuasion, and instinct. "It's poker, chess, and checkers all rolled into one," explains White, who is egg-bald with a jutting chin and a warm, ironic smile.

Scouts' casinos, however, are remote amateur ballfields, where they sit in bleachers or grab chain-link fences, surrounded by the patter of parents and high school students.

With blank expressions, they quietly read volumes into minu-

tiae, develop mental checklists of players' strengths and weaknesses, speculate about other scouts' preferences, and never, for
a moment, let on what theirs might be. And yet, since they can
directly observe only a fraction of the available pool of talent,
and often for just a game or two, they inevitably rely on biases,
or "gut feelings"—for example, a sentimental comparison to a
childhood hero.

In the final weeks before the 1990 draft, the East Coast
scouting scene was abuzz with talk of pitcher-shortstop Frankie
Rodriguez, a senior on Zitter's YSL team. The Red Sox wound
up picking Rodriguez in the second round. Before the draft,
scouts from around the country traveled to Brooklyn to see
Rodriguez, many of them fretful because of the traffic-clogged
roadways, dangerous neighborhoods, and unpredictable
weather that made trips to New York City seem more burden-
some than bountiful. As one scout noted, "Scouts prefer the
landscape of the suburbs and rural America, where they can
dine at Cracker Barrels and IHOPs, to poor urban neighborhoods. In fact, they would rather go to the Dominican Republic, where it's easy to get around. It puts urban athletes at a
distinct disadvantage." Word was, Rodriguez was worth the
headache.

At the time, Manny, a junior at George Washington and YSL
teammate of Rodriguez, was still unknown nationally. He was,
however, recognized by New York City's local scouts, often
called bird dogs—the ground-level talent hunters who send
monthly reports to executive decision makers.

Before the trip, fellow Mariners scout Joe Nigro told White
that Manny was "the best young hitter [he had] ever seen." So
White paid careful attention to Manny, who, at age sixteen, was
slight, showing no physical hint of his power. But the fluid
movement of his swing, the speed with which the bat cut over
the plate, as if gravity and all other natural forces were momen-

tarily suspended, gave White chills. "God," he said to himself. "I'm seeing a young Roberto Clemente."

That image of Manny lingered until White became scouting director for the Indians the following year. White had made the promise to himself, sure, but he also had the motive of self-preservation. More than at any other time in his career, he needed to sign an impact player. White, who had spent his scouting career on the road, driving from ballfield to ballfield, was for the first time scouting director—a club's drafting maestro—and he had something to prove. White knew that his first top pick would be the measure of his performance in the press and in Cleveland's executive offices. Could he handle prime time scouting decisions? Would he waste a high first-round draft pick—they would have the thirteenth overall pick—on a long shot, a head case, an overhyped prospect, or someone prone to injury, as many of his predecessors in Cleveland had? Or would he help turn the floundering club around?

The Indians were in the third decade of a playoff drought that would become known as "The Thirty-year Slump." The farm system was weak, with only a couple of promising prospects. The club's first-round draft choices in 1988 and 1989 had turned out to be unmitigated disasters, leading to the sacking of White's predecessor. And attendance was woeful at the cavernous, seventy-four-thousand-seat Cleveland Municipal Stadium, which was built in the 1920s as both a symbol of and a venue for mass civic entertainment but had become known as the "Mistake by the Lake." Many professional players shuddered at the thought of being traded to Cleveland.

White was hired by a cadre of new baseball executives in Cleveland who had migrated from the Orioles. Perhaps the biggest obstacle, though, was getting young players to come to Cleveland. Getting a player's assurance that he would sign if drafted was crucial, especially for high school players who had the option of not signing and going to college, where their value might grow with maturity.

White had decided early after moving to Cleveland that Manny would be one of his top picks. But he kept his intentions quiet, telling only one or two front-office executives. "Scouting is such a rumor mill and, with a slip of the tongue, the next day everyone could be on your guy or taking a second look," he says.

Meanwhile, Manny was putting on one of the best performances in the history of New York City high school ball. Still, few scouts were showing sustained interest—both a blessing and a cause for self-doubt. The weather in New York was especially cold in the spring of Manny's senior year, making the journey less appealing to many scouts. There were also "communication issues," as the Indians phrased it to White—that is, Manny spoke very little English and seemed exceptionally shy. Wouldn't that complicate minor league coaching and development? Although major league teams were stocking their rosters with Dominicans, much of that talent could be imported directly from the island at a fraction of the cost.

Still, the swing was the swing. The stats were the stats. Why weren't other teams on Manny's trail? "I had that question in the back of my mind," White admits. He wondered—just a little—whether his affinity for Clemente had led him to overestimate Manny's chance of making the majors.

White believes scouts have always drawn on statistics and pattern recognition to inform their decisions. "*Moneyball* created a folk legend of Billy Beane, but most of the concepts presented in that book go right back to what Ted Williams wrote about in *The Science of Hitting*," he says.

Long before social psychologists (and author Malcolm Gladwell) gave scientific credibility to the simple concept of following one's gut, White was steeped in the trade. Harkening to his days as a keyboard player, White notes that he tries to sense a player's *harmonic resonance*. "Success is both instinctive— having my antennae properly geared—and having the nuts to go with those instincts," he says.

Even so, White was aware that Manny's harmonic resonance was anything but certain. Only about one of every four first-round picks makes a significant contribution to a major league team; and a mere 5 percent become stars. Even if a player beats the odds and becomes a major league contributor, this accomplishment generally emerges only after years of obscurity in the minors. As if those odds weren't daunting enough, Indians' general manager Hank Peters and director of player development Dan O'Dowd had been pressuring White all winter to pursue college pitcher Aaron Sele, a six-three right-hander from Washington State. College players are, in general, a safer bet. They come with more statistical data and spend less time in the minors before being called up. Indeed, Manny had only two hundred at-bats over the course of his George Washington High School career. Economist John Burger and his colleagues found that high school draftees are less likely than their collegian counterparts to become contributing big leaguers (27 percent versus 43 percent).

To offset the risk of drafting a high school player in the first round, White instructed his local scout, Joe DeLuca, to go to as many Washington Heights and YSL games as he could. After each game, DeLuca provided detailed reports: not just on Manny, but on other major league scouts who were watching him.

DeLuca had been keeping tabs on Manny long before he got White's call. And he had already gained some valuable insights into how difficult it would be to reach Manny.

In 1988, DeLuca was in Prospect Park's Parade Grounds in Brooklyn, watching a YSL first baseman with talent but a reputation for drug problems. Alongside DeLuca, who was in his early sixties, was a brawny Dominican catcher-turned-scout, Eddie Diaz (no relation to Edwin Diaz, who lived in the same apartment building as the Ramirez family). Diaz always accompanied DeLuca into New York's roughest neighborhoods or when he scouted Spanish-speaking players.

DeLuca would have been an easy target for troublemakers: A short, slight man with carefully combed silver hair, he wore leather loafers and pressed khaki shorts. On scouting trips, he drove a blue Cadillac that attracted covetous stares in neighborhoods like Catona Park in Brooklyn or St. Mary's Park in the Bronx. When he parked his car in those neighborhoods, he was invariably approached by men demanding five or six dollars—a sort of parking fee, although it was never explained. DeLuca never asked why; he handed over the money. The reason was clear to him: It was a fee to keep his car from being stripped or stolen while he was scouting. "You were taking your life in your hands when you parked your car in some of those neighborhoods, and a lot of scouts wouldn't go to those places," he says.

Diaz, who grew up in Washington Heights and knew how to distinguish real danger from street bluster, provided a measure of comfort. He was also bilingual, an invaluable asset that August day in Prospect Park when DeLuca first made contact with Manny.

The first baseman DeLuca was scouting lived in a Brooklyn crack house, rumor had it. The boy's whippet-thin frame and ringed, sunken eyes seemed like a sad confirmation. DeLuca scanned the cluster of baseball fields, looking for other prospects. On a nearby field, a younger YSL team played. Manny was batting. Just as White would later, DeLuca immediately noticed his bat speed. "Eddie, see who that kid is when he comes in from center field," DeLuca told Diaz, handing him a business card on which to write the boy's school and phone number. "After you get back, I want you to watch his swing and tell me if you don't think it's pretty damn good."

Diaz came back and reported: "He's in the ninth grade at George Washington High School," handing DeLuca the card with Manny's address and a phone number. Sensing DeLuca's interest, Diaz ran to the car, retrieving an old pair of batting gloves from his days playing for Cleveland's minor league teams. He returned to the dugout to give them to Manny as a gift. Little did Diaz know that he was crossing into Zitter's territory.

After the game, Zitter, famously leery of scouts whom he suspected of preying on his players' naïveté, stomped over to DeLuca. "Joe, god dammit, you don't give my kids anything," Zitter chided. "I don't even want you near the kids. You think you're going to sign my kids for a pair of batting gloves? It's not going to happen."

DeLuca apologized to Zitter and quietly told Diaz he had made a mistake. That was typical Zitter, DeLuca explained: surly, protective, and confrontational. DeLuca admired it. A lot of these kids had no one else to protect them from the small enticements scouts might provide. Still, Zitter's attitude made a scout's job tougher. It almost made a scout feel as if he had to be sneaky if he wanted a mere word with one of Zitter's kids.

But Zitter had not forbidden DeLuca to phone Manny. The next weekend, DeLuca called the home number Manny had provided. He got an automated message: The number was out of service. In fact, Manny's family had no phone in their apartment. Perhaps out of embarrassment, he had rattled off a random set of numbers. That brief interaction set the stage for Cleveland's complicated courtship of Manny years later, during which DeLuca would play a key role.

During Manny's senior year, DeLuca or one of his associates watched Manny play nearly every weekend at his Youth Service League games—a huge commitment, considering that DeLuca was responsible for grading every prospect in New England and New York. Low-key was the order to his associates who scouted Manny: no Indians caps, no gabbing with other scouts, no flashing your business card around to impress coaches and parents.

DeLuca kept submitting monthly reports listing Manny as the top prospect in the region. He regaled White with stories about monster home runs, like the one Manny hit when George Washington played rival John F. Kennedy. DeLuca still blushes telling the story, drawing a diagram of the left-field fence and the twenty-five-story building beyond it. Manny hit the ball to the twentieth story of that building.

George Lazarik, the Indians' East Coast scout, came to New York to watch Manny. He was impressed, too. But a first-round draft pick? "Joe, I love this kid, but he ain't ever gonna be a first-rounder," said Lazarik, a Cuban immigrant who was also drafted by the Indians out of George Washington.

"Why do you say that?" DeLuca asked.

"Because no Latin-American immigrant kid has ever been drafted in the first round."

Other teams might have been thinking the same thing. Billy Blitzer and Buddy Paine had been unable to prevail on their teams to look closely. And no other scout DeLuca spoke to, except for Herb Stein of the Minnesota Twins, was projecting Manny higher than a fifth-round pick. Billy Blitzer's team had its sights set on Doug Glanville

But Stein, an old-school scout who had signed Frank Viola and George Washington alum Rod Carew, followed Manny as religiously as DeLuca did. Leading up to the draft, Stein pushed the Twins to take Manny with their third overall pick. But he was rebuffed by his bosses—a source of bitterness even today. The Twins chose Stanford first baseman David McCarty, who wound up hitting 36 career home runs and batting .242 in eleven major league seasons of part-time duty.

Less than one month before the draft, DeLuca and White needed to convince John Hart, Cleveland's director of baseball operations (who became general manager one year later) that Manny was for real. DeLuca picked up White and Hart from LaGuardia Airport. The YSL game had already begun when they arrived. White sprinted from the parking lot to a small break in the tarp lining the right-field fence. Manny was coming to bat.

Manny looked stronger than he had as a junior, his frame filling out. Within seconds, White saw what he'd come for: that swing. Manny's torso whipped around at the first pitch, hitting it toward the shortstop with so much force that by the time the ping of the aluminum bat reached White's ears, the infielder's glove had fallen to the grass. The ball had literally taken the shortstop's glove off his hand. Manny hit a triple off the left-field fence his next time up.

No other scouts were in the stands. Suppressing his excitement, White didn't say a word to Hart about Manny for the rest of the scouting trip. Hart broke the silence when they boarded the plane back to Cleveland. "What do you think?" he asked White. "I'm taking Manny," White said, without blinking.

"Why?" Hart asked.

"Well, because he's the best fucking hitter I've ever seen."

"That's a pretty bold statement."

"Believe me," White said. "As many times as I've seen Clemente, that bat works like his."

Hart never raised another question.

In the weeks leading up to draft day, DeLuca tried talking to Manny. Gauging Manny's commitment was especially important, given Cleveland's recent history with first-round picks.

In 1989, the Indians picked high school player Calvin Murray eleventh overall, even though Murray had declared he was going to college. When he kept his word, the organization looked foolish. "The local scout had not done his homework," DeLuca said.

In 1990, Cleveland drafted Tim Costo eighth overall, without knowing what kind of money he was expecting. When they made their first offer, he balked, as if it were an insult. Cleveland paid $300,000 to salvage its pick. Worse, Costo turned out to be a bust, amassing only 134 major league at-bats and hitting .224 with 3 home runs and 14 RBIs.

Hank Peters vowed the Indians would not repeat those blunders. Peters's assistant and vice president of baseball operations, Tom Giordano, promised to visit their prospective number-one choice. There would be no surprises on draft day. In the interest of secrecy, DeLuca tried arranging a meeting with Manny without approaching him at the ballpark, where other scouts might be watching, and without going through Zitter, who might use their interest as a bargaining chip in negotiations with other teams.

But arranging a meeting with a boy from a poor immigrant family was no easy task. This was not like the sit-downs DeLuca had set up through high school baseball coaches at preparatory schools in Connecticut, or with savvy suburban parents weighing the pros and cons of a college education. It was not as simple as making a call, or naming a time and a place.

DeLuca can't remember the young man's name, but one of Manny's teammates at George Washington said he could help set up the meeting. The three could meet at George Washington one day after school, the teenager told DeLuca. But when DeLuca met the boy at the school at the appointed day and time, Manny didn't show up. DeLuca tried again, setting up another time through this same friend, who apologized for the mix-up. Same thing again. And again. After the third time, DeLuca realized it was a lost cause. Perhaps there was a cultural gap that he couldn't bridge. He knew Manny was timid. Perhaps talking to a middle-aged Italian guy from Long Island about a career in professional baseball was an experience too foreign, too intimidating for Manny to handle alone.

Around the same time, DeLuca got an unexpected call from Zitter.

"Joe, what's going on here?" Zitter barked.

"What do you mean?"

"Joe, you've been buggin' Manny."

"Mel, I've got to fill out papers."

"You want to sit down with him?" Zitter asked. "Make an appointment. I'll be there."

"Why do you have to be there, Mel? Don't you trust me? What do you think I'm trying to do here?"

"I don't know what you're up to, but whatever, I want to be there."

They agreed to meet at a diner near Prospect Park, a twenty-four-hour greasy spoon called George's. Giordano came, too. Sitting in a booth in George's, the three men made small talk as they waited for Manny. DeLuca felt relief when he saw Manny through the diner's windows, hopping off a bus across the street. When Manny sat down, DeLuca suggested that he order something to eat. He could see the boy was shy. He kept his eyes down, and the only words he spoke the first ten minutes were to order a bowl of soup, a hamburger, and a soda. When DeLuca tried to engage him with questions about school and family—"Do your parents work?" "Do you have brothers and sisters?" "Are you doing okay in school?" "Do you really want to be a baseball player?" "Do you have a girlfriend?" "Are you serious about her?"—Manny responded with "uh-huhs," looking to Zitter for cues before answering.

Little by little, he let his guard down, answering questions with more than one word between bites. "I could see that if he felt you weren't the enemy, if he got comfortable, he would open up a little and talk," DeLuca says. But mostly Manny concentrated on eating and let Zitter speak for him. When Manny was done eating, Giordano asked if he wanted more food. Manny shook his head but Zitter knew better. "Give it to him all over again," Zitter instructed the waitress. Manny finished the second round of food in short order. "Now look," DeLuca told Manny after he finished. "You know why we're here. If we should draft you, would you play for the Cleveland Indians?"

"Fine, Manny, go ahead, you can answer that," Zitter said.

"Yeah, I like the Indians," Manny said.

"We would be fair to you," DeLuca said. "We want you to know that. We're not here to cheat you. Because I don't want to walk into a ballpark someday and have you say, 'I remember you. You're the guy who screwed me out of $40,000.'"

Giordano interjected, looking at Zitter.

"Mel, we're going to have to put down on paper what it's going to take."

"Well, what round are we talking?" Zitter asked.

"According to what Joe's been telling me, we're talking the first round," Giordano said. DeLuca remembers looking across the table to gauge Zitter's reaction. What he saw told him that no other team had talked to Zitter about making Manny their top choice: Zitter's jaw dropped in disbelief. Then Zitter pulled out papers he had brought with him, a list of the signing bonuses for the previous year's draft picks. Zitter told Giordano and DeLuca that a starting point would be $10,000 more than Cleveland's first-round pick the previous year, plus 10 percent. Later, in a report Giordano submitted to Hart, DeLuca estimated the final price tag would be around $300,000 after negotiations.

"That's fine with us, but if you need more, let us know," Hart told DeLuca in a phone conversation a few days later. Hart was eager to reach a final agreement with Zitter. DeLuca consummated the deal the next Sunday, an unusually hot day in early

June, just days before the draft. Manny was playing a YSL doubleheader. In a late show of interest, the Seattle Mariners' top scout and assistant to the general manager attended. Seattle's pick was eleventh, two ahead of Cleveland's. DeLuca felt a wave of panic.

After the game, Seattle's reps talked to Zitter for ten minutes on the right-field line. They passed DeLuca on their way to the parking lot, exchanged greetings and said, "Good luck"—shorthand, DeLuca believed, for, "We're going to pass on Manny. He's all yours." DeLuca approached Zitter. He told him that, as per Hart's orders, he had to come to an agreement that day.

Zitter went to his car, looked in his notebook, and told DeLuca, "Okay. You give us $250,000, he signs."

DeLuca smiled. "Mel, that's ironclad. That's my word. That's Cleveland's word. I'm gonna see you tomorrow if we draft him."

"Good luck," Mel said. "Go draft him."

Since Manny was still a minor, however, they would need a parental signature to consummate the deal. To lay the groundwork for this, White had a different idea—what he called his "secret weapon." His name was Winston Llenas.

Born in 1943 in Santo Domingo, Llenas was a member of the Dominican Hall of Fame and a hero on the island. White had met Winston while rooming with Winston's younger brother, Gus, during White's two-year stint as a minor league catcher for the Phillies. In 1991, Winston had been coaching the Aguiles Cibaeñas, but had some relatives living in Washington Heights. Llenas, accompanied by Giordano and DeLuca, would arrange the visit. "The three of us went to Manny's apartment and visited with his grandmother [Pura], to give the deal the finishing touch," says Llenas. "It was like in *The Godfather*, when the guy goes all the way over to Sicily just to show his face to the Family. I told her I had relatives in Washington Heights." He laughs. "I mean, what Dominican doesn't have relatives in Washington

Heights? But, you know, we had a wonderful time. Manny's grandmother made me a great cup of Dominican coffee."

As Llenas sipped the dark roast, he offered reassuring answers to Pura's questions. "She asked me, 'Where is he going?' 'What's he going to do?' 'Is he gonna be okay in Cleveland?' I told her, 'Manny's gonna see a lot of places in his life. He will be treated well. We like him. We're gonna develop Manny not only as a ballplayer, but as a man.'"

This was not the first visit by scouts to their apartment. "A lot of people had already come from Santo Domingo to our apartment, to see if they could get him to sign a contract. They would show us some papers, but Manny would never sign," Pura says.

This visit was different. Manny was ready, and Pura was charmed. "I knew this would help seal the deal," chuckles White, "but I also knew that twelve clubs had to walk by him for me to get him."

The Yankees, who had finished in last place the previous year with 95 losses, had first pick. Manny was a known quantity among New York scouts and had even developed a cult following among *New York Times* readers, since reporter Sara Rimer had chronicled his accomplishments in a series about Manny and his high school team.

But the Yankees had their eyes on Brien Taylor, a six-foot-four-inch lefty pitcher from Beaufort, North Carolina. In fact, Taylor-talk had dominated the draft and the media that spring. His fastball averaged an astonishing 95 mph and often registered 98 or 99 mph. In the 88 innings he had pitched for the East Carteret High School Mariners that spring, he had struck out 213 hitters and walked only 28. Yankees owner George Steinbrenner, serving a suspension for paying a gambler to dig up damaging information on Yankee player Dave Winfield, told reporters that if the Yankees let Taylor get away, they should be "shot."

But drafting Taylor turned out to be a catastrophic move. Taylor's hard-nosed agent (Scott Boras, who now represents Manny) and tenacious mother famously finessed a historic $1.5 million signing bonus out of the Yankees. Then, within three years, Taylor's career came to crashing halt when he damaged his shoulder in a trailer park brawl.

Taylor's contract, at the time, was the largest ever given to a draft pick. It had surpassed the well-publicized (and criticized) $1.2 million the A's had paid high school pitcher Todd Van Poppel—the fourteenth overall pick—the previous year. As a point of reference, Ken Griffey, Jr., the top pick just three years earlier, had signed with the Mariners for $160,000. Manny eventually signed for a $250,000 bonus—an inconceivably high sum to a teenager from anywhere, let alone Washington Heights. The Indians also handed Zitter a $10,000 check for the YSL.

Over time, though, Manny and his friends began to feel that Zitter had negotiated a bum deal. Zitter likely could have gotten more from the Indians, but available data suggest that Manny's bonus was not aberrantly low. It was comparable to what the top overall pick of the previous year, Larry "Chipper" Jones ($275,000) had received from the Atlanta Braves. Then again, there were the Taylor and Van Poppel bonuses, not to mention the $700,000 bonus that the second overall pick, outfielder Mike Kelly from Arizona State, had received.

DeLuca believes Manny's bonus was fair. "Think of the risk the Indians took," he said. "We were really the Christopher Columbus of that time, signing a kid with a green card in the first round and giving him that much money."

Zitter also sees it differently. "I wanted Manny to sign when I was with him, cause, yes, he is naïve, and I didn't want someone whispering in his ear the minute I stepped away. The reality was that everyone knew Manny wasn't going to graduate from high school, and he was certainly never going to be playing at a four-year, Division I school. I mean, we weren't talking [Mike]

Mussina." That's Zitter's way of saying Manny was not going to be able to feign interest in attending college, thereby leading the Indians to increase their offer, so Manny would play for them instead. Pitcher Mike Mussina, in contrast, was an academic achiever. He graduated from high school just a few decimal points shy of valedictorian and earned an economics degree from Stanford in just three years.

Zitter believes Manny came to perceive him as an inept agent and a stingy accountant—though Zitter assumed the roles of agent and accountant out of necessity. This led to the downfall of their relationship. Eventually, Manny pulled away from Zitter and did little to help the YSL later in his baseball career. But their rift took years to open.

In contrast to Zitter's hands-on approach, Macaco sat quietly in the background while Manny was courted to play professional ball. Their relationship remained locked around the element that bonded them—the simple acts of throwing, catching, and hitting a baseball. They talked about Manny's games, as always. But they rarely, if ever, spoke about the contracts, salaries, and negotiation that lay in his future. "Manny never talked about himself," Macaco says. "Always about baseball." Macaco believes that is a primary reason their relationship remained strong through the next phase in Manny's life, during which money would complicate friendships.

On draft day, Manny was flying high. A local news station had even managed to get a few words out of Manny during an interview in Zitter's kitchen. The spot showed Manny dressed in stark white sneakers, jean shorts, and a white T-shirt, swinging the bat at a local field. Neighborhood friends passed on the news through breathless phone calls, more than a few of which were received at Macaco's apartment. Macaco was in Santiago, visiting family and old friends as he did every summer, but his sister, who took the calls, knew that Macaco would be waiting for the news.

When she called Macaco in Santiago, he whispered into the receiver, "Oh my God!"

The next morning, a beaming Manny signed the contract, with its eventually controversial $250,000 bonus, in Zitter's living room. Manny had already packed his bags, which waited for him at his apartment in Washington Heights. DeLuca took him back to his neighborhood, the long-awaited contract in his hands. Later that day, after a flight back to Cleveland, when DeLuca walked into the press room to announce the signing, executives and beat writers erupted in applause—with a hint of cynicism, given the previous two years.

Riding with Manny from Washington Heights to the airport in his blue Cadillac, DeLuca tried to lighten the mood with a joke that fell flat. "Manny, I don't know if you're quick enough to hit those fastballs in the major leagues," he said with a laugh.

An earnest Manny took him seriously. "Oh, no, Mr. DeLuca," he said. He began describing a kid in the Connie Mack tournament who threw in the mid-nineties. "And I hit him pretty good," Manny concluded.

DeLuca grew more serious. "I was only kidding, Manny. But, let me ask you this. Where does it come from? This quick swing. Where does it come from?"

"Well, Joe, every day since I'm little, I swing the bat two hundred times every day," Manny said, imparting advice that DeLuca has since passed on at countless youth camps and to his own grandchildren.

"Well, I've never seen anyone swing the bat like you swing the bat, Manny. And a lot of our people say the same thing. So I know we're on the right track. The rest is up to you."

CHAPTER 9

Minor Adjustments

Since the amateur draft occurs after minor league rosters are set, the gap year in Rookie Ball is mostly a finishing school, teaching the etiquette of major league ball. Like the military and residential colleges, the minor leagues are a contained world where players can begin to make the transition to young adulthood under the supervision of caring adults. No longer stars of their high school shows, separated from parents and friends, players from different cultures and worldviews get thrown together. The abrupt transition was too much for Manny.

His first stop was a two week minicamp on the outskirts of Cleveland, held at Baldwin-Wallace College. The camp was meant to give recent draftees a whiff of life in the majors. They would practice at Cleveland's Municipal Stadium and attend Indians games. They also would be taken on a tour of the city, including a visit to the Rock and Roll Hall of Fame.

Omar Ramirez, drafted out of a junior college in Texas, recalls wondering who among the other young men lugging duffel bags through the Cleveland airport was the Indians' first-rounder from Washington Heights. But Manny barely spoke during the van ride from the airport, as the other draftees chatted, subtly sizing up one another. "We didn't know who the first-rounder was. We knew he was going to be there, but we didn't know who he was," Omar Ramirez said. "He was real quiet in the van. I mean, he didn't say a word, not a word." After about twenty-five minutes, Manny heard Omar mention that he was from the Dominican Republic. "Finally, he said to me, 'I'm Manny Ramirez, and I'm from the Dominican Republic.' From then on we became close friends. We had something in common and he felt more comfortable." Omar and Manny became hotel roommates during the minicamp.

Manny spent hours on the phone, calling New York. "Every day after practice, I mean every single day, he was calling his family and friends from the hotel room and talking for hours. He kept saying to them, 'I miss you guys. I miss New York. Cleveland is weird, it's so different.' He was so homesick. I think it was the first time he had been away from his family for any length of time." Manny also had bouts of self-doubt. "Those first few days he just kept saying, 'I don't know why I got drafted because I'm not that good.' I'd say, 'What do you mean?' And he'd say, 'Omar, really, I don't know why they gave me that much money. I don't deserve that much money.' And then we started playing a few games, and it was like 'Oh, my God!'" Omar would hear Manny repeat those same doubts on minor league teams in Kinston, North Carolina, in 1992 and in Canton, Ohio, in 1993. "I don't know if it was a joke or what," says Omar, now a coach for the Kansas City Royals' minor league team in Burlington, North Carolina.

One of the escorts during the minicamp was George Washington alum Rod Carew, who had recently been inducted into the Baseball Hall of Fame.

Carew had joined the Indians training staff to coach the art of stealing bases. Although Manny was never destined for base stealing, he and Rod shared some important similarities that drew them together. Both were Spanish-speaking immigrants, though Rod had journeyed from Panama, where, in 1945, he was named for the stranger who delivered him in the back of a segregated train. Rod and Manny had both attended George Washington High School, though Rod had managed to accumulate enough credits to graduate. And each stood out among the best players of his era. Rod, who had won Rookie of the Year with the Minnesota Twins in 1967 and earned seven batting titles on the way to a .328 lifetime batting average and 3,053 hits, could look back at an illustrious career. Manny could only dream of the triumphs that lay ahead.

When the rookies took batting practice with the major league players, Carew approached Manny and offered some words of encouragement.

"I wanted to be positive, to let him know how much they thought about his talent, to let him know that he could be on the fast track," Carew said.

"I just told him, 'I haven't seen you, but everyone raves about you and the talent that you are. You're gonna get a chance to get to the big leagues and work there so pay attention to what you're doing.' He got that shy smile, and he just said, 'I hope so, I'm going to work hard.'

"He's got that quietness about him," he said. "It's that side of him I like. He's just a good guy."

Carew took Manny under his wing, serving as gatekeeper and interpreter to a hungry Cleveland press. "I can understand what he's going through. We have the same kind of makeup," Carew told an Associated Press writer in 1991. "I was quiet and he is quiet. All of a sudden this is put upon him."

Rockies general manager Dan O'Dowd, who at the time served as director of player development for the Indians, recalls Manny that first week. "He was painfully shy and so out of his element. But as soon as we put a bat in his hand and let him stand at the plate he was right at home. I could see his whole body relax. And that swing! After the first round of batting practice we were all speechless. In my twenty-six years of doing this, I still have never seen a more naturally gifted hitter."

By late June, Manny had launched his professional career with the Burlington Indians, the organization's rookie-level Appalachian League team in Burlington, North Carolina. The league also includes teams in Tennessee, West Virginia, and Virginia. Each team in the league plays sixty-eight games, thirty-four at home and thirty-four on the road, in a season that runs from mid-June (to accommodate graduating high schoolers) to late August.

Burlington's three-thousand-seat stadium remains something of a small-town classic, with a vintage look that earned it a cameo in the movie *Bull Durham*. The park was originally located in Danville, Virginia, about fifty miles north of Burlington. Built in 1945, it served as the home of the Danville Leafs (named in honor of the town's lucrative tobacco trade). When the Leafs folded after the 1958 season, the city of Burlington bought the entire stadium for a mere $5,000 and moved it, piece by piece, down the highway to the east side of Burlington, where it was reassembled in time for the 1960 season.

To this day, the park's entire steel structure and roof can be traced to that original Danville ballpark. Plaques of famous players adorn the stadium's outside cinder-block Wall of Fame, including Manny, Brian Giles, Steve Olin, Bartolo Colon, Jim Thome, Richie Sexson, and CC Sabathia. Red Sox legend Luis Tiant and Yankees legend Mel Stottlemyre also played there.

The city of Burlington was a far cry from Washington Heights. Built around the railroad and cotton industries (it was home to Burlington Mills), Burlington retains its southern flavor. As its current website boasts, "Burlington . . . is home to major industry, to growing retail and residential development, and now it is facing up to a new challenge—the growing presence of Hispanics in the population mix."

Unlike nearby Graham, whose quaint main street looks like a faded 1950s photograph, Burlington is a charmless sprawl of strip malls, factory outlets, and tired apartment buildings. A Circle K gas station that became familiar to Manny still stands at one nondescript intersection, behind which is Hawthorne Court, a shabby apartment complex in which Manny rented a unit with two Dominican teammates: Jose Colon and Fernando Hernandez. "When I signed, I was scared," recalls Manny. "I said to myself, 'What if I don't make it?' The first month [playing minor league] I was homesick."

Although the roommates helped ease some of his pain, Manny struggled to adjust to his new life. Dave Keller, his bilingual team manager, was well aware of Manny's distress. "I remember my manager Dave Keller who helped me a lot. I would always tell him, 'I can't do this. I'm going home,'" recalls Manny. "I spent a lot of time those first few weeks trying to convince Manny not to quit," Keller says. He also mixed in doses of discipline. In early July, when Manny showed up over two hours late for treatment of a bruised thigh, Keller demanded to know why he was late. Manny's answer—"I don't know"—was unsatisfactory. Keller benched him that night. The next day Manny doubled twice and scored two runs.

Manny spent most of his time at the ballpark or his apartment. When they didn't splurge on a cab, Manny and his two roommates walked 4.5 miles along the gravel shoulders of Burlington's desolate streets. Manny rarely spoke, preferring to listen as Colon and Hernandez bantered about the night's game. "I lived with Dominican guys. It was fun, but it was also the time in our lives when we were becoming men," recalls Manny. The three young men did what they could to create some sort of domestic life in their $469-a-month, two-bedroom apartment. Hernandez, who would later pitch just two major league games, amassing an ERA of 40.50 (he gave up 6 earned runs in 1.3 innings), cooked many of the meals. He was hard-pressed to find Latin-American ingredients in the nearby supermarket. Most nights their dinner was warmed-over hot dogs and pizza, downed at the concession stands after the games. Colon pitched just three games for Burlington and never advanced past the rookie year.

Both Hernandez and Colon had signed with the Indians as amateur free agents for $5,000—2 percent of the bonus Manny fetched. Zitter knew this discrepancy would leave his protégé open to exploitation. So he advised Manny against installing a phone in their unit, for fear that it would become a honey pot for his homesick Dominican roommates. Instead, Zitter established a calling-card account for Manny, suggesting he walk to the nearby Circle K if he needed to call home. What Zitter didn't anticipate was that the pay phone would become Manny's home away from home. Each night, after the game, Manny trudged across the Circle K parking lot. He punched his well-worn sequence into the phone—first his calling card and then his girlfriend Kathy Guzman's number.

Guzman, whom Manny had been dating since the start of his junior year in high school, was as steady as a rock. There had been no shortage of girlfriends, but Guzman seemed different—not just to Manny, but to Pura, Onelcida, and his sisters. Indeed, family photo albums spanning the early 1990s contain more photos of Guzman than of Manny. "We all loved her like a sister," recalls sister Evelyn. "She was the best, no difference between her and my other sisters. She did things all the time for my mom, she lived with her when Manny went off to play. She even helped Mom pay the rent." Manny's friend and high school teammate Richie Lopez, aka "the muffin man," describes her as "the 'one,' the perfect match for Manny, simple and relaxed."

Listening to the familiar sound of Guzman's voice over the

pay phone helped melt away some of the day's anxiety. It didn't matter what she talked about. He just needed to hear her soft Spanish words; the familiar beats of city traffic; the wail of a passing ambulance. It helped drown out the stiff silence that engulfed Burlington on those lonely summer nights. "My wife and I would drive by and there he'd be, every night, on the phone talking with her," said Keller. "I think a lot of time there must have been long silences or something. I mean, he was never much of a talker." Keller eventually discussed the situation with the manager of the Circle K, explaining that Manny was a good kid, just homesick, and if any problems arose, to please give him a call.

The only problem that arose was financial. Zitter, who managed Manny's money that first year, remembers getting the twenty-five-page, $1,300 phone bill. Zitter had to rein him in, which meant, too, that he took heat from relatives and friends who felt they had a claim on Manny's bounty.

Zitter's efforts had unintended consequences. As he explained: "Manny, at least at that point, was a very giving person who never wanted to say no, especially to his relatives. Certainly, I have seen this with many young men who, previously having nothing and now having some money and fame, become targeted by all their 'loving family' and all their 'best friends.' This is what happened with Manny. If I had said yes to everyone, he would have very quickly been broke. Basically, I probably let Manny use me to be the bad guy, and I had no problem doing so, because I knew what I was doing was protecting Manny. Having said that, it was inevitable that some people (not all, but some) would try to turn Manny away from me, with bullshit about the 'us versus them' nonsense. Looking back, and understanding how impressionable Manny was, I was fighting a losing battle and, sooner or later, someone was going to get in Manny's ear and move him in different directions, and away from me being involved in handling his money." Within a year, Manny had deputized his sister Clara to manage his money.

Meanwhile, Keller and his wife became de facto dorm parents to the players, all of whom were between seventeen and twenty-two. They were youngsters who hailed from small towns in Texas, Washington, and Arkansas. Only five would eventually reach the majors. Keller and his wife provided instruction on how to run a load of laundry, shop for groceries, and tip appropriately.

The nearby Holly Hill mall, located less than a mile and a half from Manny's apartment and anchored by a JC Penney and a Sears, was where Manny fell in love with American malls. In fact, Macaco has pointed out that Manny's lack of anonymity at shopping malls was one of his primary dissatisfactions with life in Boston. "Manny always wants to go to the shopping mall," says Macaco. "Sometimes we'll go two or three times a day."

Manny's desire for a 2005 trade to the Angels, Macaco insists, was partially fueled by a leisurely afternoon at the La Brea Mall. Clara, who along with Onelcida, accompanied Manny and his wife on their Maui honeymoon, admitted that "going to the mall" was at the very top of their activities list. At Holly Hill in North Carolina, Manny liked roaming the stores with cash in his pocket. His fifteen dollars per diem and $800 monthly salary made him feel like a king, despite Zitter's fiscal reins.

Manny got his first professional hit—a two-run homer—on opening day in Burlington. But his slump over the next few games (.200 after his first 20 at-bats) reflected his adjustment to unfamiliar surroundings. "One day," recalls Keller, "he came into my office in tears. 'I can't hit. I can't hit. What am I doing wrong?' I was like, 'Hold on, pal. You're a star.' But it wasn't what he was used to. He was used to going 4 for 5, 5 for 5."

Manny's drought was especially hard for Mickey White, who followed Manny's early at-bats like a jittery investor follows his portfolio. The outlook, at first, was grim. Hank Peters, still the general manager, accused White of squandering the first-round pick. When Manny's average hit .167, a concerned Peters sent White on a fifteen-day road trip to "re-evaluate" his draft prize. Reputation and job on the line, White traveled to Burlington.

"Things are going to be fine," Keller told White. "He's going to hit and he's going to hit big." As the two men talked, they climbed a steep staircase to the rooftop box where they could catch a bird's-eye view of batting practice. Keller continued: "He's shy, it's an adjustment, just give him time." Within seconds, White's anxiety melted as he watched his young Clemente dominate the field, launching balls beyond the back wall. Manny's batting practice successes spilled over to the game. "That night," says White, "Manny hit a home run to left and then another to right. And it seemed like every game after that it was the same story." The slump was over. So was White's career anxiety.

During an eight-game stretch in August, Manny homered 5 times, tripled once, scored 10 runs, and had 18 RBIs. His average over the week was a staggering .522.

Burlington Indians' general manager Mark Schuster watched one of the season's final games from the team's rooftop box. Families with small children had departed long before the ninth, and now the grind of extra innings threatened to extend the game past midnight. Manny, who had already hammered two balls out of the park, stood at the plate. Perhaps a third would somehow materialize, sending everyone home for the night.

It was not to be. With two outs and a runner on first, Manny whiffed to end the inning. A few more exhausted fans trickled into the parking lot, crossing pavement that still held traces of the North Carolina heat. A punishing thirteenth inning brought no relief. It was now nearly 1:00 A.M. Would this game rival the eight-and-a-quarter-hour marathon between the Burlington

Indians and Bluefield Orioles back in June 1988? In that twenty-seven-inning affair, the game ended at 3:30 A.M. In fact, the radio play-by-play call of that game by announcer Richard Musterer stands as the longest continuous single-game solo broadcast in baseball history.

By the bottom of the fourteenth, with only about fifty die-hards still in the stands, Manny returned to the plate. The Princeton Reds reliever fired a low fastball. Manny blasted it over the center-field wall, ending the game. "The outfielders never even moved," recalls Schuster. "They just stood there frozen as the ball sailed into the night. We all got to go home."

Now home beckoned Manny as well. It had been a particularly grueling season for the nineteen-year-old, beginning with the YSL and continuing through his senior year of high school. Then on to Burlington, where he had endured a more intensive season than he'd ever played. Manny's performance in Burlington, all told, was spectacular: .326 average, 19 home runs, and 63 RBIs. He won two-thirds of the Appalachian League's triple crown.

He was ready to relax. The Indians had other plans.

CHAPTER 10

Winter Ball, 1991

Just before batting practice on a late August morning, Keller called Manny into his cramped, faux-paneled office. "Sit down, Manny," he said, gesturing to the chair beside his desk, "I've got some good news."

Indians management had arranged for Manny to play winter ball in the Dominican Republic. He'd be playing for Winston Llenas's former team, Aguiles Cibaeñas, in Santiago. Manny, of course, knew all about the winter league. As a boy, he had rooted for his hometown Tigres del Licey and followed their intense rivalry with Aguiles. He idolized Pedro Guerrero, Tony Fernandez, Julio Franco, Alfredo Griffin, Juan Samuel, and George Bell.

Manny forced a faint smile, but Keller, sensing his despair, jumped into salesman mode, explaining his reasoning and the virtues of the move. Manny's rookie-year performance had convinced the club he was destined for stardom. Winter ball would develop his fielding and allow him to face a rotation of Triple-A and major league pitchers in an unpredictable array of match-ups. And finally, Keller told Manny, he would be returning to the DR, to his people and language, to the warmth of the Caribbean sun.

Keller never mentioned the Indians' biggest motive: they cringed at the notion of returning their prize investment to the streets of Washington Heights. For all its virtues, sending a rookie to winter ball was an unusual move. Most slots were reserved for Double- or Triple-A players, or even major leaguers with something to prove.

As Keller prattled on, Manny's mind seemed to drift. He needed to talk this over with Macaco, his agent, and Kathy. He needed to brace himself for more strange faces, hotel rooms, rowdy teammates, and homesickness. He consoled himself with the reminder that he'd be joining a veritable fantasy team of Dominicans: Tony Peña catching, Felix Fermin at shortstop, and Moises Alou in left field.

There was one hitch: The Aguiles, by league bylaws, were permitted a maximum of five American players on their roster. In order to maximize the number of prospects they could send to their winter league team, the Indians arranged for Manny to count as a Dominican. This meant he was paid in pesos and, consequently, his salary was significantly less than that of his American peers, all of whom were inferior prospects. Moreover, instead of staying at the hotel with the rest of the American players, Manny had to stay with a host family. It was as if he were back with Sherry Magee, playing in New Mexico.

Aguiles manager Brian Graham recalls Manny's plight that winter. "Manny had to fight for what the other guys had," he says. "Of course, Manny was not comfortable with confrontation and negotiation." With Graham's help, Manny got a pay adjustment and was moved to team quarters.

Manny worked hard for the team, but the turn of events complicated what was already a rocky transition. "He really didn't want to go," says Graham. "He went because the organization thought it would expedite his development. But he was too young, he had already played a long season, and he wanted to go home and rest."

Just fifteen days into the season, Manny quit. Here's how

Graham recalls it: "So he comes into my office, with that little smile, and he says, 'Hey. I'm going home.' 'No you're not!' I say. 'No, really, I don't want to be here,' says Manny. I tried, but in my heart, I knew it was the right thing to let him go. He just wasn't happy."

So Manny got his way. He returned to Washington Heights to a fawning entourage. His fame and wealth made him a magnet on the streets of upper Manhattan. When Manny attended private tutoring to improve his English at the urging of the Indians organization, a trail of friends tried to follow him into the tutor's apartment. "There were a lot of boys who followed him around," recalls Jose Soriano, a teacher at G-Dubs who was hired by the Indians to improve Manny's English in the off-season. "I told him, 'They can't come in here with you. They can wait for you outside.'"

Manny also received regular entreaties from agents who saw his future value. Luis Valdez, Manny's high school assistant coach, was approached by Florida-based agent Jaime Torres, who asked if Valdez could convince Manny to sign with him. Valdez succeeded and, in exchange, Torres hired Valdez, who was still a teacher at G-Dubs, as an assistant agent of sorts. Valdez would tend to Manny's every need over the next four years—buying gloves and cleats, arranging family travel, and playing watchman over Manny's money.

Valdez remembers that Manny, young and impressionable, couldn't account for where about $60,000 of his signing bonus had been spent by the time he signed with them. "When we got Manny on, we checked his accounts, and he only had $26,000. Out of all that money, that's all that was left. I said, 'Manny, where's all the money?' He said, 'I don't know.'"

Soon, Valdez got a glimpse at the number of outstretched hands surrounding Manny, as if he were a neighborhood patriarch. "When he'd go to Washington Heights, people would ask for money. He didn't know how to say 'No.' He was like, 'Valdez, everybody wants money.' I told him to tell them we don't have the money right now, but next year we'd be glad to give them money. And that's how you say 'No.' But it's a nice 'No.' And that was the thing that drove him, little by little. People crowd, they ask him, ask him, ask him, ask him. And you get tired of that."

Manny quietly gave money to several Little League baseball teams for uniforms during his minor league years and to friends, such as Jose Mateo at Peligro Sports, and, of course, to his family. "When Manny gives money, he doesn't like to talk about it," Macaco says. "If it's going to be in the newspapers, or if people are going to talk about it a lot, he'd rather not do it."

Early in his minor league career, increasingly audacious requests from some friends became a source of anxiety. At one point, a close friend whose father had passed away called Manny to ask that he pay for the funeral, Valdez says. The friend wanted to hold the funeral in the Dominican Republic, and he asked Manny to pay to fly his family there, too.

"I don't know what to do," Manny confided to Valdez, who isn't sure what Manny ultimately decided. "If it were to happen now, I'm pretty sure Manny would take care of it," he says. "But at the time, he wasn't making that much money. And you have to take care of your family."

"You have to have your friendships," Manny explains, "but you don't want them to abuse you. You can help someone, but everyone has their limit."

CHAPTER 11

Kinston, North Carolina

Manny began his second season playing for the Indians' Class-A team in Kinston, North Carolina, a small town located in the Inner Banks region where southern manners (and racial prejudices) are still a way of life. If Washington Heights was ethnically insulated from non-Hispanics, Manny found himself in a racially diverse community where color had long been a distinction of significance.

Kinston has a rich Confederate history, and only a half-century ago, the town's Granger Stadium was a crucible in baseball's racial integration. Until 1956, no black player had ever been granted the privilege of putting on a Kinston uniform. The entire Carolina League, in fact, had been off-limits to black players. Then Carl Long, a black man who grew up picking cotton and playing stickball on endless red-clay roads in Rock Hill, South Carolina, arrived in Kinston, crashing through the color barrier, inciting racial hatred across the Carolinas, and setting records that still stand today.

Long is a living storybook of perseverance over racial intolerance. "When we played in Greensboro," the seventy-three-year-old says, recalling one of many times he faced naked racism during his one year playing for Kinston, "I hit one out my first time up to the plate. The second time, a white man sitting behind home plate said to the pitcher, 'Hit that nigger in the head. Cut him down.' I got so mad, I hit it out again."

Long tallied a total of six RBIs that day on two home runs, a double, and a single. At the end of the game, a white woman approached Long's heckler and implored, "Leave those black boys alone. Every time you open your mouth, they get a hit." The next day, the man heeded the woman's advice, watching silently. Long went hitless, he says with a chuckle.

By the time Manny arrived in Kinston, outward displays of racial intolerance were less common. But the underlying racial tensions were enough to put Keller—who'd been promoted to coach the Kinston team—on edge.

"Good afternoon, this is the North Carolina highway patrol," said the officer in a thick southern accent. "I'm looking for a Mr. David Keller." Keller shot up in his chair, clenched the phone against his ear, and identified himself.

"Well, Mr. Keller," the officer drawled, "I need to inform you that I have a warrant out for the arrest of a Mr. Manuel Ramirez."

Keller knew that if the top draft choice was in trouble with the law, Keller would be in even bigger trouble with his boss, O'Dowd, a flamboyant workaholic who would snap in anger at the drop of a hat.

"Sir," the officer continued, "we clocked Mr. Ramirez going one hundred miles an hour." Keller pictured Manny flying down Highway 264 in his new, black Nissan 300ZX—his reward for a recent deal with Topps baseball cards.

As it happened, at that very moment, one of Manny's teammates was in tears in Keller's office, telling the manager about his mother's breast cancer. So Keller gathered himself and muttered into the phone, "This isn't a great time."

"Well, sir," the officer snapped back angrily, "if you're not going to cooperate, I'm just going to have to take Mr. Ramirez into custody."

At that, Keller excused himself briefly, calling upon his pitching coach, Ricky Horton, to comfort the young player. Returning to the phone, his heart heavy, he was greeted with quiet laughter on the other end of line, and then, in his familiar deep voice, "Hey, Dave. It's Dan O'Dowd."

"Dan was good at that," Keller recalls. "With him it was practical joke mania, and he had me. I was spinning. He knew I was always looking out for that kid."

Manny did, in fact, cultivate a village of caretakers during those early days, men who, along with Zitter and Macaco, helped light his difficult passage through North Carolina.

Keller remembers Manny's initial struggles, shaking his head over the difference between Kinston and Washington Heights. "KKK rallies down Main Street," says Keller. "People would yell at the players to run like there's a watermelon on first base."

Manny spent hours hitting balls. "This guy was driven," says Keller. "Unbelievably driven to succeed, from day one. But incredibly humble. He always deflected praise and attention, and wanted to practice when nobody was around."

The homesickness also faded. Manny's high school girlfriend, Kathy Guzman, left George Washington High for a year to live with Manny in Kinston. "They were like husband and wife," Kinston teammate Omar Ramirez says. "I thought for sure they were going to get married." Guzman's cooking became familiar to the Latin players on the team, who met at least twice a week at Manny's one-bedroom apartment, outfitted with top-of-the-line rental furniture and a state-of-the-art stereo system. "We'd hang out and listen to music, and we invited Latin players from visiting teams when they were in town," says Omar, who also regularly hosted dinner for the Latin-American contingent.

Manny seems to be most at ease around other Hispanic players, a result of growing up in linguistically and culturally insulated Washington Heights. When Manny was paired up to room
with Pete Rose, Jr., during the Indians' 1992 spring training
camp in Arizona, every evening he made his way to the room of
Omar Ramirez and fellow Dominican Paulino Tena. "He used to
sleep with us because he didn't feel comfortable being around
Pete Rose, Jr. At first he just didn't feel comfortable around
American players, partly because his English wasn't very good
and he just did not have much in common with them," Omar
says, adding, "People may think it's odd that we shared a bed,
but that's how Manny was. He didn't care."

Although Manny's English has improved markedly since his
minor league days, Omar thinks the language barrier contributed to Manny's reluctance to talk to the press in the minor
leagues. "He didn't feel comfortable talking in English. He
didn't feel comfortable at all." But inside the Kinston clubhouse,
Manny let his boyish personality spill out, sometimes frustrating
the more buttoned-up players and the coaches. More often, he
unwittingly entertained them. Kinston general manager North
Johnson still laughs about Manny running around gleefully
showing teammates his baseball card. And Manny always sang
along to the Dominican music playing on the Walkman or the
portable stereo he brought wherever he went: On the bus. In
the clubhouse. In the shower. He gravitated to the team
pranksters and goofballs, like pitcher Julian Tavarez, a fellow
Dominican who rose through the minors with Manny and was
one of his closest friends on the Red Sox. "Manny likes to be
around people, and when he finds a person who is always joking
around, who he feels comfortable with, he'll have him as a
friend forever," Omar says.

But in the batter's box, Manny was all business. North recalls:
"It took him about a month to come into his own. There were

high expectations, and he was one of the best pure hitters any-one had ever seen. Still, he was fairly young—just nineteen, and still immature. One night he went 3 for 4, with 2 homers and a double. To me, that was a signature game. As I watched that sec-ond homer, I knew that he was going to be the player everyone thought he was."

During one hot streak in June and early July, Manny drove in 47 runs in forty-seven games. In a single week in late June, he went 9 for 21 (.429) with 2 homers and 6 RBIs. The following week, however, Manny broke the hamate bone in his left hand, sidelining him for the rest of the season.

Fittingly, Manny's injury came on a bedazzling opposite-field home run against Orioles Class-A affiliate Frederick Keys in Maryland. It was the opening pitch of the at-bat, a fastball in the upper nineties, thrown high and on the inside of the plate. Manny hit a line drive that seemed unwilling to arc downward until the ball clanked off the scoreboard in right field. After rounding the bases, Manny told his teammates he felt pain in his wrist, and tests later confirmed it was the hamate. "We were all like, 'This is impressive, unbelievable.' The guy injures him-self swinging and he still hits a home run," recalls Omar Ramirez.

It was always like that, seemingly effortless. Teammates con-stantly asked Manny how he managed to combine finesse and power. Did he know what the pitcher was going to throw? Had he seen something in the windup that gave him a clue? Was he inside the hurler's head? As Omar explains, "He'd always say the same thing: 'I don't know. I just saw the ball and hit it.' Sometimes he didn't even know what pitch he had hit. He would come back to the dugout after scoring a run or hitting a home run, and we'd ask him about the pitch he hit. He'd say, 'I'm not sure, maybe a changeup.'"

Manny stayed in Kinston, undergoing rehabilitation in the

hopes of getting better before the end of the season. But the Indians were careful not to risk further injury by rushing out their young slugger. "We knew, even when he was nineteen, that we couldn't replace him," says Johnson, the GM. "You never want to lose a guy like that."

Although he played just eighty-one games, he managed to bat .278, with 13 home runs and 63 RBIs. Not astronomical numbers, but enough productivity to validate his status as the next great hitter in the Indians organization.

Manny returned to his friends and family and Guzman in Washington Heights during the off-season to recuperate. Privately, he was confident he would continue to move through the minor leagues. But he had no idea how fast that ascension would be.

CHAPTER 12

Moving Up

Manny began the 1993 season with the Double-A Canton-Akron Indians of the Eastern League. The team was young and talented, including Brian Giles, Omar Ramirez, and Herb Perry. And the manager was a familiar face to Manny: Graham. Graham's memories of Manny are of a young man with "a long way to go," when it came to professional behavior and appearances. Manny showed up in Canton with a new, souped-up BMW M5. Its chrome muffler and rims drew quizzical stares and ribbing from teammates. "He would be late for stretches or come out with his shoes untied or his shirt untucked," says Graham. "I think the world of Manny, but he certainly wasn't a finished product when he arrived."

Graham also recalls Manny's baffling tendency to raid teammates' lockers, a habit Keller had fruitlessly tried to extinguish in Burlington and Kinston. Some observers have chalked this up to his impoverished background; others have seen it as endearing. Charlie Manuel, Manny's Triple-A manager, recalls similar behavior: "He used to go and mess in someone's locker, grab a shirt and put it on. He'd put someone else's uniform shirt on or borrow your belt and he'd do it just to mess with you. I'd see him wearing my belt, which was way to big for him, and he'd have it pulled all funny and high around his waist. Just to show me how much he liked me, you know, for a joke or something. I can say this, in all my forty-six years in this business, Manny is the only guy who could get away with that."

His promiscuous approach to clothes has continued into the majors, including the Dodgers' locker room. As *L.A. Times* columnist T. J. Simers described, "Any chance he gets, he makes fun of himself and his reputation for being a goof. And stepping into a pair of teammate Ramon Troncoso's sneakers, while packing a pair of Russell Martin spikes for the trip to Philadelphia, how could anyone think him a goof?" Indians clubhouse assistant Frank Mancini said, "He loved to wear other people's clothes. He was the master of that. And if a piece of clothing was missing from someone's locker we'd all figure Manny was wearing it. Other Latino players have told me that it is cultural—that it's not yours or mine, it's ours. It breaks down barriers to share clothing."

Not quite, according to Manny's sister Clara. She went so far as to construct actual barriers to such sharing, only to have them broken down by Manny. During high school, Clara had a job at the Gap in the Bronx. Like many teenage workers, she was induced by her employee discount to invest much of her paycheck back into the store's inventory. "Back then baggy pants and belts were in fashion. I bought clothes from the Gap and they fit Manny, too. So he and his friends would get into my closest and take my clothes. I'd see them wearing my stuff at school. Eventually I had to install a lock on my closet door. But Manny broke in!" She can laugh about it now.

Manny's victims usually seem to laugh it off. And, in Kinston, his talent and playfulness elicited warmth and tolerance. But Manny struggled with the arduous minor league schedule. "Manny was not a big fan of riding on the bus, checking in and out of hotels," says Graham. "He was the guy who looked like he hadn't slept for days. I really doubt if he ever unpacked his suitcases in those small cities."

On the upside, Canton played against teams in towns that were bigger than the likes of Kinston. Which meant, of course, that the shopping malls were bigger, too. "We started going to the malls all the time," Omar Ramirez says. But not necessarily to buy anything. Omar notes that Manny always bought clothing in New York City or had his friends send him clothes. Manny knew where to get the best deals on brand-name clothing in New York City. At the malls they just walked, checked out girls, maybe got something to eat. At night, after games, Manny lifted weights.

Manny started the season in Canton with another slump, giving rise to a new round of speculation about whether Cleveland's rising star had hit a plateau. A newspaper story compared Manny with Cliff Floyd, the Montreal Expos' first-round pick in 1991. Floyd had begun the season on a tear. But having a few early season slumps behind him, Manny seemed more at ease than in the previous season. "He'd have an 0 for 4 night, and he'd go home and say, 'Not a big deal. I'll get it tomorrow.' Four-strikeout night? He'd say, 'I'm having fun. I'll get it tomorrow,'" Omar Ramirez says. "If he had a good game or a bad game, he was always the same. I used to get mad, I used to slam helmets or tear my batting gloves. I think that's one reason for Manny's success. He approaches baseball, and life, differently than everybody else. He's happy to be alive, and that's it."

Several weeks into the season, Manny broke into a hot streak that never really abated. He ended up batting .340 in Canton, with 17 homers and 79 RBIs in 89 games. By April 1993, the Cleveland *Plain Dealer* had anointed Manny the Tribe's "right fielder in waiting."

On July 19, 1993, Manny was called up to the International League's Charlotte Knights, the Indians' newly acquired Triple-A affiliate, where Manuel was the manager. Manuel still remembers the twenty-one-year-old's grand entrance. As the limo driver waited for his fare, Manny burst into the front office and asked Charlie for money. As the clubhouse attendant settled the tab, Manuel learned that Manny had left his suitcase and equipment at the airport. That night he went 2 for 4 in his Triple-A debut.

Manny's mind was on baseball, not the nuts and bolts of travel and money. Still, this forgetfulness and his chronically empty wallet are recurrent themes in his career. There was nothing haphazard, however, about his initial approach to hitting in Charlotte.

Manuel will never forget his first afternoon. "Manny goes up for batting practice and starts nonchalantly hitting balls to right, then to center. I turn to [assistant coach] Luis Isaac and say, 'It looks like I'm going to have to work with this kid [about his lack of intensity]. But then the game started. And the first thing I know, he hits one over the center-field backdrop, probably 430 feet. His second hit went over the left-field backdrop. I turned to Luis and said, 'Nah, I'm not going to talk to him.'"

Manny and Manuel did talk about other things. Once again, he'd found a father figure, this time in the form of a tough-minded, forty-nine-year-old former major leaguer. "He'd come and get me for lunch and we'd sit down and talk. I used to spend a lot of time with him. He was always by my side. He was like my son," says Manuel.

Somehow, after fewer than five weeks, Manny had managed to insinuate himself into his coach's inner circle. Their bond followed the familiar template: young, carefree slugger, smitten and protective older coach.

"He'd be in the cage, and he'd want to play games with me. I'd pick the balls up and he'd say, 'Nah, Coach, I don't want to hit today.' And I'd say, 'Get in there and hit.' And he'd say, 'Nah, I'm not hitting today.' So, we'd start wrestling, right there in the cage, and he'd be laughing and saying, 'No, Charlie, no.' And finally, he'd say, 'Yea, all right, you win, I hit, I hit.' That's all he wanted, to get me playing with him like that."

Manny also won over the players on the Triple-A team, including Thome, Byrd, and Sandy Alomar, Jr. With a sense of comedic timing, Manny could sometimes say one or two words that would bring down the house. "On the team bus he'd always make these perfect remarks," says Manuel. "After we won, we'd be on the bus to the airport or something, and Luis Isaac would have a few beers and then stand up and start telling all these funny jokes. Manny would wait till everyone got all quiet between jokes, and then he'd yell, 'Shut up, Luis! Sit down and have another beer.' And everyone would just crack up." Manny employed the same deadpan delivery to amuse Macaco after the first time Macaco saw him play minor league ball. Macaco and a few of Manny's neighborhood friends drove to Pawtucket when Manny was with Charlotte. Manny rewarded them with two homers.

After the game, the two embraced and Macaco asked Manny, "How are you feeling?" Macaco still giggles at Manny's response: "I don't like this league," Manny said, referring to Triple-A. "It's got too many old people in it." Because of his quick rise through the minors and because Triple-A is also where major leaguers recover from injuries, Manny, at twenty-one, was much younger than his teammates and opponents. But the experience and higher talent level did not slow his ascent. In 40 games with Charlotte, Manny hit .317 with 14 homers and 36 RBIs. His next stop was Cleveland.

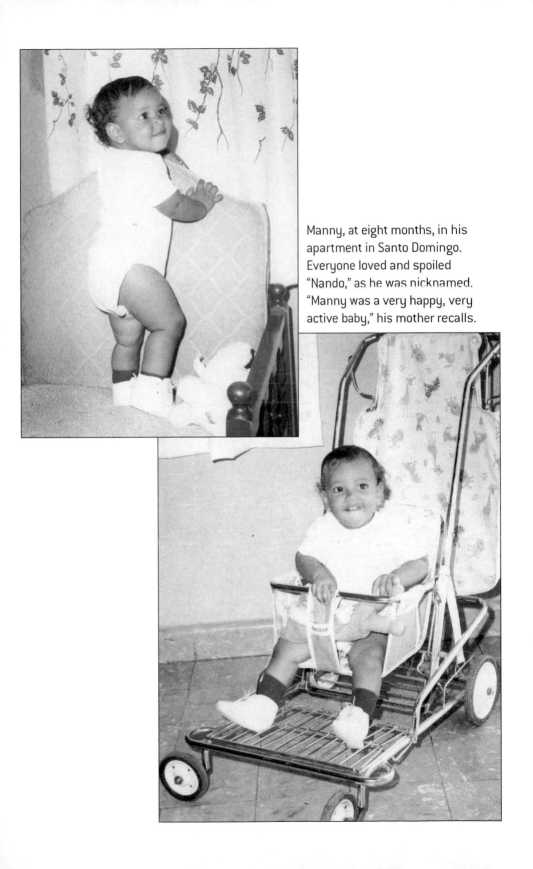

Manny, at eight months, in his apartment in Santo Domingo. Everyone loved and spoiled "Nando," as he was nicknamed. "Manny was a very happy, very active baby," his mother recalls.

By the time he was five, Manny, his three sisters, and his parents had moved into a new housing project in the El Brisal neighborhood of Santo Domingo. Although the decaying barracks now epitomize some of the most entrenched poverty in the Caribbean, it was, at the time, a symbol of upward mobility.

Manny, six, beside his paternal grandmother, Rosa Emiela Sanchez. Manny spent hours playing outside, often coming home only long enough for his favorite drink of orange juice and evaporated milk: *morir soñando* (to die dreaming).

A proud seven-year-old Manny, reading certificate in hand, poses at a second-grade literacy ceremony.

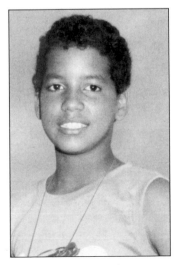

Manny, thirteen, attended New York's Eleanor Roosevelt Junior High School on 182nd Street before entering George Washington High School.

Manny, lower right, also played for the Brooklyn-based sandlot team, Youth Service League, where he met influential coach Mel Zitter. (Courtesy of Sherry Magee)

The YSL team had many strong players. Frank Rodriguez played in the major leagues with several clubs, and Jose Flores, Freddy Smith, and Trovin "Kiki" Valdez all played in the minors. *Bottom row (left to right):* Manny Ramirez, Freddy Ramos, Trovin Valdez, Carlos Puello, Nestor Cruz. *Second row:* Jose Flores, Warren Reid, Mel Zitter (coach), Ulises Velazquez, David Batista. *Third row:* Paul Rizzo, Freddy Smith, Carlos Sanchez, Unknown, Ed Aponte. *Top row:* Unknown, Frank Rodriguez, Unique Rencher, Joe Olivo.

Manny, left, seventeen, and his Youth Service League teammates twice
made it to the Connie Mack World Series Championships (CMWS)
in Farmington, New Mexico, where they stayed with host families.
(Courtesy of Sherry Magee)

Manny, eighteen, with his mother,
Onelcida. Manny slept on this sofa bed
throughout high school, waking before
sunrise for arduous runs through
upper Manhattan. Onelcida worked long
hours at a textile factory in New Jersey.

Manny, eighteen, stands in front of a
dresser in his apartment in Washington
Heights. Although Manny recalls passing
drug dealers on street corners as he
walked to high school, he and his friends
remained singularly focused on baseball.

Macaco, Julian Tavarez, and Manny in the Cleveland Indians clubhouse. Manny and Tavarez forged a deep friendship as they ascended the minors. Both were called up to Cleveland in 1991. "Teammates and friends are something different," says Manny, "but Julian is both." (Courtesy of Carlos "Macaco" Ferreira)

Manny, January 1995, outside his home in suburban Cleveland, where he lived with his expectant girlfriend, parents, grandmother, and his sister Clara and her baby. Manny worked out and devoured his mother's cooking during the off-season.

Manny met his wife Juliana shortly after his move to Boston. "I didn't know who he was," Juliana says. "In Brazil, none of my friends followed American baseball, and I wasn't somebody to sit around watching games on television. I had never heard of Manny Ramirez. But I just loved him." (Courtesy of Carlos "Macaco" Ferreira)

Manny, Sherry Magee, and Unique Rencher at Fenway Park in 2002. Manny grew close to Sherry in the early 1990s when she hosted Manny and Rencher in Aztec, New Mexico, during the CMWS. (Courtesy of Sherry Magee)

Manny and Macaco in Manny's Ritz-Carlton
penthouse before he was traded to the L.A. Dodgers.
"I go play the game, go home, that's it," says Manny.
"I don't read what people are writing about me, that's
not my style. I want people to like me for who I am,
not because I'm trying to be a person that I'm not."
(Courtesy of Jean Rhodes)

Macaco holds a baseball glove in the background, with Miguel Rodriguez and Jose Mateo
(nicknamed Peligro) in the foreground. Peligro Sports is a baseball institution in
Washington Heights. Owned by Manny's friend Jose Mateo, it is a meeting place for old
teammates to talk baseball and get behind-the-scenes reports from Macaco, who speaks
with Manny regularly and can be found at the store most days.
(Courtesy of Shawn Boburg)

CHAPTER 13

Welcome to Cleveland

The steady drone of the jet engines seemed to calm him. The fear and dread that had gripped him only moments before began to lift. It felt strange not to be with his Charlotte teammates for the semifinal series against the Richmond Braves.

Wearing jeans, black boots, a light-blue sports jacket, and a T-shirt with a gold chain around his neck, Manny waited for his plane to depart. As he sat in the plane, he replayed what had unfolded in the airport. "I just got a call from Cleveland," Manuel had confided. "They want you to play in Minneapolis tonight. You're going to the big leagues."

Manny was stunned. Manuel still remembers his immediate response: "Thank you. Thank you." And then sheepishly asking, "Coach, can you come with me?"

His 1993 totals (.333, 31 homers, 115 RBIs in Canton-Akron and Charlotte combined) had earned him a promotion and *Baseball America*'s Minor League Player of the Year Award. Still, there was debate about the wisdom of calling him up. Higher-ups believed he needed to improve fielding and base-running.

With less than an hour before the first pitch, Manny—delayed at the airport because the airline had lost his checked baggage—ran into Municipal Stadium. Still panting, he poked his head into the office of his new general manager, John Hart.

147

Minutes later, Manny had signed his first major league contract—nearly $20,000 for the remaining month of the season, a tenfold increase from what he had been earning the day before.

As Manny sat quietly watching the game in the dugout, teammates covertly affixed a large gum bubble to his brand new Indians cap. "Made me feel like part of the team," he told a *New York Times* reporter. Manny debuted the next day against the Minnesota Twins. The Twins' star center fielder, the late Hall of Famer Kirby Puckett, loaned Manny a glove for the series. "Here you go, rookie," he told Manny, handing him a glove after he heard about the lost luggage. He went 0 for 4 with three hard fly outs.

The very next day, he played at Yankee Stadium.

It was a storybook game. In front of a Dominican-flag-waving, Manny-chanting section in the left-field bleachers, Manny got the start. The owner of Peligro Sports, Jose Mateo, had reserved three hundred tickets, one hundred for each game during the three-game series, for Manny's fans in the neighborhood. The group picked up their tickets at the store that evening and walked to Yankee Stadium, just across the Harlem River. The section greeted every plate appearance with an uproar normally reserved for World Cup soccer. Fans wore Cleveland caps and held an oversized banner: "The Hit Man from Washington." They sang Dominican songs over the rattle and clang of guiras, tambora drums, and maracas. Macaco, who sat in the family section with Manny's parents and sisters, looked up at the section in wonderment.

Earlier that day, Manny had hung out in Washington Heights. His mother and sisters prepared themselves at the beauty salon, while he and his former teammates shared his traditional pregame meal of steak and fried plantains at Las Tres Marias. Local television cameras and reporters followed them around.

In his first at-bat, in the top of the second, he stroked a ground-rule double to left field off Melido Perez, the ball bouncing over the wall. Manny kept running until he reached third base. Coach Jeff Newman gently sent him back to second. His teammates laughed. When he scored, cameras caught some of them speaking to Manny and mimicking the umpire's signal for home run, reminding him what signal to look out for. In the sixth, Manny would see it after he ripped his first career big league homer off Perez to give Cleveland a 6–0 lead. Two innings later, he blasted a solo shot to left off Paul Gibson.

"It was great," Manny recalls. "All the guys from the neighborhood came. They saw me. I had my cheerleaders over there, all my friends."

The night was memorable for other reasons. Bob Ojeda pitched five innings for his first victory in the season. He had only recently come off the DL, having been severely injured in a March 22 boating accident that killed two relief pitchers, Steve Olin and Tim Crews. The tragedy still haunted the team. "We were all still in mourning well into that season," recalls manager Mike Hargrove. "We were all still trying to move on. In a way, Manny's arrival late that season helped lift us."

That night, after the game, Manny returned to Amsterdam Avenue, where a parade of hundreds had gathered along the sidewalks to catch a glimpse of their splendid slugger. The sonorous wave of "Manny" chants grew as he walked in front of the storefronts dressed in a suit, his mother at his side smiling broadly. "The whole neighborhood went crazy," Macaco says.

CHAPTER 14

1994: The Rookie

The 1989 movie *Major League* opens with a montage of the Indians' real-life misfortunes: their stunning Series sweep by the Giants in 1954, despite winning a league-best 111 games, followed by a demoralizing thirty-five-year losing streak served up by washed-up veterans playing in a decrepit, mostly vacant stadium. In the movie, the new owner tries to void her lease at Municipal Stadium by tamping out the remains of the team's dwindling fan base. It almost seemed like a good idea. Indeed, there may not have been a sorrier franchise in all of sports than the Indians when Manny arrived for his first full season in 1994.

In reality, a shrewd front office had started remaking the team in the late 1980s and early 1990s and saw Manny as one of their centerpieces. Hart and O'Dowd had cut several high-priced veterans in 1990, slashing the payroll to $8 million—a low figure back then, an unthinkable number today—and began locking young players into long-term contracts.

By 1990, pitcher Charles Nagy and outfielder Albert Belle had reached the majors. Infielder Carlos Baerga and catcher Sandy Alomar, Jr., came from San Diego in a blockbuster deal for Joe Carter. Jim Thome, a thirteenth-round draft pick, had also arrived. In December 1991, the Indians traded Willie Blair and outfielder Eddie Taubensee to the Astros for a little-known rookie outfielder named Kenny Lofton. In July 1992, they traded a minor leaguer to the Orioles for an erratic starting pitcher named Jose Mesa.

By spring of 1994, the Indians looked ready to contend. What was less clear was whether Manny would remain with the Tribe. Several club officials wanted Manny to start the year in Charlotte. At the end of the 1993 season, Hart had told Manny that the only thing that could hold him back was his defense. He sent Manny back to Las Aguilas in the Dominican Republic's winter league to work on his defense. But the off-season trip exposed Manny's lack of maturity and his occasional lapses in judgment.

Manny requested that Luis Valdez ship his beloved BMW to the Dominican Republic. When the car arrived in the port of Santo Domingo, Manny asked the Aguilas manager, Miguel Dilone, for a day off to pick up the car in Santo Domingo—a trip across the island that takes several hours. But when Manny arrived at the port, he was told he needed a document he had left in Santiago. The next day, in Santiago, he called Valdez to tell him about the problem. He also mentioned that he noticed while at the port that the car's radar detector had been stolen. "You need to get that car out of there as soon as possible," Valdez advised him, sending Manny into a spiral of anxiety.

"He panicked," Valdez said. "I thought he would just wait until he could borrow a friend's car again or take a bus on his next off day." Instead, as game time approached, Manny coaxed a driver at the stadium to hand him the keys to the "gringo bus," so-called because the small bus shuttled the team's American players between their hotel and the stadium. Manny told the driver he would pick up the players, but instead he picked up a friend and headed south across the island's fertile plains. As game time approached, the American players called the stadium to say no one had arrived. It didn't take long for the manager,

Dilone, to figure out that Manny was to blame. Manny got his car, but he created other problems.

"The team got pretty mad," Valdez says. Omar Ramirez, who was playing with Las Aguilas, remembers Manny walking into the clubhouse the next day before a playoff game as if nothing had happened. "It was like, 'Hey, I'm here.' He hadn't called the front office or the manager or anyone to tell them where he was. He disappeared. And then he just showed up. When the manager saw him in the clubhouse, he goes, 'No, I don't want you here.' Manny says, 'Oh, you don't want me here. Okay.' Manny didn't say anything else. He just turned around, went to his locker, grabbed his bag, and left." That was the end of Manny's season.

"At the time he didn't take the Dominican winter league seriously," Omar Ramirez says. "He didn't know about the Aguilas team, about its tradition. He didn't know Aguilas was about winning, winning, and winning. The fans don't accept finishing second. I mean, he made a lot of mistakes on the bases. Fans weren't happy about that. The fans expect so much from him." But Manny had formed a friendship with thirty-seven-year-old catcher Tony Peña, the team's leader who became a close friend of Manny's and, eventually, the godfather of his first son. Peña pushed Manny to concentrate on his weaknesses in Santiago, to some degree of success, before Manny's bus incident, leading Hart to sign him as a backup catcher in Cleveland.

Another relationship also sprang up that winter. Jogging in from the outfield during a game against the Tigres, Manny glimpsed a familiar face in the crowd of eighteen thousand. It was sixteen-year-old Celia, the younger sister of an old high school pal, Jose Lisaldo.

The seeds of their relationship had been secretly planted in Washington Heights, during Manny's brief respite before winter ball. After all, Manny had a serious girlfriend in Kathy Guzman. It was hardly risk-free on Celia's side: As the youngest, only daughter in a traditional Dominican family, she was guarded like a jewel by her three older brothers, including Jose. They expressly forbade friends like Manny from even speaking to her, screened her phone calls, read and discarded her mail, and took it upon themselves to discipline her if she so much as spoke to an older boy.

Manny understood these rules; he enforced the same with his own sisters, even though he was younger. Always, before inviting his friends up to the Washington Heights apartment, he dashed up the six floors to clear the deck. "Girls get in the bedroom," he commanded.

Celia's three older brothers were no less protective and were growing increasingly suspicious about her behavior. Celia's mother was also worried. What was happening to her girl? Celia now refused to speak Spanish at home; she talked back; she skipped school; she had been seen with older boys.

So Celia's mother did what many Caribbean parents do when they sense their child is straying—she sent Celia to live with relatives in Santiago. There, they reasoned, life would be simpler and safer.

Manny tried not to let Celia's presence in the stands distract him. Still, he couldn't help wondering what she was doing there, and occasionally smiled up at her. After the game, Manny bolted to the clubhouse. Before long they were trading phone numbers. When Guzman got wind of the relationship, she moved out of Manny's apartment, hastily shoving her belongings into black garbage bags as a tearful Onelcida begged her to stay.

Manny was eager to escape the drama he had created and, by spring, he had moved into a three-bedroom suburban Cleveland home with Onelcida, Clara, and Clara's two daughters, Kathy and Viannie. Macaco was also a frequent guest. The Indians found the house for Manny in North Olmstead, twelve miles west of the stadium. "It's different," Manny told *New York Times* reporter Ira Berkow. "But it is safe. I don't even lock the doors of my car. It is not like where I grew up, with the drugs and the shootings." And, of course, he had Macaco alongside him.

In spring training of 1994, Manny hit .370 with 3 homers in 21 games. Almost daily, he arrived early to work on his fielding. Charlie Manuel, to whom he had grown close while playing for Charlotte, had also joined the team as the hitting coach. He worked closely with Manny through hours of extra batting practice. Hargrove and Hart wanted him on the roster. When it became apparent that Manny had improved his defense enough to make the team, the Indians waived outfielder Ruben Amaro. Amaro didn't take umbrage. "That kid is going to be a great player," he told reporters. "He can swing the bat. Whether he's ready to play every day remains to be seen."

Hargrove announced Manny would play only three out of every four games and be replaced for defense in the late innings. Manny found a familiar niche for himself—raiding teammates' lockers, lingering around the edges of conversations, trying to fit in as best he could. His precocious ascension enabled him to occupy a familiar, comfortable role during the early part of his career—that of the mischievous youngster. "Everybody was Manny's uncle," explains Hargrove. "We all just looked out for him. He'd go around and borrow things from other guys, T-shirts, socks, but nobody would get mad—it was just Manny's way of goofing with people. Manny was ours, and we loved him."

He started the regular season hitting .429 with 8 RBIs in the first week, all from the ninth spot in the order. On April 11, he blasted two home runs against the California Angels in a 9–6 win. "We don't know who that masked man in right field was," Angels manager Buck Rodgers told the *Plain Dealer* afterward. "But we'll remember his name." Manny gave reporters a classic

Manny quotation after the game when they asked if he tended to hit homers in bunches. "I don't know," Manny said. "They just come out." He took extra batting practice, watched videos of pitchers, and discussed pitching strategies with his teammates.

Sometimes he even slept at the clubhouse, an arrangement that had less to do with his work ethic than his weariness with the cramped, day-care-center atmosphere at home. Within a few weeks, Manny left the townhouse to his family, moving to a nearby apartment complex, Fairview Village, into a unit owned by his terminally eccentric best friend Julian Tavarez. Manny had risen through the ranks with Tavarez, and the two remain best friends. "Teammates and friends are something different," Manny observes, "but Julian is both. I think he's a great guy."

They had first played together on the Canton-Akron Indians in 1993. Tavarez had progressed rapidly before debuting in Cleveland in 1993, about one month before Manny. The two men often stopped at Lozada's Restaurant for Mexican food on the way to the stadium and led each other into playful antics. On one occasion, they asked Sheldon Ocker of the *Akron Beacon Journal* if he could loan them $60,000 to buy a motorcycle. An amused Ocker checked his pockets and said he was "a little bit short." "How about $50,000?" replied a joking Manny. Years later Manny explained his logic to *L.A. Times* reporter, T. J. Simers, "I'm just playing around to keep everyone loose. When I was in Cleveland I asked a sportswriter if I could borrow $50,000 to buy a motorcycle. He wrote it like I was serious."

Manny also managed to forge a connection with Albert Belle. "Manny thought that Albert was the straw that stirred the camel's drink," recalls clubhouse assistant Frank Mancini, "and he was like a little boy around Albert." Indeed, Manny took note of Belle's every stretch, every protein shake, and every facet of his approach to the game. He also noted Belle's faith (Belle provided fans with his favorite passages of Leviticus alongside his autograph) and, notably, his aloofness with the press. But mostly, Manny was enamored of Belle's bat. "I watched his routine and tried to learn from it," Manny recalls.

Manny fell into a nasty slump in mid-May, his average dropping to .220. A few columnists called for him to be sent down. But he caught fire again and was named the AL Player of the Week by early June. "Where are all the people who kept telling us to send Manny down?" Hargrove asked the *Columbus Dispatch*. The Indians were 33–25 after fifty-eight games, ten games better than their record in 1993.

On June 17, Manny entered the clubhouse and, with a single, classic question, reduced his teammates to tears of laughter. The team was huddled around the NBA Finals, the New York Knicks against the Houston Rockets. Suddenly, game coverage was interrupted by a special report. Dozens of police cars were following O. J. Simpson down California's Interstate 405. Manny, when informed that the police were "chasing O.J.," asked innocently, "What did Chad do?" His reference was to Indians pitcher Chad Ogea.

But Manny also showed a limit to his sense of humor that season. During a series on the road at Yankee Stadium, the Indians held their annual hazing. The MLB fall ritual involves confiscating rookies' clothing and forcing them to don silly costumes from the ballpark to the airport to the hotel. As is most often the case, Cleveland dressed their rookies as busty prostitutes. Tavarez and three others begrudgingly obliged, boarding the bus outside Yankee Stadium in tight dresses, fishnet stockings, and high heels. But, as the jubilant players say idly in the bus outside the stadium, team personnel frantically searched for one last player. "Where's Manny? Where's Manny? Manny's nowhere to be found," Luis Valdez said to Onelcida, as they both waited near the bus. A nearly naked Manny had made a dash for the team gift shop where he was found purchasing a large team shirt. Tony

Peña still laughs about the episode. "When we found him, he said, 'I will not put on those clothes. If you make me put them on, I will not make the trip.' And that was that. The whole team had to wait in the bus while we found Manny's clothes and he put them on. And I look back on that and I think, that's Manny. He's always been the guy who does his own thing and that's it. He doesn't talk much, but when he has to, he's going to express his opinion. With Manny, nobody can say what he's going to do next."

But the team had plenty of other reasons to smile. They were in first place in mid-June, the latest they had topped the standings since 1974. The Indians were one game behind the Chicago White Sox when the season ended on August 11 because of the players' strike. Manny's final stat line in 290 at-bats: .269 batting average, 17 homers, and 60 RBIs. He finished second in American League Rookie of the Year voting to the Royals' designated hitter Bob Hamelin, who hit .282 with 24 homers and 65 RBIs.

Meanwhile, they had hatched a plan for Celia to join Manny in Cleveland, which was executed on a sunny September school day when a scared and defiant Celia boarded a flight to Cleveland. "But she's so young, she doesn't even know how to cook," her worried mother later objected to Manny over the phone. "It doesn't matter," Manny countered. "I love her. We'll eat at Taco Bell, we'll eat McDonald's."

Celia's appetite would soon be growing. By October she was pregnant with Manny's first son.

CHAPTER 15

1995: World Series Season

Manny and Celia returned to Washington Heights during the off-season. The neighborhood rallied around him. He had become a folk hero and a model of what was possible. Sales of Indians merchandise flew off the shelves at Peligro Sports. "Manny has made everyone here a Cleveland fan," the store's owner told the *New York Times*. But Indians coaches worried about drug dealers and gang violence. "You never know what can happen back there," Hart told the *New York Times*. "We believe in Manny as a person. And we feel he has a tremendous future, so we'd like to try to protect him the best we can."

Manny did, in fact, have an eventful off-season. New York City police arrested him for driving under the influence of alcohol. Manny was driving a friend back to her mother's apartment after taking her out for a birthday dinner at Jimmy's Bronx Café, next to Yankee Stadium. The left-turn signal on his Supra hadn't been working since he had commissioned work on the car's lights and stereo at a body shop in New Jersey. The car, with its darkly tinted windows and a spoiler, was an easy target in Washington Heights. The officer who stopped Manny said he smelled alcohol when Manny rolled down the window. In fact, Manny's blood alcohol turned out to be .07 percent, below the threshold for driving while intoxicated but high enough for him to be charged with driving while impaired.

Luis Valdez remembers getting a call early that morning to go downtown to pick up Ramirez, who found himself with fans in the lockup. "The guys in the cell, they recognized him. They said, 'Ah, Manny Ramirez, come sit over here,'" Valdez says. Not long after, Valdez said, he got several calls from a district attorney in the Bronx, who said he would love to introduce his son to Manny Ramirez. Convinced the meeting would help in court, Valdez urged Manny, "We gotta meet this guy. But of course, we never did. Manny was too shy."

Manny eventually paid a $250 fine and served five days of community service teaching baseball to kids on Long Island. But after the incident, which had been covered by the New York City press, Manny "went into hiding" from Indians executives who wanted to get the full story but could not get Manny to return their calls for about a week. John Hart turned to area scout Joe DeLuca, who called Manny's apartment and spoke with Evelyn.

"Joe, I don't know where Manny is," DeLuca remembers Evelyn saying.

"Evelyn, I just want you to know that John Hart is on his side, and I'm on his side and we're trying to help him. He's not in trouble at all. You talk to him and tell him that I want to speak with him," DeLuca responded.

"Can you hold on a minute?" Evelyn asked, before a sheepish Manny came to the phone. DeLuca told Manny not to worry but to call Hart. He did. Hart told Manny he was sending plane tickets for him to fly to Cleveland.

The incident, combined with the October 1993 murder of Roberto Ceballos, tapped into the Indians' worst fears about the dangers of having their young prodigy let loose on the streets of Washington Heights. And it would touch off another transition in Manny's life. At the Indians' behest, Manny, Celia, and his extended family returned to Cleveland. Manny worked out by morning and devoured his mother's cooking by day. He showed up to spring training with ten extra pounds of muscle. By 1995 the team had several Latino players on the roster, including Tony Peña, Carlos Baerga, Sandy Alomar, Jr., Jose Mesa, and, of course, Julian Tavarez, and Manny's comfort zone continued to expand.

His dependence on Macaco quickly grew stronger, as he cut ties to his old neighborhood. As the 1995 season commenced, he began calling Macaco every morning, a routine that would continue through Manny's time with the Red Sox. "Did you watch the game?" Manny would ask in Spanish. Macaco invariably had, and he awoke ready to impart some advice.

Manny also asked Macaco to visit him in Cleveland or to meet him on the road at every opportunity—which meant every other weekend, Macaco's only time off from work at the hospital.

"We really got close at that time," Macaco said. "It got to the point where I wasn't sure I was going to stay in Washington Heights or move to Cleveland. Every time I had a weekend off, I had to fly."

On and off the field, Manny still had his goofy moments, and the press loved them. In the opening series of the 1995 season, he left his paycheck in a boot underneath his locker in the Rangers' visitors' clubhouse. The Indians had to call a Texas clubhouse attendant to have someone pick it up and ship it to Manny. But Manny's performance at the plate during the season's first two months overshadowed his mental lapses. He began the season on fire and was named AL Player of the Month for May, hitting .394 with 11 homers and an .808 slugging percentage.

There were bumps along the way. In a May 19 game against the Red Sox—a game Manny would win with a home run in the ninth—Manny, standing at second, misjudged a blooper and stayed at second when it fell for a hit. Later in the inning, he was thrown out at home after misjudging yet another fly ball that fell in for a hit.

It certainly wasn't the last time Manny would err on the basepaths. On July 1, he was doubled off first base when he sprinted all the way past second on an obvious pop out. He made the same mistake later in the same game, resulting in another easy double play. Indians' coach Dave Nelson told the *Plain Dealer*, "I haven't seen anything like that in a while—not at all, actually, not from one guy in one ball game."

Regardless, Manny made the first of his twelve All-Star teams. Celia and the two-week-old Emanuel made their debut at the game. As Lyle Lovett crooned the national anthem, Manny smiled at his namesake. He had a beautiful girlfriend, a baby boy, and he was thriving in the majors.

A few days later, on July 16, he made the leap from All-Star to MVP candidate. In the bottom of the twelfth, he came to the plate against Oakland's legendary closer Dennis Eckersley. The A's were protecting a 4–3 lead. There were two outs, but Baerga was on first. Eckersley's first two pitches were strikes. Manny took a fastball outside—1-2. Eckersley threw a nasty breaking ball over the inside part of the plate; Manny pulled it foul into the dugout. Same thing on the next pitch. It remained 1-2. Another ball made it 2-2. Manny stepped out of the batter's box to calm himself. When Eckersley threw his next pitch—an inside fastball—Manny slammed it to the left-field bleachers. As Eckersley turned to watch the ball fly over the wall, cameras caught him mouthing "Wow!"

The Indians won 5–4, their thirteenth win in their final at-bat and their league-leading twenty-fourth comeback win. They led their division by fourteen games. The Indians cruised into the playoffs for the first time in forty-one years with a major-league-best 100–44 record. All told, Manny batted .308 (.402 OBP) with 31 homers and 107 RBIs.

Manny finished twelfth in the MVP voting. The Indians swept the Red Sox in the first round, but Manny went 0 for 12.

The local press turned against him. Taking his cue from Belle, Manny stopped talking to reporters. In Game 1 of the American League Championship Series, the Indians lost 3–2 to the Mariners. Manny went 1 for 4, raising his postseason average to .062.

Manuel, who'd been promoted from Triple-A manager to Indians hitting coach, encouraged Manny to open up his stance—that is, move his left leg slightly toward left field. The goal was to create a deeper bend in the knees. Whether it was the tinkering or the natural up-and-down progression of baseball, Manny exploded in Game 2. He went 4 for 4 with 2 homers in a 5–2 win behind starter Orel Hershiser. Manny also broke up a potential double play with a takeout slide at second base on a Paul Sorrento ground-out in the fifth, with the game still scoreless. Sorrento later scored on a two-run single. The game turned the series, which the Indians went on to win in six games.

In the World Series, they faced the Braves, the National League juggernaut that had lost the Series in 1991 and 1992. The Braves had the best starting rotation in baseball, led by Cy Young winner Greg Maddux, Tom Glavine, and John Smoltz. Although the Braves had more than enough talent hitting, it was billed as a test of the baseball cliché that good pitching beats good hitting. The cliché proved right. The Indians hit just .179 as a team against Atlanta, falling in six games. Manny hit his first World Series home run in Game 4, in a brief flash of his future postseason power. After the game, he gave the ball to Valdez. Manny finished the series 4 for 18 with 4 walks, his .222 average good for second among Cleveland's regulars. (Belle was 4 for 17.)

Said Baerga: "We've got to learn from our mistakes and be ready the next time we get here." Baerga wasn't the only one who thought there would be a next time. The Indians entered 1996 expecting to make the playoffs.

CHAPTER 16

1996: Great Expectations

Baerga's confidence was understandable. The 1996 Indians were loaded. The club re-signed Manny to a four-year, $10.15 million deal one year before he would have been eligible for arbitration. Securing Manny gave the Indians the best out-field in baseball: Speedy center fielder Kenny Lofton was coming off three consecutive seasons of batting at least .310 and stealing at least 54 bases; right fielder Belle had hit 50 homers and 50 doubles in 1995. The Indians also signed White Sox right-hander Jack McDowell to bolster an aging staff.

Manny arrived at spring training weighing 225 pounds, thirty pounds over his playing weight from the year before. Hart called Manny "the only red flag" on the team. Hargrove was also angry. "It fries me that he let four months of the off-season go by," the manager told the *Plain Dealer*. "He lifted weights, but he also didn't push himself away from the table."

Onelcida's cooking was irresistible to Manny. And it still is. To this day, she lives with and cooks for her son during long stretches each season. She also drives by his home to drop off dinners during the off-season. Her *caldo de gallina* (chicken noodle soup) is his comfort food. Back in 1996, Manny admitted, "I did nothing but eat and lift weights," and nicknamed himself "El Gordo," Spanish for "the fat man." But he promised to work it off before the season—and he did. After the team's morning workouts, Manny was ordered to ride a pink bike around the spring-training complex under the watch of Fernando Montes, the team's strength coach. Teammates and reporters mocked him for riding a girly bike. (When Manny arrived at spring training in shape in 1997, he said it was because he never wanted to ride the bike again.) By early March, Manny had shed half the extra pounds; Hart pronounced that the red flag had been lowered.

When the *Sports Illustrated* baseball preview hit newsstands on March 27, Manny was on the cover. But the next day brought some bad news for Manny. He accidentally struck a five-year-old boy with his car as he was pulling out of the Indians' spring-training complex. The boy suffered a broken pelvis. But police did not cite Manny. The boy was standing unattended where he wasn't supposed to be, while his parents clamored for auto-graphs. Manny sent a teddy bear and a get-well message to the boy in the hospital. But privately, Valdez was relieved that he had taken steps during the off-season to clean up the spotty driving record Manny had left in New York City—the kind of detail that had the potential to magnify the controversy. Manny had so many unpaid tickets in New York—seventeen—that offi-cials in Florida had blocked him from getting a Florida license in the off-season. Valdez appeared before a judge in the weeks before the accident, paying $1,700 in fines and clearing Manny to get his Florida license shortly before the accident.

The Indians moved into first place April 13 and never left. They were twenty games over .500 by June 13. But Manny con-tinued to have a hustling problem. The *Plain Dealer* wrote about Manny's tendency to stay in his outfield crouch and not even turn around if an opposing hitter smacked a homer. Hargrove said he didn't mind, but Wayne Kirby, Manny's backup, said he would always turn and hustle as "a courtesy to pitchers." In addi-tion, Manny had recently turned a 325-foot line drive into a single by not breaking hard out of the batter's box. He had assumed it was a home run.

On June 11, Manny displayed his best and worst. In a comeback 6–5 win over Oakland, he reached base five times and won the game with a sacrifice fly in the fourteenth. But in the eighth, he committed a major base-running gaffe. After drawing a one-out walk, Manny sprinted to third on a single by shortstop Omar Vizquel. The throw beat him easily, but he was safe when A's third baseman Jason Giambi dropped the ball. Lofton flied out to left, easily deep enough for Manny to tag and score. Manny tagged up and lollygagged home. But the A's left fielder, Phil Plantier, saw Vizquel trying for second, threw there, and gunned Vizquel down. Manny had been running to home so slowly that he didn't score before Vizquel had made the third out. "When that happens, you bite your tongue to stop from going berserk," Hargrove said to the *Plain Dealer* afterward.

But as usual, Manny offset his mental errors with staggering statistics and clutch hits. In fact, he had several huge at-bats as the Indians surged in September. He did it while occasionally batting fifth, a big step for Manny, who preferred the shelter of the sixth and seventh spots. One of the biggest at-bats came September 10. He came to the plate with two outs in the bottom of the ninth. The Tribe trailed the Angels 5–4. Pinch-runner Casey Candaele was on third, Julio Franco on second. Manny smashed a 429-foot homer to center off feared Angels closer Troy Percival to win the game. His teammates jumped up and down and pounded his head when he stepped on home plate. The Indians clinched their second straight division title one week later. Manny finished the season hitting .309 with 33 home runs and 112 RBIs. They faced the Orioles in the first round.

The Orioles crushed starter Nagy and the Indians 10–4 in Game 1 in Baltimore. Manny, batting sixth, went 3 for 4 with a home run—the only Indians player with more than one hit that day. The Orioles won the next day, too, 7–4. The winning pitcher, reliever Armando Benitez, mowed down the 5–6–7 spots of the Cleveland order with no outs and the bases loaded in the eighth. Benitez's clutch performance included striking out Manny, hitting sixth between Franco and Alomar, on a split-fingered fastball.

Staving off elimination, Cleveland rallied to win Game 3 by the score of 9–4 behind a Belle grand slam in the seventh; Manny also homered in the second. But the season ended one day later. The Indians lost the next game, 4–3, when the Orioles' Roberto Alomar—brother of the Indians' Sandy—homered in the top of the twelfth to break a 3–3 tie.

All things considered, it was a solid season for the Indians. Their 99–62 record was the best in baseball; they won the AL Central by 14.5 games. But after the World Series loss in 1995, Indians' fans—and players—had championship expectations. The entire organization was disappointed. It entered 1997 believing that anything less than a title would be a failure.

CHAPTER 17

1997: World Series Redux

Albert Belle signed with the White Sox for $55 million over five years, making him the highest-paid player in the majors. To fill the void, the Tribe signed third baseman Matt Williams and shipped Lofton to the Braves for right fielder David Justice and center fielder Marquis Grissom. While none of these players could match Belle at the plate, all three were defensive upgrades.

Manny came to camp in good shape; he bequeathed the pink bike to the hefty Kevin Mitchell, the 1989 MVP, who, now thirty-two years old, reported to spring training weighing 260 pounds. In his first ride around camp, Mitchell bent the front rim beyond repair while trying to pop a wheelie.

Belle's departure meant Manny would have to hit fourth or fifth in the new lineup. Initially, Manny resisted the change. "I like hitting sixth or seventh," he said during spring training. "That way, people forget about me." Manny prevailed, batting sixth in the opening-day lineup. Thome hit third, Williams hit cleanup, and Justice hit fifth.

Manny's baserunning blunders continued throughout the season. He blew a chance at the cycle on June 21—his second day batting cleanup—when he failed to hustle from the batter's box and turned an easy triple into a double. The next day, he stopped running on an attempted steal when he realized he was going to be out easily. Both gaffes occurred in Jacobs Field against the defending champion Yankees. "I don't have any idea what he was thinking," Hargrove told reporters. In a July 1 game at Houston, during the first season of interleague play, Manny gave up on a drive down the line, assuming the ball was foul. It wasn't. It bounced around the Astros' bullpen bench and the batter, Tim Bogar, sprinted to an inside-the-park home run.

But as usual, Manny was starting to hit. Between June 20, his first day in the cleanup spot, and July 6, he hit .436 with 4 homers and 16 RBIs. "I don't worry about batting cleanup any-more," he told reporters.

But the mistakes kept coming. On August 13, with the Indians trailing 13–2 in the eighth, Manny singled in a run to make it 13–3. With Thome at the plate, Manny stole second. Thome swung and missed, and the ball rolled a few feet from home plate. Thinking the ball had been fouled off, Manny headed back to first. The Tigers tagged him for the second out of the inning. Hargrove looked mystified.

In the next day's paper, columnist Terry Pluto of the *Akron Beacon Journal* suggested Manny needed "a brain transplant." Pluto added, "The guy has been in the majors for four years, and it's becoming obvious that if he hasn't figured out where first and second base are now on the diamond, he never will." The next day, Manny went 3 for 5 and hit his nineteenth home run, keying a 12–1 victory. After the game, he made a joke of the previous day's baserunning incident. "When I hit the homer," Manny said, laughing, "I was thinking about going back to first."

Manny also continued to get into trouble off the field with his reckless driving. In mid-August, police stopped his car and ticketed him for having tinted windows that were too dark and blaring music too loudly. As Manny said good-bye to the officer, he made an illegal U-turn and earned another ticket.

Still, Hargrove credited Manny's ability to stay carefree in situations that would unnerve other athletes. "Manny has the ability to put the past in the past and stay in the moment," the manager said. In fact, Hargrove was Manny's staunchest defender in 1997. He constantly reminded reporters of Manny's stats, often rattling them off from memory. He told the press how Manny was the only hitter he gave the green light to on a 3-0 count, knowing Manny wouldn't take it as an invitation to swing at bad pitches.

His teammates were also protective. "He's a young guy," Alomar told Steve Herrick of *The Sporting News*. "He learned how to play baseball in the big leagues. Not many guys make it to the big leagues when they're twenty-two or twenty-three. He was learning how to play up here. That's a lot of pressure." And, while his approach might have seemed lackadaisical to others, Hargrove casts it in a more positive light, "I think he cared too much," he says. "Early on, there were times he'd make plays in the outfield and fans thought he wasn't hustling. I go and look at those tapes now and I realize that he cared so much about what people thought of him that he didn't want to look foolish in front of them. So he wouldn't lay out because he didn't want to make a mistake. But, over time, I think he got beyond that."

There was also growing pressure on the home front. Midway through the 1997 season, Manny's mother called Macaco, summoning him to Cleveland. Manny had gone AWOL for a week, she cried, not even calling to tell them where he was. Celia and his parents knew he was in town, however, because they could see him on television each night. As Macaco recalls, "I went to the stadium and he ran up to me and gave me a hug and said 'Macaco! Who told you to come to Cleveland?' and I said, 'No, forget that. Tell me what happened.' He said the wife of another player told Celia something, gossip, you know. They get together and talk too much. He told me he didn't want to go to the house, didn't want to live with her anymore. I told him, 'Okay. We'll talk about this after the game.'" "Macaco," Manny said, before returning to the basement weight room, "you're the only one who listens to me." After the game they sat in the living room with his mother, and Macaco said to Manny, "'Listen, if you don't want to be with Celia, then sleep in the living room or on the floor, but promise me you won't do that to your mother again.'" As Onelcida listened, wiping tears from the corner of her eyes, she managed a smile.

Despite any domestic turmoil, Manny ended up hitting .328—a career high, good for fifth in the AL—with 26 homers and 88 RBIs. The power numbers were not extraordinary. Not until 2007 would he have another season with fewer than 33 homers and 102 RBIs. But Manny actually had an outstanding season by Sabermetric measures. His on-base percentage of .415 was sixth in the AL; his OPS of .953 ranked seventh.

Cleveland finished with an 86–75 mark. It was their worst record in the past three seasons, but it was still good enough to win the AL Central by six games. They faced the Yankees—who won the wild card with a 96–66 mark—in the first round.

The series had special significance to Manny because he was playing against his hometown team, and he knew his performance would be closely watched by friends in Washington Heights. But Manny again started cold, going 2 for 9 with 1 RBI as the teams split the first two games. The Yankees won Game 3. In Game 4, they were four outs away from winning the series. Their All-Star closer, Mariano Rivera, took the mound to protect a 3–2 lead with one out in the bottom of the eighth. He got Williams to fly out. Alomar was up next. He took the first two pitches for balls, then lined Rivera's next pitch just over the right-field wall to tie the game. The Tribe won in the bottom of the ninth when Vizquel singled in Grissom, who led off the inning with a single and was bunted to second by second baseman Bip Roberts. Thanks to Vizquel's heroics, the series was tied 2–2, setting up a do-or-die Game 5 in Cleveland.

Manny's drought continued as he entered Game 5 at 2 for 17.

He grounded out in his first at-bat against Andy Pettitte, but with two outs in the bottom of the third, Manny came up with runners on second and third. The game was scoreless at that point, with Indians starter Jaret Wright matching Pettitte's zeros on the scoreboard.

All series long, the Yankees had been busting Manny inside. And it was working, even though Manny knew the inside pitches were coming. Again, Manny waited on an inside pitch. But this time, he drilled it, ripping Pettitte's cut fastball over the head of Yankee center fielder Bernie Williams. Grissom and Vizquel scored and the Indians took a 2–0 lead. The hit would become critical to the Indians' 4–3 series-winning victory. "I didn't want to see happen what happened last year when we didn't get past the first series," Manny told reporters after the game.

So the Indians moved on to a playoff rematch with the Orioles. After getting shut out in Game 1, the Indians went on to win the series 4–2.

The team returned to the World Series for the second time in three years. This time, their opponent was the Florida Marlins.

The teams split the first two games at Dolphin Stadium in Florida. The Marlins pounded Hershiser in Game 1, and the Tribe returned the favor against Marlins ace Kevin Brown in Game 2. In the two games, Manny was 1 for 8. Florida took a 2–1 series lead with a 14–11 win in Cleveland in Game 3. Manny went 1 for 5 with an RBI; his lone hit—a slow roller to third— gave the Indians a 5–3 lead in the fourth. The game was tied 7–7 after eight until the Marlins blew it open with a seven-run ninth.

It was snowing in Cleveland for Game 4. Wearing his red stockings up to his knees, in a trend Thome had started, Manny mashed a one-out, two-run homer in the bottom of the first against Marlins lefty Tony Saunders. "That set the tone for the evening," said Matt Williams. Indeed, Saunders was a disaster that night, yielding six earned runs in two innings of work. The Indians won 10–3. Manny's first-inning blast was his only hit. His average for the series now sat at .176 (3 for 14).

His slump continued into Game 5, another 1-for-5 effort and the Marlins prevailed 8–7.

Facing elimination in Game 6 in Miami, the Indians' pitchers stepped up. Ogea held the Marlins to one run over five innings and the Indians won 4–1.

In Game 7, Wright, the winner of Game 4, took the mound for the Indians; Al Leiter, who got shelled in Game 3, took the mound for the Marlins. Both pitched well. Wright left the game with one out in the seventh and a 2–1 lead. It remained 2–1 Indians until the bottom of the ninth, but the Marlins managed to stay alive. The game entered extra innings, tied 2–2.

Manny, 4 for 25 in the Series, struck out swinging in the tenth. It would be the last World Series at-bat for Manny until 2004.

The game remained tied 2–2 until the Marlins scored in the bottom of the eleventh.

It was an incredibly frustrating Series for the Indians. They held leads in all seven games, but could not muster enough offense to overcome the Marlins, a club that had been in existence for only five years. It was also the last time the Indians made it to the World Series.

CHAPTER 18

1998 and 1999: Two Years of Near-Playoff Runs

The 1998 season was a tumultuous one for Manny, at least outside the batter's box. Unsatisfied with his agents, he left Jaime Torres and Luis Valdez for good. He also began showing signs of frustration in the clubhouse. After a spring-training game against the Tampa Bay Devil Rays, in which Manny was lectured by Hargrove for lack of hustle in the outfield, Manny slapped Indians' clubhouse attendant Tom Foster. The dispute started when Manny swiped two bats from the equipment room, where players were forbidden to go. Manny was trying to give the bats to Marcus Giles, a minor leaguer and younger brother of teammate Brian Giles. Foster berated Manny, adding an insult "questioning his intelligence," Hargrove later told the *Plain Dealer*. The Indians dealt with the matter internally. Hargrove played down the incident, saying the team didn't want to turn a "molehill into a mountain."

Then there was Manny's home life. He and Celia broke up, with Celia and Emanuel moving to a new home in Pembroke Pines, Florida. Manny moved, too. He lived in a modest unit in Westlake, Ohio. With its small living and eating area and two bedrooms, the second-floor walk-up was nice but hardly extravagant. The unit was furnished with rental couches and a bed, and dominated by a sixty-inch television in front of which Manny diligently analyzed game videos.

Once again, he managed to pull a caring father figure into his orbit: This time, it was a then-seventy-three-year-old former varsity football coach and teacher who lived in the unit below. Bill Quayle introduced himself to Manny one morning in their shared garage space, issuing an impromptu invitation for breakfast. For the next couple of years, Rose Quayle cooked up big platters of bacon and eggs for Bill and Manny, who sat at the table discussing sports. Bill showed Manny the medals he had earned as a B-24 bombardier in World War II. Quayle also had a trove of Indians artifacts, including autographs from the legendary slugger Rocky Colavito. Quayle told Manny about the demoralizing 1954 World Series—the last one the Indians had appeared in before 1995. Manny heard Bill describe Willie Mays's infamous over-the-shoulder catch in Game 1.

Manny also joined the couple for occasional steak dinners. And sometimes Rose walked up to the second floor with a fresh batch of homemade cookies. "I make a pretty good sugar cookie. And oatmeal raisin, and peanut butter. I'd take a plate up to him that had all three kinds," she remembers. To childless Rose, Manny was the perfect surrogate son. And mother him she did, taking his car in for repairs and occasionally lending an ear when he wanted to sit and talk. Mostly, however, Manny was drawn to Bill: his stories, his warmth, and his advice.

At the plate, Manny established himself as a premiere power hitter, and a key to the Indians' playoff hopes. The Indians went 18–10 in May and were ten games up in the AL Central by early June. Jaret Wright and Bartolo Colon gave the Indians two young arms in the rotation. Along with Charles Nagy and Dave Burba, the Indians had four starters who would each give the team at least 190 innings. The fifth starter was the thirty-three-year-old Dwight Gooden, who also had a solid season, pitching 136 innings with an 8–6 record and a 3.76 ERA.

The Indians puttered along in July and August, going 29–27 but holding a steady lead in the Central. The highlight was a seventeen-inning victory over the Mariners on July 30. The game lasted nearly five and a half hours. Manny put the Tribe ahead for good with a three-run homer off Bob Wells in the top of the seventeenth, breaking a 6–6 tie that had lasted since the twelfth inning. The Indians moved to 62–45, 11.5 games ahead of the Twins in the Central.

On September 15, Manny began the greatest power streak of his career. He hit three home runs in a home game against the Blue Jays to reach 40 for the season. Hargrove called him an MVP candidate. The next day, Manny hit a home run in his first at-bat against Minnesota, giving him homers in four straight at-bats, tying a major league record. He homered again in the fifth inning of the 8–6 win, making it five homers in two games, also a record held by twenty other major league players. The win clinched the fourth straight division title for the Indians, upping their record to 84–66 and giving them a 12.5-game lead over the White Sox.

Manny homered again the next day, becoming the first player to slam six in three games since the Phillies' Mike Schmidt in 1976. He went homerless in his next game before slamming two more in a loss against Kansas City. That made eight round-trippers in five games. Manny now had 45 homers and 141 RBIs. Manny refused to analyze what was happening. "I don't know how I'm doing it," he told reporters. "I'm staying the same, looking for the ball, and it's jumping off my bat."

He finished the season with 45 homers and 145 RBIs, both fourth-best in the AL. His .599 slugging percentage, a career best at that point, was also fourth-best in the league. However, his .377 OBP was the lowest since his rookie year and is the lowest for his career as of 2008. Great as his season was, he had room to improve. But his progress was undeniable.

"The goofy things that used to happen to Manny on the field all but stopped this year," *Plain Dealer* columnist Paul Hoynes wrote. "Umpires no longer had to tell him to take first base on ball four or to go back to the dugout on strike three. He has played a Gold Glove right field and run the bases without major incident."

It was perhaps indicative of Manny's reputation for brain cramps among the writers that one complimented him for not being picked off since the All-Star break. Manny partially credited his work with Charlie Maher, the team psychologist, who continued to preach staying in the moment and blocking out larger worries.

No one would mistake Charlie Maher, the rumpled, fifty-nine-year-old psychology professor, for a Zen master. Yet his Brooklyn-inflected pearls of wisdom have a Buddhist ring. "Don't attempt to control your thoughts," the Indians' team psychologist reminds players. "Just notice them, and change the dial."

Manny couldn't resist this logic. Nor was he immune to the Zitterlike charms of this gruff, middle-aged Jewish man. "Sometimes I'm going to be a little anxious," he had Manny repeat to himself, "but I'm just going to watch that, and let it go." Over time, this logic steered Manny's "no worries" worldview into a powerful, consistent philosophy that sets him apart from most other players.

Maher is that baggy breed of eccentric far more common in academia than corporate offices. His long-winded emails, invariably sent between 2:00 A.M. and 5:00 A.M., seem lofty and esoteric to the BlackBerry set. For years, Maher worked with emotionally disturbed students in urban public schools. At each level of his career ladder—first as a teacher, then as a school counselor, assistant school superintendent, and organizational psychologist—Maher gained new vantage points for understanding troubled students. Over time, he formulated innovative ways to address students' needs. Students' "Individualized Development Plans" (IDPs), he argued, must be situated within the broader context of school and family systems.

Maher's career in sports psychology was launched by chance in the mid-1980s. A White Sox bullpen coach happened to be assigned one of his articles while working on a master's degree in psychology. On a whim, the coach picked up the phone and caught Maher in his office. They began talking baseball—Maher had coached local high school and college teams—and played with how the IDP approach might be applied to player development. By the end of the conversation, Maher had been hired to consult with White Sox players and management.

When Mark Shapiro, who was in charge of the Indians' minor league operations at the time, got wind of the White Sox' secret weapon, he wooed Maher to Cleveland. Since then, Maher has been plying his trade in Cleveland. From Rookie League onward, managers are charged with maintaining IDPs, which efficiently communicate a player's physical, fundamental, and mental performance. In theory, a player must redress all limitations before moving up in rank.

Of course, if a player is off the charts in one area, as Manny proved to be, he skips a grade or two. Maher didn't need an IDP to know where Manny needed to improve. "My focus was on two things," Maher says. "His development as a person, not in terms of clinical problems, but in terms of his strengths. And two, his performance. This is what I tell all young players: 'Look, if you want to be a big league performer, you've got to be a big league person, too.'"

Manny was also, according to Maher, a victim of a Cleveland

press that cast him as an ethnic stereotype: "When he came in he was—like many Latin-American players, very quiet, laid-back. And as a result, sometimes there's an interpretation made that they don't care, they're not engaged, not really 'with it.' He had that stereotype. He comes across as not caring, as everything is 'nice and easy.' And, to a certain extent, that's how he is cultur-ally. But people interpret it as laziness. Obviously he had talent, he had natural talent. In fact, I'll go so far as to say he's the best right-handed hitter I'd ever seen. But he actually cares a hell of lot. In fact, I'll use the term 'overcaring.' He wanted to do a lot; he wanted to do really well. And I needed to work with him to slow his mind down, slow his game down."

Indeed, long before Manny met Maher, even before he was a teenager, his friends in the Dominican Republic had given Manny the nickname Pancho, which means "calm" or "unruf-fled." Although Maher's calming, mindful approach shares much with Eastern philosophy, Maher's approach to working with players, Acceptance Commitment Therapy (ACT), draws on a rich literature in cognitive psychology. Cognitive psychologists focus on the way we think, analyzing the internal conversations we have with ourselves and how they shape our behavior. The basic premise behind cognitive psychology is, to quote Hamlet, "There is nothing either good or bad but thinking makes it so."

In other words, verbal processes can set us free or entrap us in negative self-evaluations. Unlike other cognitive approaches, the ACT approach isn't set on changing how people think about their experiences. Rather, the goal is simply to recognize these internal conversations for what they are—thoughts—instead of binding realities. In doing so, we distance ourselves from the thoughts and disrupt their negative effects on behavior.

Maher's approach encourages players to acknowledge their thoughts but then to keep on moving. Although logical, this approach is more difficult than it seems. One of life's most frustrating paradoxes is that its most vital features—falling asleep, urinating, even sexually climaxing—occur most freely when we relax our forceful effort and let our natural processes unfold. The same holds true of Maher's approach. It is only when we can relax enough to simply notice and accept our thoughts that we can untether ourselves from their punishing consequences.

This approach appealed to Manny on an intuitive level. "A game is ultimately about having fun," says Manny, "not for you having so much pressure." In contrast to tightly wound players who smash down their helmets in frustration, Manny's worldview enables him to approach his performance with a Zen master's sense of detachment. This approach gained momentum during his years with the Indians. After meeting with Maher, Manny commissioned red T-shirts with "Indians" on the front and "Baseball Is a Mind Game" on the back.

In the first round of the playoffs, the Indians, who finished 89–73, faced the wild card team, the Red Sox, who finished 92–70 but still lost the AL East to the Yankees (114–48) by twenty-two games.

Manny was a monster at the plate. He crushed two home runs in Game 3, sparking the Indians to a pivotal 4–3 win in Boston and helping the Tribe take a 2–1 lead in the series. His second homer was a solo blast off Eckersley in the ninth that extended the Indians' lead to 4–1—an insurance run they'd need when their bullpen allowed two runs in the bottom half of the inning. This home run raised Manny's series average to .500 and his OPS to a staggering 1.915. Manny went 0 for 4 in Cleveland's series-clinching win in Game 4, but still finished with a .357 average and 1.400 OPS for the series. Thus the Indians advanced to the ALCS, giving Manny the chance to face his hometown Yankees in the playoffs for the second time in two years. The Yankees had swept the Rangers in the ALDS.

In Game 1, the Yankees lit up Wright for five runs in the top of the first. Yankees starter David Wells shut out the Indians for eight innings. Manny (2 for 4 that day) hit a one-out two-run home run in the ninth, before Yankees reliever Jeff Nelson retired third baseman Travis Fryman and Jim Thome to seal the Yankees' 7–2 victory. Game 2 went to the Indians, tying the series 1–1 and sending the teams back to Cleveland.

The Indians sent the young Bartolo Colon out for Game 3 against the Yankees. The game turned out to be, arguably, the high point of Colon's career. He pitched a complete game, holding the Yankees to one run—a Bernie Williams RBI single in the first inning, driving in Chuck Knoblauch, who had led off the game with a single.

The Yankees starter was Andy Pettitte, whose performance belied his reputation as a clutch player. The Indians scored six runs—two in the second, four in the fifth—en route to their 6–1 victory. Manny went 3 for 4, lifting his series average to .417 (5 for 12) and his OPS to 1.500. With the Indians leading 2–1 in the fifth, Manny belted a solo shot. All of a sudden, the 114-win Yankees trailed 2–1 in the series.

Game 4 pitted Gooden against Cuban defector Orlando "El Duque" Hernandez. Gooden was no match for Hernandez, who pitched seven shutout innings. The series was tied 2–2, heading for the final game in Cleveland. Manny had gone 0 for 3—three strikeouts—with a walk.

Yankees pitching reigned supreme again in Game 5, with the team winning 5–3 behind Wells and Rivera.

So, the series returned to Yankee Stadium for Game 6. The pitching match-up was David Cone against Nagy—the two starters who had pitched well in Game 2. But Nagy simply didn't have it. The Yankees pounced for six runs in the first three innings. The Indians rallied for five runs in the fifth to close the lead to 6–5, but the Yankees extended the lead to 9–5 with three runs in the sixth. Yankee relievers combined for four shutout innings in relief to preserve a 9–5 victory.

Though Manny was not charged with an error in the Yankees' key sixth-inning rally, it was arguably one of his miscues that helped the Yankees seal the game—and the series. With runners on first and second, shortstop Derek Jeter came to the plate. Jeter ripped one to right-center. Manny sprinted to the wall, as if he were going to attempt a warning-track leap. But the ball landed at the base of the wall. Manny actually hadn't needed to jump at all.

"I took a peek at the ball and ran right toward the wall," Manny told reporters. "I saw the ball. I didn't think it was going out, but I thought it was going to the wall. I turned and saw it hit. I was surprised where it landed."

Manny wound up with good numbers for the series: a .333 average (7 for 21) with 2 home runs and 4 RBIs, not to mention a 1.090 OPS. But his MVP-caliber offensive numbers made his fielding gaffes at clutch moments all the more glaring. A solid defensive right fielder might have caught Jeter's ball and kept the Indians in the game and the series. No one was blaming Manny for the Indians' loss, but baseball analysts pointed out that a great all-around outfielder would never have misread the defense in a big postseason moment.

The Yankees went on to sweep an overmatched San Diego Padres team in the World Series, cementing their status as arguably the greatest single-season team ever. The Yankees were primed to win two more championships in 1999 and 2000—the last two years of Manny's contract with Cleveland.

In spring training 1999, the Indians wore shorts with the slogan "100 +: Go hard or go home," a reference to the team's goal of winning more than one hundred regular-season games and reaching the World Series. Manny, gearing up for his contract drive, hit .337 with 7 homers and 30 RBIs in his first twenty-two games. He earned Player of the Month honors and *USA Today* called him "a complete player" in a May sports section profile.

The profile focused on how hard Manny worked on his defense in spring training. But whether Manny had truly become a better defensive player was, in reality, questionable. His range factor—the measure of how many put-outs a defensive player makes per game—marked him as at league average or below. And his defensive miscues continued. On May 7, Manny dropped two routine fly balls against Tampa Bay, including one where it appeared he tried to catch the ball without looking at it. The ball glanced off his glove and two runs scored on the play. The Indians rallied to win the game 20–11.

The Indians joked about the drops the next day. When Manny showed up at his locker, he found a new glove—actually two gloves laced together for extra range. That kind of humor is possible on a winning team, and the Indians were winning. The 20–11 victory upped their record to 20–8, good for a 5.5-game lead in the Central.

By mid-May, the media speculated whether Manny, with 53 RBIs after thirty-eight games, could break Hack Wilson's 1930 record of 191 RBIs in a season. The Indians were threatening to be the first team to score one thousand runs since the 1950 Red Sox.

The only trouble spot for Manny came on June 20, when a pitch from his old YSL teammate, Seattle righty Frankie Rodriguez, hit Manny's left hand. Manny left the game and missed the next six, slowing his RBI pace, at 79 after fifty-six games. Still, Manny returned strongly and reached 96 RBIs (batting .333 with 25 home runs) by the All-Star break, at which point the Indians were 56–31, 13 games up on the White Sox in the Central. Manny addressed his contract status directly for the first time September 8 when he told reporters, "I want to stay in Cleveland. I think it's the best place to play. I don't know what kind of offer they'll make. We'll just have to wait and see."

He finished with 165 RBIs, tied for thirteenth all-time with Lou Gehrig, Al Simmons, and Sam Thompson, a nineteenth-century player. No player had hit that many RBIs since Jimmie Foxx in 1938, and no one has passed that mark since. Sosa batted in 160 runs in 2001 and Alex Rodriguez drove in 156 in 2007. After the season, Manny received the AL's Hank Aaron Award as the league's outstanding hitter.

With the Indians (97–65) winning the Central by 21.5 games over the White Sox, there was an argument for Manny as MVP. He led the league with a .663 slugging percentage and was second with a .442 on-base percentage; his 1.105 OPS led the AL as well. Then there were his old-school stats: His .333 average ranked fifth, his 131 runs ranked fourth, his 44 home runs ranked third, and his RBIs led the league. Yet Manny finished third in the AL MVP voting, tied with his first-year teammate, second baseman Roberto Alomar. Rangers' catcher Ivan Rodriguez won the award, edging Red Sox starter Pedro Martinez.

Rodriguez slammed 35 homers and drove in 113 runs, both career highs, but he walked only 24 times and finished with a .356 on-base percentage—more than eighty points lower than Manny. Martinez, for his part, had a historic season, going 23–4 with a 2.07 ERA that was almost exactly three runs below the league average. He struck out 313 batters in 213 1/3 innings. He led the league in wins, ERA, strikeouts, and strikeouts per inning, and allowed the fewest base runners per inning (walks plus hits per innings pitched, or WHIP). Still, Rodriguez won the MVP, in part because of his ability to gun down would-be base stealers—and because two sportswriters left Martinez off their ballots altogether, arguing pitchers were undeserving of the MVP award. Interestingly, Manny would have the chance to face Martinez in the ALDS. The Red Sox (94–68) had won the wild card once again, finishing four games behind the Yankees.

The Indians prevailed 3–2 in Game 1 and took Game 2 with ease, 11–1 on a day that had little to do with Manny. He went 0 for 4 with a walk, scoring on Thome's fourth-inning grand slam. After two games, Manny was batting .000 in the series. He remained hitless in Game 3, too, going 0 for 5 in the Red Sox' 9–3 victory in Fenway Park. For Game 4 at Fenway, the Indians sent Colon out on three days' rest to try to avoid a do-or-die Game 5 at Jacobs Field. But Colon didn't deliver. He gave up seven runs in the first two innings. After five innings, the Red Sox led 18–6. They went on to win 23–7. Manny went 0 for 3. After four games, he was still batting .000 for the series. He was 0 for 15 with seven strikeouts.

Manny would finally end his drought with a double in Game 5, but the Indians fell short of their preseason goal of returning to the World Series.

All told, Manny was 1 for 18 in the series, a .056 average. It was the second straight year he had ended the playoffs on a disappointing note, given his fielding mistake in 1998 against the Yankees. But the prevailing question for many baseball fans was whether the postseason performances would diminish Manny's value on the open market. In one more season, the baseball world would get its answer.

CHAPTER 19

2000: Last Season in Cleveland

Hargrove had led the Indians to five consecutive postseason appearances, but no championships. Hart fired Hargrove and replaced him with Charlie Manuel. Hargrove's wasn't the only transition Hart had to handle. Manny was also history after the 2000 season. Everyone knew it, but no one could admit it. Manuel saw Manny's price jumping and almost begged him to stay. "I need you, son," he told Manny through the *Plain Dealer*'s Paul Hoynes. "Take care of Daddy. Stay in Cleveland." Hart, however, had already begun to manage his fans' expectations. "Clubs have different agendas," he told Hoynes. "The Yankees are going to have three guys with double-digit salaries. The Dodgers have two guys at $15 million per year." The message was clear. We are not the Yankees or the Dodgers. Be prepared to lose Manny.

Meanwhile, the Indians ownership board approved the $323 million sale of the team to Larry Dolan, an attorney who had built his wealth on stock in his brother's company—Cablevision. It was unclear what the deal meant for the team's financial future, and it cast more uncertainty over re-signing Manny.

Manny's contract was the lead story of spring training. Hart said to Hoynes, "We're prepared to make Manny the highest-paid Indian, but we can't do something ridiculous." In his public statements, Hart put the onus on Manny to wrest control of negotiation from his agent, Jeffrey Moorad, who Hart insisted had no desire to get for Manny anything other than the most lucrative deal, as opposed to a "creative" solution that could keep him in Cleveland.

Not surprisingly, talks broke down for the next month and a half. During this time, the Indians got off to a so-so start. A six-game losing streak dropped their record to 34–30 on June 17, 7.5 games behind the White Sox in the Central. The team struggled with injuries. Wright and Nagy started only twenty games combined. Lofton, Richie Sexson, and Sandy Alomar all missed major chunks of the season.

Manny joined the crowd on the disabled list on May 31, two days after straining his hamstring while running out a ground ball in a May 29 loss to the Angels (which dropped the Indians to 25–22). At the time, Manny was hitting .322 with 13 homers and a team-leading 47 RBIs.

Team doctors said Manny might be able to play again in a week. It didn't happen, and the fallout from the two-month recovery process hurt Manny badly in the press. Initially, there was no rush, despite the team's slow start; the Tribe had won nine of its first eleven without Manny to reach 34–24 and close within two games of the White Sox.

Then the six-game losing streak began. It coincided with Manny's reinjuring the hamstring on his rehab assignment in Double-A. Manny wound up missing all of June. By July 4, the Indians were 42–39 and trailed the White Sox by ten games.

Hart was not sympathetic. "If Manny isn't going to come back until he wants to, we've got to get another piece," he told the *Plain Dealer* on July 4, apropos of the July 31 trade deadline. Hart vented again a few days later. "Manny's killing us by not being in the lineup," he said in the July 7 *Plain Dealer*. "It has put pressure on everybody else."

Manny and Hart met later that week and Manny agreed to rehab with the Triple-A Buffalo Bisons. Manny finally rejoined the club as a designated hitter July 13, blasting a homer in a 4–3 win over Pittsburgh. The crowd gave him a loud ovation when he left for a pinch-runner in the eighth. He remained hot, hitting four more homers in the next seven games as the deadline approached.

On July 25, Moorad revealed he wanted an escalator clause in Manny's deal that would increase his salary any time a free agent signed for more money than Manny. The media reported the Indians were discussing Manny trades with the A's, Mets, and Rockies. Fans were getting worried. A group started a website called keepmanny.com even as others worried the Indians would raise ticket prices to generate Manny money.

On July 27, the Indians offered a five-year, $75 million deal, of which $25 million would be paid out in small increments until 2025, but Moorad declined. The deferred money was a deal-breaker. "I guess the Indians can say they offered Manny $15 million a year over the next five years," he said sarcastically to Hoynes. "But you have to say the real value of the proposal is impacted dramatically by the deferred money."

On the field, Manny reinjured his hamstring August 5 in a home-plate collision against Anaheim. He was still out one week later. By that point, he had missed forty-three of the Tribe's last sixty-four games. In the twenty-one games he did play, he hit .355 with 11 homers and 26 RBIs.

Manny played nearly every day after mid-August. But the Indians sputtered and never got within six games of first until the last week of the season. They played their final home game October 1, and the fans knew it might be their last chance to cheer Manny. The crowd of 42,594 gave him a standing ovation when he stepped into the batter's box in the bottom of the seventh against the Blue Jays' John Frascatore. On the second pitch of the at-bat, Manny smashed a 452-foot home run into the center-field picnic area. He leaped out of the dugout for a curtain call, and the fans chanted his name in both the eighth and ninth innings as he stood in right field.

The homer capped a dominant season obscured by the injuries and hand-wringing over his free agency. He set career highs with a .351 batting average, .457 on-base percentage, and .697 slugging percentage—best in the American League. For the second year in a row, only Todd Helton in the National League had a higher OPS than Manny's 1.154. Manny also homered 38 times and had 122 RBIs in 118 games. Moreover, the Indians, while missing the playoffs for the first time since 1994, finished a respectable 90–72, five games behind the White Sox, but only one game behind the Mariners for the wild card spot.

On October 16, Cleveland papers reported the Indians were likely to offer a six-year, $90 million deal, comparable with what Chipper Jones had signed for with the Braves a year earlier. That likely wouldn't be enough. The Blue Jays had just signed their star first baseman Carlos Delgado to a $17-million-per-year deal. Moorad hinted he was seeking a longer deal, possibly up to ten years. "He's twenty-eight. You figure it out," Moorad told the *Plain Dealer*.

A few weeks later, Manny signed a deal that would change the course of baseball history.

CHAPTER 20

Next Stop, Boston

Manny and his downstairs neighbor Bill Quayle were driving through morning traffic to fetch Manny's Impala from the mechanic. The topic of his contract came up. "Bill, what should I do?" asked Manny. Quayle listened carefully as Manny laid out possible options. "Manny," Quayle reassured, "you have more money than you'll ever need. Fans love you, the team loves you, you're happy. Fifteen million, twenty million—after a certain point, what difference does it make?"

Manny nodded in agreement. "Yes," he told Bill. "I'm staying in Cleveland. The money isn't everything."

Moorad continued to hint at a ten-year deal worth more than Delgado's. Indians executives anonymously told the press they didn't believe Manny was worth that much, even though he was younger and better than Delgado. The *Plain Dealer* reported Moorad had asked for a ten-year, $200 million deal that would have made Manny the highest-paid player in the game.

On November 9, the last day the Indians had exclusive rights to negotiate, the team offered seven years for $119 million. The deal would have made Manny the highest-paid player in history, though everyone knew that distinction might last only until Alex Rodriguez, Mike Mussina, and Mets' ace Mike Hampton inked new deals.

Manny rejected the offer on November 11. To this point, the

Red Sox had not entered the negotiations, at least publicly. They were looking for pitching and zeroed in on Mussina. The Orioles' ace had gone only 11–15 the year before, but his 3.79 ERA was well below league average and he was a reliable fifteen-win, two-hundred-inning starter. Teams considered him the jewel of the free-agent pitchers, along with Hampton, and he had already proven he could pitch in the AL East.

On November 30, the Yankees signed Mussina to a six-year deal worth nearly $90 million. The Red Sox became serious quickly, possibly out of desperation to sign a big name after losing out on Mussina. Red Sox general manager Dan Duquette flew to Miami on December 5 to meet with Manny and Moorad. Pedro Martinez and Nomar Garciaparra phoned Manny and urged him to sign with Boston. Martinez reassured him that fans would embrace a minority player.

On December 7, Duquette made his move. He offered Manny $122.5 million over seven years, just $3 million more than the Indians' offer. It was still higher than the eight-year, $120 million deal Hampton was expected to sign with the Rockies.

On December 10, Duquette upped the offer to eight years and $144 million, or about $18 million a year. Hart, meanwhile, had re-emerged to make his final offer: eight years, $138 million. It was a leap from the previous offer and a fair-market deal, though perhaps it may have also been a publicity tactic, a contract offered with the knowledge that Manny was unlikely to accept it.

The ESPN series *Outside the Lines* provided a behind-the-scenes look at the eight-week bidding frenzy: offers, counteroffers, leveraging, and high-stakes brinkmanship. Moorad played Boston and Cleveland against each other like an auctioneer.

The stage was set for Manny to consider the nuances of the two offers. It would be a tough choice. In his heart, he wanted to stay in Cleveland, but as his agents argued, why not go for the highest possible salary? Manny was torn. He spent the day phoning friends, including Macaco, Frank Mancini, Pedro Martinez, and Wil Cordero. Moorad stayed up until 5:00 A.M., putting together the deal. An hour and a half later, Gene Mato, one of Manny's agents, phoned Moorad with the news that Manny had made up his mind. He would take the Red Sox offer.

But Manny's acceptance hinged on one final, somewhat bizarre request—that Boston hire Mancini, the Indians' clubhouse assistant. Moorad laughed. "Are you kidding me?" he said. With nearly $200 million on the line, the high-powered Moorad was suddenly thrust into Manny's world: Moorad had to take seriously the importance of Manny's relationship with a clubhouse assistant, a man whose job involved setting up pitching machines, fetching towels, scraping clay from players' cleats, and replacing bats.

Moorad recalls, "I called Duquette and I said, 'Listen, it's still alive but it's going to involve hiring a clubhouse attendant from Cleveland.' Duquette asked me, 'How am I gonna do that?' I said, 'I have no idea, but you can. I mean, we're talking twenty million a year—how much extra would this cost us, maybe fifty grand at most. So he agreed.

"But the ironic thing is that Mancini wouldn't come anyway."

Mancini's loyalty to Cleveland ultimately trumped this endearing request, and Manny joined Boston with explicit plans to befriend new assistants. But this episode, in which Manny was prepared to make a major decision based on his attachment to a friend, provides another glimpse into the role that these ties play in his life.

Mancini is a gentle forty-six-year-old Ned Flanders type. He offers upbeat, religion-infused assessments of life and likes to answer questions with a deferential, "Yes, sir," or, "No, ma'am." He holds a degree in computer science from Cleveland State University and says he has been to more than eighty-five countries "because of my passion for travel." But his greatest passion has always been the Indians. He grew up dreaming of playing for the team, honing his pitching skills on Little League and high school fields. Cut from his college team, his big break came in 1989, when his younger sister was hired as an Indians ball girl. Through her connections, he eventually befriended the equipment manager, who, within a year, offered him a job in the clubhouse.

Although he was hired to work with all the players, he was quickly absorbed by the demands of Albert Belle. "I became close to Albert in 1990 and through time, I got incorporated into Albert's daily routine," he said. When Belle was traded, Manny made his move on Mancini. "Could you stretch me the way you stretched Albert?" Manny asked. "Every single day we went to the batting cage together. And Manny felt that, whatever I did with Albert, he could learn from me. He knew that I was always there for Albert, and that I would always be there for him."

Mancini believes another key factor in earning Manny's trust was bilingualism. Eventually, the two men began to address spirituality. "When I saw him getting down on himself, I'd get on his case and I'd say, 'Manny, God gave you this ability. Don't question it. Don't be afraid. Don't lack faith. He'll get you through this. He will, you know that. He always has in the past. You wouldn't be here if he didn't give you this ability.' And Manny would look at me and say, 'Yeah! You know, you're right.' And he'd be a lot more happy. I could always tell if something was bothering him, and we'd work it through. I think I was a good support for Manny, but in the end, I just couldn't leave Cleveland."

The basic sentiment was that Manny wanted to stay, but had been hijacked by a heartless agent. "You have to understand that when it gets down to decisions of that magnitude, most of these guys are uncomfortable in that setting and that forum," explains current Indians' GM Mark Shapiro, who was assistant general manager for the Indians when Manny was drafted. "They're going to follow the advice of the person that they trust. It's not going to be the team, because the team's interests can be pitted against them. It's going to be a person who is their business advisor. And he got offered more money. And it's not fair for a player to have to stand up alone and make those decisions. It's hard on any player, let alone one that doesn't have a ton of education. Remember, when he was forced to make that decision, you're talking about a twenty-eight-year-old without a strong educational infrastructure and a complicated set of life experiences. . . . He hasn't been married, he hasn't made occupational decisions, he hasn't made geographical decisions. This isn't just Manny, this is every young player. He's made no major life decisions. You don't choose if you'll get drafted, you get drafted. You don't choose who you'll get drafted by, you'll get drafted by whatever team picks you. You don't choose when or if you'll move up. You don't choose when you'll play. So, you're not making decisions your whole life, and all of a sudden you're faced with making a $120 million decision. I don't know what guy in the world wouldn't listen to an advisor in that situation."

And to players who have risen from poverty, it would seem a supreme luxury to consider anything but the highest bid. They are not like, say, Trot Nixon (a college-educated physician's son), who could have made his fortune in other venues, and will likely have a bright, professional future well after his body passes its prime. For Manny and others, the invitation into this gilded world of wealth and power has been issued only because they happen to be able to hit, catch, throw, and run. The sense that they will be just as quickly ushered out the door when this narrow reservoir dries up fuels a sense of urgency and cynicism. "Baseball is like a factory. It's just a job, if you don't give them hits, you're gone," Manny says.

Players like Manny are thus, to a much greater extent than their middle-class counterparts, at the mercy of their agents. Like sharks, these agents have been selected for their capacity to snatch up as much of the money that is floating around the deal as possible. So long as the player is as singularly focused and unsentimental as the agent, their interests are aligned, and the partnership is mutually advantageous. But this equation breaks down when sentimentality creeps in. Monetary value cannot be assigned to a player's sense of comfort and connection with his teammates and managers. And there are other intangibles. What agent wouldn't want to tout a $200 million deal?

By all accounts, Boston and Manny were never well suited to each other. The more relaxed Cleveland atmosphere would have remained a better fit. For Boston, baseball is not so much a game as a blood sport. The fans may indulge in a few refrains of "Sweet Caroline," but as anyone who has ever soaked up the Fenway ambience knows, it's back to business when the music stops. *Boston Herald* sportswriter Mike Barnicle once quipped, "Baseball isn't a life-and-death matter, but the Red Sox are," and Manny's first few seasons in Boston played out like a Shakespearean tragedy cum comedy of errors.

CHAPTER 21

2001: Two Managers, One Marriage

Manny arrived in spring training February 17, four days before the mandatory reporting deadline. He seemed gregarious, greeting his new teammates with loud calls of, *"Qué pasa?"* on his first day and joking that he had to prove he could "make the team." He stayed in the same hotel as the Red Sox minor leaguers.

The Red Sox were coming off a second-place, 85–77 season in which they finished only 2.5 games behind the Yankees for the AL East title. The pitching staff was the best in the AL, with a 4.23 ERA. Led by Pedro Martinez, they carried a mediocre offense that outscored only two AL teams, the Twins and Devil Rays. Manny had the potential to change that, sliding into the lineup behind Garciaparra.

But his presence created a logjam in the outfield. The Red Sox believed that Trot Nixon, who turned twenty-seven early in the 2001 season, had a future as the team's right fielder and therefore preferred Manny in left field. Incumbent left fielder Troy O'Leary, the hero of Game 5 of the 1999 ALDS against Cleveland, seemed like the odd man out—provided Manny could and would play left field for Boston. Three days into spring training, Manny declared he was not ready to play left field for the first time in his career in front of Fenway Park's Green Monster. Red Sox manager Jimy Williams told the press he would follow Manny's wishes. "He has to feel good about where he plays," the manager told reporters.

Manny was also preparing himself for the fans, whose intensity was going to be a shock to his system. Martinez had warned him that Boston's microscopic lens was, perhaps, its biggest drawback. As Leigh Montville described in his biography of Ted Williams, "To play baseball in Boston was to be analyzed and scrutinized, laid out on a municipal laboratory table and picked apart. To be a star, a star of the magnitude Williams became, was to have the process increased by a factor of ten." Manny expected he'd be fine, but almost immediately, he was not.

As Manny recalled to T. J. Simers of the *L.A. Times,* "The first time I stepped foot in Boston, I said to myself, 'Whoa.' I told Pedro Martinez, 'Damn, man, I just want to get traded and get out of here; this place is not me.'" The intensity was just too much for the slugger whose successes relied on maintaining an emotional even-keel and who had always avoided the spotlight. "When you're playing for a team like Cleveland, Detroit, Anaheim, life is smoother," observes Manny. "It's like, you played the game, it's over. But not in Boston. In Boston, everyone goes crazy over it."

"The first years in Boston, it wasn't comfortable," Macaco recalls. "The people, no privacy. But I told him, 'Number one, they are fans. Number two, you are the superstar of the team. And number three, besides Ted Williams, you are one of the most famous players to be in Boston. Boston doesn't have too many famous players like you.'" Manny took the advice to heart and did his best those first few months to ignore his anxiety, the annoyance, and his craving for privacy and to reach out to his new fan base.

•   •   •

Manny opened the regular season as a designated hitter in an away game against Baltimore. After twice striking out looking against Orioles' starter Pat Hentgen, Manny hit a 390-foot shot off the right-field wall at Camden Yards. It looked like a sure double, but Manny felt a twinge of pain as he rounded first. Williams pinch-ran with reserve outfielder Darren Lewis. Manny would remain the designated hitter for the next fifty-three games of the season.

The Sox scored just five runs in losing two out of three games in Baltimore and returned home to face the then-hapless Devil Rays. Red Sox starter Tomo Ohka gave up three runs in the top of the first. In the bottom of the inning, Manny came up with one out, Nixon on second, and Jose Offerman on first. Manny drove a three-run homer over the Green Monster in his first Fenway Park at-bat.

Macaco watched in joy from the family section behind home plate. He had seen Manny hit a home run in his last at-bat in Cleveland and now he was closing the loop in Boston. "I'll never forget that, how he closed with the old team and opened with the new in the same way," Macaco says.

Manny stayed hot, helping to push the Sox into first place at 16–8 at the close of April. At that point in the season, he was hitting .402, with 7 home runs, 26 RBIs, and a 1.166 OPS. Better still for Red Sox fans, who began chanting his name when he came to the plate, Manny had gone 14 for 30 against the Yankees, including key hits off Rivera and Mussina. He set club records for the most home runs and RBIs in the opening month of a season. But he shrugged off his early success with characteristic mellowness: "I ain't trying to do nothing," he told a *Boston Globe* reporter. "Sometimes it happens. Sometimes it doesn't happen. We've still got like 150 games left. I think nobody's going to remember about April. I know there's a lot of energy [in the crowd when I come up to bat], but I'm just trying to pace myself."

Manny notched 50 RBIs by his fortieth game, the fastest any Red Sox player had done so since Walt Dropo in 1950. Opposing managers began taking extraordinary steps to keep him from beating them. On May 13, A's manager Art Howe walked Manny intentionally with nobody on and one out in the tenth inning of a 4–4 game. On June 5, Tigers' manager Phil Garner ordered four intentional walks to Manny in an eighteen-inning Sox win, tying the AL record for most intentional passes in a game. Following that game, Manny led the AL in all three Triple Crown categories, with a .388 average, 20 homers, and 63 RBIs. His OPS was 1.201.

Manny, appearing modest to Red Sox fans and menacing to opposing teams, was quickly becoming a Fenway favorite.

On June 23, Manny hit two monstrous home runs, both solo shots, over the Monster, his twenty-second and twenty-third of the season, in a 9–6 loss to the Blue Jays. His first homer was the first ball ever to hit the Fleet Bank sign above the wall in left-center, an estimated 463 feet. His second homer cleared the famous Coke bottles and clanged off the lights hanging above. The length of the second home run was officially put at 501 feet, a foot shorter than Ted Williams's famous 1946 blast whose spot is still marked by a red seat in Fenway's right field. The estimate was a gesture of respect to Williams, considered by many to be the best hitter ever. In fact, no one could say how far Manny's homer would have sailed because it hit the left-field light tower while still rising. Based on measurements of past home runs in Fenway and the trajectory of Manny's home run, the best Sox PR could say was "It was close to the longest home run [Williams] ever hit at Fenway Park." The display of raw power along with a sky-high batting average in the first several months in Boston showed that Manny had the potential to be among the most elite hitters ever to play in Fenway's hallowed grounds. His thoughts on that subject: "I got lucky and got two [homers]. But anybody can have a good game," he said after the game. Manny was now hitting .351 (1.113 OPS) and had 72 RBIs. Boston was 43–29, two games ahead of the Yankees in the AL East.

Not surprisingly, Manny was voted to the All-Star team, but he blew off the mandatory media day on July 9. He showed up the next day and told one group of reporters he skipped the media sessions because his grandmother was sick. He told another pack of scribes his grandmother had died. "I don't know why he says things like that," bemoans his older sister Evelyn. "My grandmother says to him, 'Manny, use something else.'"

Manny continued to hit, but the Red Sox fell apart for reasons beyond his control. Off the field, there was a distracting feud between Duquette and Jimy Williams. More important, Martinez missed two months because of a rotator cuff injury. A wrist injury sidelined Garciaparra, who played only twenty-one games. And Lowe struggled as the closer, losing 10 games and saving just 24. On August 15, Duquette fired Williams, even though the manager had kept the ship afloat and led the Sox to a respectable 65–53 mark—five games behind the Yankees in the East, but one loss behind the A's in the wild card race.

The team struggled under the new manager, promoted pitching coach Joe Kerrigan. Following nine straight losses between August 25 and September 4, the Red Sox (71–65) were nine games behind the Yankees and nine and a half behind the surging A's. ESPN's Peter Gammons reported that Manny had told teammates he wished he had never left Cleveland. "Now Manny's teammates say he repeatedly tells them that all the discord, front-office interference, and dysfunctional atmosphere so bother him that he wishes he never signed with Boston in the first place," Gammons wrote on ESPN.com. Manny denied Gammons's report. "I'm very happy here, and I don't want to be anywhere else," he told Gordon Edes of the *Boston Globe*.

Where does the truth lie? It was several years ago, but Mancini recalls that Manny missed Cleveland badly—not just in 2001, but in all of his Boston seasons: "It didn't take long for him to realize he'd made a mistake. Every single year I'd see him he'd say, 'Frank, get John Hart to call me, I'd like to come back. Frank, I'll tear my contract up right now.'"

"He didn't want to go to Boston before he came," says former agent Gene Mato. "He blamed me for telling him it was a good opportunity. But I felt it was my job to put the deal before him, tell him that it was a better market, and let him make the decision. I'll never understand why, but I can tell you he wanted to leave from the start."

If Manny missed Cleveland, that was no crime. It was a defendable emotion, given how poorly the Red Sox season had turned out. It was harder to defend Manny's absence before the Sox final home game against Baltimore, a game honoring Orioles legend Cal Ripken, Jr., for his record of playing 2,632 consecutive games. Manny did show up at Fenway, at noon. Then he left and showed up again at 3:30 P.M. Then he left for good. Kerrigan initially told reporters he decided to leave Manny out of the lineup. Hours later, he and Duquette changed the story, saying Manny was excused to miss the game for "personal reasons." The Sox lost the game 4–2 and fell to 76–75, fourteen games behind the Yankees.

Manny did not play in the final nine games of the season. The stated reason for his absence was a bruised left hand he suffered when hit by a pitch on September 28 against the Tigers. But no one knows whether Manny could have played had the Sox been in a pennant race. The last game of the season was a 5–1 win in Baltimore to give the Sox a final record of 82–79. But all told, the Red Sox superstar nucleus of Martinez, Garciaparra, and Manny did not play one game together during the entire season.

Manny had had another outstanding year, though his numbers were down from his landmark 1999 and 2000 seasons. His OPS of 1.014 was fourth in the AL, though his .609 slugging—also fourth in the AL—was significantly lower than his .697 the year before. His power numbers—41 homers (fourth) and 125 RBIs (fourth) in 142 games—were unassailable, but his .306 batting average was his lowest since 1998.

In some ways, Manny was a victim of his own torrid start. His numbers accumulated nicely, but certain breakdowns told a different tale. As reporters pointed out, Manny hit .414 in forty-four games through May 23, with 15 home runs and 56 RBIs, and seemed on track to win the American League Triple Crown. But in the eighty-five games that followed, he hit only .251—far below his norm for any three-month stretch in Cleveland—with 24 home runs and 57 RBIs.

Manny was, however, having clear success in his personal life. He met a twenty-two-year-old Brazilian woman named Juliana Monteiro while working out at Bally Total Fitness on Winter Street near the Boston Common. "I came up to her and started talking to her," he told the *Globe*. It's possible, however, that Manny had already seen or spoken to Monteiro at Joe's American Bar and Grill in Boston's Back Bay, where Manny, living only blocks away at the Ritz-Carlton, was a regular customer. Monteiro was a hostess there.

Either way, what's clear is that Juliana Monteiro didn't recognize him as a superstar. "I didn't know who he was," Juliana says. "In Brazil, none of my friends followed American baseball, and I wasn't somebody to sit around watching games on television. I had never heard of Manny Ramirez. But I just loved him. He would show up every week at the restaurant with these huge bouquets of flowers and we would go out and have fun. My manager was like, 'Do you know who that is?'"

Juliana has thick, long black hair, green eyes, a dazzling

smile, and a friendly demeanor. She grew up the second oldest
of five children of a civil engineer and stay-at-home mother. She
first visited Boston during the spring break of her freshman year
in college (where she was studying tourism), staying with her
uncle near the Malden-Everett line outside Boston. (The
Boston area has the second largest Brazilian population in the
United States, many of whom are young and college educated.)
She returned home just long enough to pack her bags and bid
farewell to her disappointed parents. With plans to eventually
return to college, she found a job at Joe's.

"When I met her the first time, I liked her," says Macaco.
"She was nice and sweet." Although a native Portuguese
speaker, Juliana worked hard to pick up enough Spanish to communicate with Manny's mother. "She speaks Spanish so much
better than I do," says Manny's high school teammate Carlos
Puello. "Plus they're both Catholic." Puello was also impressed
with how Monteiro was already taking charge of Manny's life
beyond Fenway. Onelcida, who met Monteiro briefly in August
2001, agreed. "This is it, Manny," she proclaimed. "She is going
to be your wife. She is just like an angel." Clara says, "Juliana
was very sweet to my mom, and she would talk with me and call
me 'sister.'"

And, unlike other women, Juliana was not afraid to set limits
with Manny. They hit a rough patch in August, shortly after
Juliana had quit her job at Joe's to work for a car rental agency
near her apartment in Brighton. Until then, their dates had been
confined to Boston's Back Bay neighborhood, whose gridded and
alphabetically ordered streets provided easy passage between
Manny's apartment and Joe's. With Juliana's change of venue,
Manny would have to learn to navigate some of the winding,
one-way roads that make Boston a famously difficult place to
drive. But instead of driving Juliana all the way home, Manny
would simply pull over near Fenway and insist that she walk to

her apartment. "One night I said, 'Manny, it's far, drive me all the way home,'" Juliana recalls. "But he said, 'Baby, I don't know my way on those streets. If I go over there, I'll get lost.' I said, 'Okay, but that's it, if I get out here, I won't come back.'" Manny did not bend, and Juliana slammed the car door behind her as she marched toward Beacon Street. For the next two weeks a contrite and desperate Manny searched for her. It wasn't until he tracked down Juliana's roommates, got directions, and drove himself to her apartment to apologize that Juliana relented. As the relationship deepened, Manny beckoned Onelcida from Florida to help seal the deal. "Every day Manny and his mother would show up at my work with a homemade lunch. It was very sweet."

By the end of September, Manny had proposed to Juliana. "We were lying in his mom's bedroom, and his arms were around me," Juliana remembers, "and he says, 'Baby, you know I love you so much, right? And you know I want to have a family with you, right?'" Almost immediately the young couple began making plans for a big wedding. Manny ordered his mother subscriptions to wedding magazines so that she could be in on the festivities. But one morning, as Juliana and Onelcida sat at the kitchen table, surrounded by bookmarked magazines, guest lists, and to-do lists, an impatient Manny walked in and announced, "Let's just forget about all this and get married." Within an hour, a gleeful Manny and Juliana headed to his familiar Pembroke Lakes Mall, where they hastily purchased two gold bands.

The October 21st wedding was a low-key affair, just Manny's mother and Clara at the Weston City Hall. Manny invited Macaco with one week's notice, but he could not get his shifts covered. After making their vows, the young couple paused for a photo under the city's makeshift wedding arch—white lattice panels affixed to a sky blue wall and adorned with an autumnal garland of straw hats and faux leaves.

Manny wore white pants, a white belt, and a pink-and-white shirt, which clung tightly to his broad shoulders. Juliana looked radiant in beige slacks and a maroon striped shirt. The next day the young couple embarked on their weeklong honeymoon to Maui. They brought Onelcida and Clara with them. "He was so happy," recalls Juliana. "I think he just wanted everyone to be part of it."

Manny and Juliana moved into a fourteen-thousand-foot Mediterranean-style home along a labyrinth of man-made lagoons in a gated Weston, Florida, community. Weston is situated just six miles from Pembroke Pines, where Manny had purchased a house for his parents, Pura, Clara, and Clara's two teenage daughters.

Macaco has a room in the Ramirez Florida home and an open invitation—not only to visit but also to stay as long as he wants. What does Juliana think of this Little League coach, who seems to have come into her life part and parcel with the man she married?

"When I think about Macaco, it just fills me with a sense of happiness," she says. "He's like a father figure," Juliana says, referring, in particular, to Macaco's role as marriage counselor during the early stages of their marriage. "Things were new," she recalls. "So many adjustments and distractions. And we hit some tough times. We asked Macaco to come up to Boston and help us work it out. He listened to us and helped us find a way out. We weren't looking for him to take sides, to say who was right, who was wrong, only to help us figure out a way out of our difficulties. We still call him whenever we hit a rough patch. He knows how to handle our problems in ways that make sense. Macaco has given our lives stability."

Juliana echoes Manny's observation that Macaco is one of the few people in the world Manny holds "close to his heart." As she explains, "Macaco has helped Manny with life. He's advised him to stay away from drugs and the streets when so many in his neighborhood ended up there. Manny can call him any time—4:00 A.M., 6:00 A.M.—and Macaco will pick up and be there for him. I feel bad because I know he works the night shift and needs his sleep, but Manny knows he won't mind. Manny can say, 'I need you to be here,' and as long as Macaco doesn't have to work, he's on the next plane to us."

Like Macaco, Juliana is disheartened by the media portrayals of Manny. She does concede, however, that Manny sometimes says one thing and means something else. "Like, when I first met Macaco, Manny told me he was his uncle. Eventually, I found out that he was his Little League coach. Manny says things from his heart. And he's kind of childlike, not in a bad way, but he just doesn't get all that caught up in worrying about things. He's just living his life and trying not to get it all complicated. He has such a good heart—I'm so proud of him."

She adds, "I get really angry with the way that he's portrayed in the media. He could be outside playing golf, enjoying this beautiful weather and instead what is he doing? He's working out. During the off-season when he's here, he gets up at 5:30 in the morning and goes to the gym. He comes home for lunch and in the afternoon helps with the boys—taking them to the batting cage, or picking them up from karate or something. He's a very devoted father. Or he's analyzing videos, or upstairs on his computer with a program that looks at his swing. He says, 'Mama'—he calls me that—'come up here and look.' He wants me by him all day. He says, 'Come to this meeting, Mama, you're my secretary.'"

Juliana possesses some of the same qualities Manny has come to rely on in Macaco. Manny needs to feel that someone loves him apart from his fame and fortune. This litmus test explains why one of the most important people in his life, Macaco, still lives in a subsidized housing unit, supporting his mother, sister, and adopted son on paychecks earned through arduous night shifts in an operating room. "We try to send him some money," Juliana explains. "I say, 'Macaco, would you please take this gift,' and he says, 'I don't need it. I have a lot.' He works hard, and he should retire soon. If he wants to move in with us, I'd be happy. But he has his mother, and sister, and nephew who depend on his paycheck. He's waiting for his pension. Money complicates things."

Money complicated things for Yankees superstar Alex Rodriguez and his mentor, Eddie Rodriguez (no relation). Although he was only eight years old when he met Eddie, Alex had already moved three times and had recently been abandoned by his father. Forced to work two jobs, Alex's mother enrolled her three young children in the Hank Kline Boys and Girls Club in Coconut Grove, Miami. Alex was primed for the sort of support and stern guidance that the club's baseball coach, Eddie, had to offer.

For the next eight years, Alex never missed a day at the club, spending countless hours under Eddie's supervision. A bond was forged. Like Macaco, Eddie has a passion for baseball. He grew up playing in Cuba and then spent eight years in the minors. There was a time when Eddie had a guest room in his protégé's Florida manse and received phone calls from Alex each day.

Sitting in the family section at Yankee Stadium in 2004, Eddie sounded like an overinvolved parent when he told the *Daily News*, "The games are so hard for me. I don't believe you can enjoy the game when you are watching someone you love. You can feel the joy when they do something great. But when they strike out, you die a little." And, in a tribute to his mentor two years later, Alex credited Eddie with instilling in him the confidence and determination to achieve. "I don't make a big decision without talking to Eddie. Baseball, business, life—I trust him completely. It's a nice relationship to have after all these years. It's very pure."

Pure? Yes. Like Manny, Alex Rodriguez took comfort in knowing that at least one important relationship in his life was unspoiled by the seductive forces of his enormous paycheck. And in 2004, Rodriguez began to give back to the Boys and Girls Club, including a $1.8 million gift to establish a learning center.

But by 2007, Eddie and A-Rod suffered a painful falling-out, apparently over what Alex perceived to be Eddie's overreaching requests for charitable contributions to the center. Eddie doesn't deny being persistent. "Alex Rodriguez?" he says. "I don't like to answer questions like that—he gave me a lot of money. I raised it for the kids. But, listen, I am my own man, and I'm *never* going to let famous rich people tell me what to do. I run the show. My way, or the highway. I don't care how much money you have."

It would be hard to imagine a scenario in which Macaco would banish anyone to the highway, but the unraveling of the A-Rod–Eddie relationship sheds light on the symbolic meaning of money for stars like Rodriguez and Manny. It also explains how Manny and Macaco have maintained their bond. As Manny's former agent Gene Mato observed, "Macaco is probably the only person who has never asked Manny for anything."

Then again, Manny's relationship to money and possessions is unusual. According to his managers and teammates, Manny, for all his Ritz-Carlton living, remains modest about his wealth and retains simple tastes and habits. "Manny would be just as happy at Burger King as at a Ruth's Chris Steak House," recalls Brian Graham, his minor league manager. Gene Mato has other explanations. "In some ways, I think Manny sees money as the root of all evil, and with good reason. He has been hurt a lot because of money. That's part of it. And he may not fully grasp how much he has."

One thing's for certain: Throughout his career in professional baseball, Manny has carried little or no money. Brian Graham describes how Manny would sometimes ask to borrow fifteen dollars to buy lunch, only to drive off in his tricked-out $30,000 car. Mancini recalls: "He'd say, 'Frank can you grab me some sushi?' But he'd never have any money. He'd hop in a cab with another player, and the player was making one-hundredth of what he was making, but would still have to pay for the cab ride. 'Cause he never had a penny on him. He just doesn't think about it."

And Omar Ramirez, Manny's minor league teammate and friend, recalls that, when he visited Manny in Cleveland, Manny would sometimes leave the table just as the check was delivered, never to return. "I think it was a joke," he said, adding that Manny always picks up the tab when they go out with friends more recently. Manny pays with a credit card.

Nobody seems to begrudge Manny this absentmindedness, even if it is a passive-aggressive form of parsimony. Still, his spending patterns are curious. In their study of people's money attitudes, psychologists have described the symbolic meaning of money and how it can provide feelings of security, freedom, or power. For some people—and Manny falls into this category— there is a strong thread of distrust running through their encounters with money: suspicion and doubt regarding others' intentions. Such suspicions are often marked among those who've risen from poverty. Given money's symbolic value for everyone, spending habits can often provide a lens into one's personality. As psychiatrist David Krueger once wrote, "Money is probably the most emotionally meaningful object in contemporary life; only food and sex are its close competitors as common carriers of such strong and diverse feelings, significances, and strivings." From this perspective, Manny's approach to money, which carries vestiges of his economic background and social distrust, is no different from his approach to many things in life.

Manny recently had an opportunity to give back to Macaco without actually having to reach into his wallet. He agreed to be the subject of *Payback*, a series that runs on Speed TV, a cable channel for car enthusiasts in which celebrities work with a team of car specialists to customize a vehicle, which he or she later bequeaths to an unsuspecting mentor. "I'm blessed to be in this show and to do something real special for him," Manny explained in footage filmed beside his mother's swimming pool. Manny selected a Cadillac Escalade EXT pickup truck because, he reasoned, it would provide ample room for Macaco's softball equipment. "He's gonna go nuts," Manny says. "Nobody's done something special like that for him in his whole life. So when he sees this he's gonna go crazy."

Indeed, as his new car rolls down the ramp of a truck, parked beside the City of Palms Park in Fort Myers, Macaco exclaims, "You're joking! I can't believe it! Oh, my God," and, after he's handed the keys, "Ah, come on, that the truth?" Manny beams, as he points to the embroidered "Carlos" on each of the front headrests. Macaco raises his face toward the sky, eyes closed and hands pushed deep into the front pockets of his jeans. "No more train, no more taxi." He looks ecstatic, yet mystified, particularly as the show's announcer officiously describes some of the car's more outrageous features—rare, "moonshine-white" ostrich-leather seat cushions, a built-in cooler over the right wheel, a custom exhaust system. The two men embrace as Macaco declares, "My blood pressure is probably too high right now to drive it."

Macaco has not yet driven the car; he doesn't even have a driver's license. Although it sits in Manny's Weston garage, Macaco likes to describe his car's many special features and he still shows the *Payback* episode, downloaded onto the computer at Peligro's sports apparel shop, to anyone who will watch. He scrolls to his favorite segments, where Manny says things such as, "I'm like his son, man, he's always with me. He always was there to give me support, you know, and to show me the right path."

CHAPTER 22

2002: New Ownership

As a member of the Indians, Manny had avoided the media by slipping out the back door of a large clubhouse. But he couldn't hide in Boston, where he was the main attraction, where the media were more ravenous, and where the size and structure of the clubhouse made it more difficult to scurry away from reporters. Actually, Moorad spoke to Duquette about changing the layout of the Red Sox clubhouse. Duquette said he was considering it. Trot Nixon, who has played for both Boston and Cleveland, noticed the difference. "Boston's clubhouse is definitely smaller and more intense. There are fewer places to hide," he observes. "I mean, in Cleveland, you probably have maybe four, at most six, reporters at night here, and they don't really bother you. And there's a lot more places to go in Cleveland where the media can't get you." Moorad also indicated that Manny had been unhappy in his first year in Boston, despite Manny's denials during several interviews in 2001. In hindsight, those denials were not a surprise, given Manny's aversion to confrontation. Moorad also implied that the clubhouse commotion and the controversies had contributed to Manny's late-season decline. "Manny prefers a comfortable clubhouse, and it was anything but last season," Moorad told reporters at winter meetings. "Manny performs better in a relaxed environment. . . . He was not comfortable, especially toward the end of the season."

In discussions with his agent, Manny decided to take a break from speaking to the media. "To the extent that he was pushed into a more primary role in terms of being expected to be a spokesperson on the team, I think there were challenges that went along with that," Moorad said. "And it's fair to say that he's still adjusting to the challenges of playing in Boston."

During a mid-February workout, Manny approached John Henry, one of the many business partners who had just purchased the Red Sox from the Yawkey family's trust-holders. Henry was determined to put a face on the new ownership and was excited to meet his team. He couldn't get a full sentence out before Manny begged him for a trade out of Boston. "I hate it," he told Henry, according to *Feeding the Monster* by Seth Mnookin. "I hate the clubhouse, I hate the pressure. I gotta get out of here." Henry promised Manny to look into a trade and contacted the Phillies about a possible swap involving their third baseman, Scott Rolen. But Henry did not want to trade Manny and didn't pursue the deal seriously.

Henry kept the exchange and trade talks secret from the press. But that only kept Manny out of the headlines for a few days. On February 20, Kerrigan scheduled the team's first workout and planned to address them about showing up on time and acting like professionals. Manny was a no-show. His teammates had no clue where he was. "He's probably in the U.S. somewhere," Lowe told the *Globe*.

Trot Nixon criticized Manny in a candid interview with the *Hartford Courant*. "You want to know why the Yankees win so many championships?" Nixon asked. "I'll tell you why. Everybody shows up ready to play baseball. They don't come strolling in, pimping around and doing this and that. Bernie Williams showed up. Derek Jeter made $20 million. He shows up. [Manny] had enough time in the off-season. He should be here."

Dan Shaughnessy interviewed Nixon for the next day's *Globe*, and the outfielder stood by his comments.

With the new ownership group in place, neither Kerrigan nor Duquette survived spring training. The new CEO, Larry Lucchino, hired Grady Little as the new manager. Little had been the Indians' bench coach. He had served the same role in Boston in the late 1990s. His easygoing approach helped both the team and Manny, at least early on. At the end of April, Manny was hitting .346 with a 1.174 OPS, 7 home runs, and a team-leading 22 RBIs. Boston was in first place at 16–7, one game ahead of the Yankees.

On May 11, Manny was hitting .366 with a 1.163 OPS, 9 homers, and 35 RBIs in just thirty-two games. But it all unraveled during the second inning of that night's game in Seattle. Manny was on first with no one out. Third baseman Shea Hillenbrand doubled to left. Manny chugged toward third and saw third-base coach Mike Cubbage waving him home. He sped toward the plate, where catcher Dan Wilson waited to gather the shortstop's cutoff throw. Manny dove headfirst. As he slid, his left hand jammed into Wilson's shin guard. He was out at the plate, and his left index finger was fractured.

The team estimated Manny would miss between four and six weeks. About one month later, the Red Sox sent Manny to Triple-A Pawtucket for a rehab assignment. Little had wanted him to go to Atlanta with the Red Sox, but Manny pressed for Pawtucket, partly so he could see an old friend, catcher Luis Rodriguez, with whom he'd roomed during spring training two years previously. "We went to the malls. We did a lot of things together. He's a funny guy. We're going to enjoy him the next couple of games here," Rodriguez told the *Globe*.

Pawtucket's longtime owner said the eleven days Manny spent there were the most fun he'd had in thirty years. He often told the story of how Manny was down the street getting his hair cut when he was supposed to be at batting practice—an indiscretion that could be laughed off in Pawtucket but would be damning in Boston. And people were amused when Manny lost his diamond earring while sliding into third base, causing the entire grounds crew to rake the infield in search of it between innings. Manny struggled in his Triple-A stint, going 3 for 30. And some of the more wound-up citizens of Red Sox Nation wondered whether Manny was worth the team's investment.

On June 20, the Red Sox were in the middle of a nine-game road trip against National League teams. Because Manny was playing left field in Pawtucket, some of the Red Sox reporters questioned why he couldn't do so for the Red Sox. They believed Little and Lucchino were coddling Manny, just as the Duquette administration had. "The Red Sox pay Manny approximately $3.3 million a month," wrote Gerry Callahan in the *Herald*. "They should able to dictate which Sox uniform he wears."

Duquette's replacement, General Manager Mike Port, announced on June 21 that Manny would rejoin the lineup when Boston returned home to face Manny's old team, the Indians, on June 25—an occasion that prompted columnist Michael Holley of the *Globe* to proclaim that the Red Sox should have heeded the wacky stories from Manny's days in Cleveland before signing him. "They told us in December 2000 that we could never understand the quirks of their star. They told us that we were too hysterical to embrace the complex package that is Manny Ramirez. You'll devour him whole, they said. Manny is a dynamic right-handed hitter, they said, but he is not dynamic in a vacuum. He is a calm Ohioan hanging out in New Yorker's skin. New England is nice, but it's not his scene. If anyone in Cleveland finds out about the last few weeks, they'll say they were right. Unfortunately, they have a case."

The Sox finished the road trip 3–6 and fell to 45–27, a half-game behind the Yankees. Their record without Manny was 21–18. In his first game back, Manny went 1 for 5. He struck out with two outs in the bottom of the ninth and the tying runs on base. After the game, he told reporters he was not 100 percent healthy.

Manny hit just over .260 in the next month. His average had dropped to .319, his OPS to 1.024. His power was below his high standards but respectable: His totals stood at 17 home runs and 57 RBIs, meaning he'd hit 8 home runs and logged 22 RBIs in his thirty-three games back. By the July 31 trade deadline, the Yankees had opened up a four-game lead in the East. Seeking to bolster the lineup for the playoff run, the Red Sox acquired slugging outfielder Cliff Floyd from the Expos in exchange for two minor leaguers. The move enabled the team to move Manny to DH.

On August 6, the A's (64–48) came to Boston for a three-game series, trailing both the Sox (65–45) and the Angels (65–45) by two games in the wild card race. Boston was still four games behind the Yankees (69–41). Oakland took the first two games of the series to pull even with Boston (but still 1.5 games behind Anaheim). The second loss was especially gut-wrenching. Manny came up in the ninth, Boston trailing 3–2 with two on and two out. He had already sliced a solo homer around the Pesky Pole in right field in the fourth; he had also singled and scored in the eighth. This time, Manny laced a line drive into the gap in right-center. It appeared to be headed for the stands until sprinting A's center fielder Terrence Long reached over the fence and pulled the ball back in with a leaping catch.

Over the next twenty-two games, the Sox went 11–11 and fell to 76–58, 7.5 games behind the Yankees in the East and five games behind the Angels for the wild card. The A's, meanwhile, were in the midst of an astonishing twenty-game winning streak that propelled them to an 86–51 mark, best in the AL. Those were the circumstances under which the Red Sox entered a three-game series at Yankee Stadium on September 2. The Sox won the opener 8–4, scoring three runs off Mussina in the third to take a 3–2 lead that they would hold on to for the win.

But the final two games were close losses—4–2 and 3–1—and Manny was among the goats. He hit into rally-killing double plays in the eighth inning of both games. He had otherwise had a decent series at the plate, going 3 for 10.

The season fell apart for the team a few days later. In the first game of a four-game series in Tampa on September 9, Manny hit a grounder right back to Tampa pitcher Tanyon Sturtze in the bottom of the third. Manny failed to even jog from the batter's box as Sturtze tossed the ball to first.

Manny returned to the dugout and apologized to Little and the players. Little considered removing him from the game. He decided to leave him in. Though Manny rewarded the team by hitting a solo shot in the top of the seventh to break a 3–3 tie—in a game the Sox won 6–3—the press was appalled by Manny's laziness and Little's failure to bench him. It didn't help that Manny was involved the previous night in another controversy over a rap song he selected to be played at Fenway Park when he came to bat. Due to a short delay by the opposing pitcher, the song, Styles's "I Get High," played longer than usual. An expletive in the song blared from the Fenway speakers, embarrassing Red Sox brass. "I didn't know. I didn't even hear it," Manny told the *Boston Herald* after the game. "I was focused on the pitcher."

With the team fading from contention, Manny hit .396 (1.263 OBP) with 9 homers and 31 RBIs in September and October. He wound up winning the American League batting title with a .349 average in 120 games, beating out Kansas City's Mike Sweeney, who posted a .340 average. Manny also led the league in OBP (.450) and ranked second in slugging (.647). He had 33 home runs and 107 RBIs. But his performance was not enough to lift the Red Sox into the playoffs. The Sox finished 93–69—a respectable mark, but still ten games behind the Yankees and six behind the Angels for the wild card.

In the final game of the season, Manny appeared as a pinch-hitter in the seventh inning. He drew a walk and preserved his .349 average. Then he left the ballpark before the game was over. So he didn't speak to the media about his feat. That was nothing new. He hadn't spoken to the press since his failure to hustle in Tampa. Even in a moment of triumph, he was not about to make himself available to a press corps that had vilified him not five weeks earlier.

CHAPTER 23

2003: Almost Paradise

Before the 2003 season, the Red Sox hired Theo Epstein, only twenty-eight at the time, to be the new general manager. He was the youngest GM in baseball history. Epstein wasted little time. He brought in veteran third baseman Bill Mueller to challenge Shea Hillenbrand, traded for Reds' second baseman Todd Walker, and snatched former Marlin outfielder Kevin Millar from a Japanese team that had agreed to pay him more than $3 million per season. In addition, he paid $1.25 million for a castoff from the Twins named David Ortiz, who was not yet twenty-eight.

The team raced to an 18–9 mark at the end of April, only three games behind the 21–6 Yankees. The team played .500 ball in May and June. After seventy-four games, they were 42–32. The Yankees had slowed down as well, so Boston was only two games out of first, but in third place overall in the East, since the Blue Jays had won nine of their last eleven and were only one game out.

The battle for the AL East came to a head on July 4 in the first game of a four-game series at Yankee Stadium. Entering the game, the Red Sox (48–35) trailed the Yankees (52–31) by four games and the Blue Jays had faded to third. However, the Red Sox were in the thick of the wild card race with the A's (48–36), giving the four-game series the feel of a playoff preview.

It was Manny's biggest series yet as a member of the Red Sox, and he rose to the occasion. He hit his twentieth home run of the season in the first game as the Sox pummeled David Wells en route to a 10–3 victory. The two-run blast off Wells in the third gave the Red Sox a 5–2 lead. The ball landed in the upper deck in left field. According to Sean McAdam, then of the *Providence Journal*, Yankee experts could remember only two balls ever reaching there before—homers by Jose Canseco and Cecil Fielder.

The Sox battered the Yankees again the next night 10–2, chasing Roger Clemens in the sixth. Clemens plunked Millar in the second inning. Manny came out of the Sox dugout and strode toward Clemens, yelling at him. A brawl did not ensue, but Manny's actions on this night are worth recalling, if only because he's so often cited as a player who is indifferent to his teammates.

The Yankees won the final two games of the series to stay four games ahead of the Red Sox. But the Sox had proven they could play with the former champs. And they were starting to roll. They were 63–44 at the end of July and finished the season 95–67, six games behind the 101-win Yankees but two games ahead of the Mariners for the wild card spot. The Red Sox would move on to play the AL West champion A's (96–66) in the ALDS.

The 2003 Red Sox had personality, especially in contrast to the buttoned-up Yankees, who banned facial hair and prided themselves on their strict code of professional conduct. The Red Sox were different, and perhaps none more so than Manny. He wore baggy pants and dreadlocks that stuck out from under his cap. Trot Nixon's batting helmet was so covered in pine tar you could barely make out the B underneath. Center fielder Johnny Damon had grown his hair out, too.

Meanwhile Millar and Ortiz, always japing and cursing, were the class clowns. Ortiz spat into his batting gloves between pitches and exchanged man-hugs with everyone. Millar became a beloved goofball. One of his old college roommates (from Lamar University in Beaumont, Texas) had found an old videotape of Millar singing Bruce Springsteen's "Born in the USA" in what looks like a dorm room or college apartment. Like Springsteen in the song's video, Millar had his sleeves rolled up and pumped his right fist above his head to the song's drumbeat. Beginning in August, Fenway technicians played the video on the stadium JumboTron during games with the words "Rally Karaoke Guy" on the screen.

The silly video came to symbolize the team. They really seemed to enjoy playing together. But the season had its share of Manny controversies. And the most damaging involved Boston's nemesis, the Yankees. In an April 29 interview with ESPN that only appeared online, Manny told Joe Morgan that playing in pinstripes "is one of my biggest dreams right now. I know I've got a big contract here in Boston, but maybe when it's over, I'll go out there and try it." On August 31, with the AL East still on the line, the Yankees were in Boston to play the third game of a three-game series. The Sox lost 8–4 with Clemens outdueling Tim Wakefield and fell 5.5 games back. But that quickly became a secondary story.

Manny was excused from the game and the previous two by team doctor Bill Morgan because of severe throat inflammation. Morgan sent Manny home to rest and recover. But Manny was spotted with Yankees infielder (and former Indians teammate) Enrique Wilson at the city's other Ritz-Carlton hotel on Arlington Street—not far from where Manny lived. Questioned about the rendezvous, Wilson said Manny had come to his room and they chatted in the lobby for five minutes but that Manny was not drinking at the bar, as was initially reported.

Thus began the fiercest round of criticism Manny had ever faced from players, fans, the media, and the front office. And it was compounded by Manny's silence. The closest he ever came to explaining that night was during a radio interview about a year later, when Manny said, "Enrique, man, you know Enrique is my brother, man. You're my brother, you're my brother no matter what, no matter if you play for the Yankees or whoever." Wilson later told the *Boston Herald*, "We didn't do anything [wrong] at that time. . . . They made a big deal about that, but he didn't do anything."

The fiasco encapsulated everything that made Manny unhappy in Boston: the this-is-more-than-a-game attitude when the Yankees came to town, the intense scrutiny of his every move, and the media frenzy that followed a perceived misstep.

Little benched him for the next game in Philadelphia, which the Sox won 13–9 by scoring six runs in the ninth. Manny refused to pinch-hit in the game, saying he was still too sick. Johnny Damon, meanwhile, was starting in center field, two days after a vicious collision with reserve outfielder Gabe Kapler, who'd been subbing in left field for Manny. Epstein damned Manny by praising Damon: "We really appreciate the way Johnny Damon sucked it up and got in the lineup. That's the kind of effort we need from everyone on this club in September as we try to make the playoffs," he told Michael Silverman of the *Boston Herald*.

The criticism kept coming. Millar promised not to "question anyone's integrity" but later pointed out that there "are gamers and nongamers. There are different kinds of players. We'll be great when [Manny] is back in the lineup, but I like having Dave McCarty in there, Gabe Kapler, Damian Jackson. . . . We're not going to skip a beat," he told Silverman.

Even Ortiz, already Manny's closest friend on the team, offered some backhanded criticism. "I'm the kind of guy, you've got to put me down to make me quit," Ortiz told Gordon Edes of the *Boston Globe*.

The 2003 Red Sox led the AL in runs (961), OBP (.360), and slugging (.491). Manny led the team with 37 homers and a .427 on-base percentage. His 104 RBIs were one behind Garciaparra for the team lead; his .587 slugging was second only to Ortiz (.592); and his .325 average was one point behind Mueller, who won the AL batting title, which was remarkable since he was the team's number-nine hitter. The Sox broke major league records for team offense in three categories: slugging, extra-base hits (648), and total bases (2,832). Ortiz's 31 homers and 101 RBIs were a large part of it.

The Red Sox, under first-year GM Epstein and second-year manager Little, won the wild card and faced the A's in the ALDS. It was Boston's first playoff series since losing the ALCS to the Yankees in 1999—the year Boston had eliminated Manny's Indians in the ALDS.

Manny went 0 for 5 in Game 1 in Oakland, stranding five runners with two inning-ending groundouts. His three other outs were also the last out of the inning. Still, Boston led 4–3 going into the ninth. Boston's shaky closer, Byung-Hyun Kim, was one out away from sealing the game when the A's Erubiel Durazo came to the plate with runners on first and second. Little lifted Kim for lefty Alan Embree. It was a strange move if only because Durazo, a lefty, actually hit lefties (.283) better than righties (.247) in 2003. Durazo slapped a shot to left. Manny hustled for the ball but it dropped at his feet and the tying run scored.

The A's eventually won the game in the bottom of the twelfth on a two-out, bases-loaded bunt single. The true hero of the game was Oakland closer Keith Foulke, who no-hit the Red Sox in the ninth, tenth, and eleventh innings.

Game 2 was not much better for Boston. The vaunted Red

Sox offense was stifled by A's lefty Barry Zito in a 5–1 A's victory.

Manny was not to blame for the loss, but he didn't acquit himself well in the bottom of the second, when Oakland's lead was only 1–0. With runners on first and second and no outs, A's center fielder Eric Byrnes hit a fly ball to left. The ball bounced behind Manny on the warning track and both runs scored.

Manny was not charged with an error, but it was clear he had misread the ball's trajectory; he broke slowly and half-turned over the wrong shoulder. He also struggled to corral the bouncing ball. Without question, a more mobile left fielder would have made the out or prevented both runs from scoring. On top of this, Manny was innocuous at the plate. He walked and singled but again made two inning-ending outs, going 1 for 3 overall and 1 for 8 in a series the Sox were suddenly one game away from losing.

The Sox' season almost ended in Game 3. The game went eleven innings. From the sixth inning on, it was tied 1–1, the result of a pitching duel between Derek Lowe and A's starter Ted Lilly. But the Sox prevailed, 3–1, surviving to see Game 4.

Manny, however, went 0 for 4 and was now batting .083 in the series, 1 for 12 with eleven runners left on base. Ortiz was still hitless, while Mueller's average stood at .183.

Manny came to life in Game 4. He went 2 for 4, and one of his hits buoyed a season-saving rally in the eighth, when the Sox trailed 4–3 and were six outs away from losing the series. Foulke had entered the game to nail down the series for the A's. Manny came up with two outs. He singled to left. It was arguably the most clutch hit of his career, to that point.

The score remained 4–3 Oakland, but now runners were at the corners with Ortiz at the plate. Ortiz was 0 for 16 in the series. He worked a full count against Foulke. The Red Sox' season was one strike away from ending. Then Ortiz lined a double over the head of leaping right-fielder Jermaine Dye. Garcia-parra and Manny scored the winning runs.

Game 5 was on. It was Martinez, who had had a no-decision in Game 1, against Barry Zito, the dominant victor of Game 2. After five innings, the score was 1–0 Oakland. The Red Sox charged back in the top of the sixth. Jason Varitek tied the game by leading off the inning with a solo shot. With runners at first and second, Manny, 3 for 18 in the series, ripped a pitch deep into the left-field seats, giving Boston a 4–1 lead. As he ran to first, he turned toward his teammates, smiled impishly, and pointed at them. The Red Sox went on to win the game 4–2, with Lowe earning the save. The Red Sox were bound for the ALCS for the first time since 1999, when they also faced the Yankees after overcoming an 0–2 deficit in the ALDS. This ALCS would be one for the ages.

The Red Sox turned to Wakefield in Game 1. He gave up two runs in six innings. Mussina, starting for the Yankees, looked good until the fourth, when Manny singled and Ortiz followed him by blasting a two-run shot to right, making it 2–0 Boston. Walker homered to lead off the fifth, and Manny hit his own solo blast later in that inning to make it 4–0 Boston. The Red Sox won 5–2. Manny finished 4 for 5 with three runs scored.

The Yankees evened the series behind Pettitte in Game 2 with a 6–2 win that saw Manny go 1 for 4, bringing his average to .556 for the series. Game 3 pitted two of the best pitchers of their eras, Martinez and Clemens, against each other. The Sox got to Clemens in the first. Damon, playing in his first game of the series after his nasty collision with Damian Jackson in Game 5 of the ALDS, led off with an infield single. Walker doubled to left, and there were two runners in scoring position for Garcia-parra. Garciaparra struck out and Manny came up with a single to center, scoring two runs. It was 2–0 Red Sox.

But Martinez could not hold the lead. The Yankees scored runs in each of the next three innings, building up to a moment that would illustrate the bad blood between the two rivals.

It was 3–2 Yankees and Karim Garcia came to the plate. With first base open, Martinez zipped a fastball at Garcia's head. Garcia ducked; the ball plunked him in the back. Garcia shouted at Martinez, and Varitek put himself between the two. Jorge Posada jumped up the dugout steps and screamed at Martinez. Cameras caught Martinez pointing at his head, then at Posada. The announcers and the Yankees thought Martinez was threatening Posada, but later Martinez said he was signaling that he would remember what Posada had said.

Play resumed, with Garcia at first. Soriano hit a double-play grounder but Nick Johnson scored to give the Yankees a 4–2 lead. On the double play, Garcia slid hard into Walker at second base, upending him. The two players had to be separated. As Garcia returned to the dugout, he and Martinez kept shouting at each other.

Manny had the unenviable task of leading off the bottom of the fourth against Clemens. On a 1-2 count, Clemens threw a fastball at eye level but over the plate. Manny screamed at Clemens and took a few steps toward the mound with his bat still in his hand.

The benches and bullpens immediately cleared in one of the ugliest, highest-profile brawls in recent baseball history. The Yankees' stocky bench coach, Don Zimmer, then seventy-two, charged at Martinez. Martinez later said he was afraid Zimmer was trying to injure his pitching arm. The pitcher stepped slightly to his left, placed his left hand on the side of Zimmer's head, and shoved him stomach-first onto the ground. It was a gentle shove, but it was still a shove, and the Yankees were appalled Martinez had even touched Zimmer given his age.

When play resumed after a ten-minute stoppage, Clemens

struck out Manny. He retired Ortiz and Millar with ease, and after four innings it was 4–2 Yankees. The score stayed that way until the seventh, when the Red Sox cut the lead in half with their last run of the game.

It was a 2–2 series after a Red Sox win in Game 4, with Wakefield accountable for both victories and Mussina, though he hadn't pitched terribly, for both Yankees losses. Manny went 0 for 3 in Game 4, lowering his series average to .375. In Game 5, the Yankees started David Wells for the first time in the series, whereas the Sox returned to Lowe, the loser of Game 2. Wells was superb, holding the Red Sox to one run in seven innings. The one run was a Manny solo homer in the fourth. Lowe lasted seven and one-third innings, pitching well until he left the game in the eighth, trailing 4–1. The Yankees took a 3–2 lead in the series, which now returned to the Bronx for the final two games.

Game 6 was a seesaw affair, but the Sox prevailed and it was on to Game 7. Manny was batting .333 for the series.

The final game of the series was a rematch between Martinez and Clemens that would break the hearts of Red Sox Nation. The Red Sox led 4–0 after four innings. Martinez was cruising, having surrendered only two hits. By the bottom of the eighth, Martinez was pitching with a 5–2 lead. He had struck out Alfonso Soriano on his one hundredth pitch to end the seventh and pointed to the heavens as he left the mound, indicating to Sox fans familiar with the gesture that he believed he was done.

So Sox officials and fans were surprised when Martinez strolled out for the eighth inning. By the time it was over, the score was 5–5 and the Red Sox knew they'd blown their best chance—because now they'd have to face Rivera.

The great closer shut down Boston in the ninth, tenth, and eleventh in a relief performance that only further sealed his lock as the best closer to ever play the game. Out of reliable relievers, the Sox turned to Wakefield for the tenth and then the eleventh. When third baseman Aaron Boone led off the eleventh, Wakefield tossed a knuckleball that stayed relatively straight, and Boone hacked at it. It was clear immediately the ball was high enough and far enough to get over the fence in the left-field corner. The only question was whether it would be fair or foul. As it sailed to the right of the foul pole, Boone raised his hands and sprinted toward first. Wakefield walked off the field with his head down, no expression on his face.

A few Sox players, including Lowe, Martinez, and Ortiz, sulked in the dugout as New York celebrated its latest clutch victory over Boston. Manny had been a nonfactor in the game, going 1 for 5 and grounding out in his final two at-bats, in the eighth and tenth. He still batted .310 for the series, but his OPS was only .885. Overall, he was 13 for 49 in the postseason with 3 home runs and 7 RBIs in twelve games.

And as draining and disappointing as the ALCS was for the Red Sox, the off-season would be even more tumultuous—for the team, but especially for Manny.

CHAPTER 24

2004: Conquering the Yankees

Little was fired after the Game 7 disaster. That was just the beginning of the housecleaning. On October 29, the Red Sox placed Manny on waivers, making him available, for a $20,000 fee, to any team willing to absorb the last four years and nearly $100 million left on his contract. Teams had forty-eight hours to act. Manny was coming off a season in which he had hit .325 with 37 homers, 104 RBIs, and a 1.009 OPS.

No team claimed Manny. Reports surfaced in early November of a possible three-way deal in which the Sox would send Garciaparra, a free agent after the 2004 season, to Anaheim to free the shortstop position for Alex Rodriguez, whom the Sox would obtain from the Rangers in exchange for Manny. Officials from all three teams furiously denied the rumors.

By early December, officials from Boston and Texas had asked the league for permission to discuss the possibility of restructuring Rodriguez's gargantuan contract—usually prohibited under league rules. The Sox met a representative from the players' union about adjusting A-Rod's contract. The union would have to approve any such deal, and they were strongly opposed to any player's taking a voluntary pay cut because of the precedent it might set for the rest of the union's members.

On December 17, the deal was set to go. The Sox would send Manny and lefty pitching prospect Jon Lester to the Rangers for A-Rod. They would then deal Garciaparra to the White Sox for outfielder Magglio Ordonez, a hardworking slugger who would go on to have several injury-prone years. The Sox essentially were betting that an A-Rod–Ordonez combo would outperform Manny and Garciaparra.

The Rangers demanded the Sox pay at least $25 million of Manny's salary over the length of his contract. The Sox hoped to recoup some of that cash by having A-Rod restructure his contract. A-Rod, desperate to get out of Texas, was willing. He offered to lop $29 million off his deal in exchange for some minor concessions. The union countered with a plan that would cut A-Rod's deal by about $12 million and grant him increased marketing powers. The difference amounted, then, to $17 million the Sox would have to pay to set off the cascade of deals that could have changed the course of Manny's career—and Red Sox history.

The Sox said no. The union said it could offer no sweeter restructuring of A-Rod's contract. And with that, the deal was off. The Red Sox were furious at the players' union. "The Players' Association's intransigence and the arbitrary nature of its action are responsible for the deal's demise today," Larry Lucchino told the media.

Meanwhile, Macaco tried to focus Manny, who felt unwanted outside Boston and unhappy within it. "I told him, 'You have to forget about leaving Boston. You have to start over, change your point of view. Stay focused on baseball, but try to talk to the press every once in a while. It won't hurt you.'" Manny would heed his advice.

Manny arrived in camp on time and met immediately with Sox officials, who reassured him about his value to the team. He strolled around the locker room telling everyone, "This is the year!" When the season began, Manny had no problem shrugging off the off-season snubs. He hit a two-run homer off Yankee Javier Vazquez on April 25 in the Bronx, giving Martinez all the support he needed in a 2–0 win. The victory clinched a sweep for Boston (12–6), which had beaten the Yankees (8–11) five of six times to open up an early 4.5-game lead over their rivals. Manny was hitting .392 with an OPS of 1.122.

On May 10, Manny took his first day off to fly to Miami and take the U.S. citizenship test. Although Pura had been a citizen for many years and frequently advised her grandchildren to follow suit, changing immigration laws had created a new sense of urgency. The next day at Fenway, he sprinted to left field in the top of the first inning carrying a miniature American flag as the crowd roared. He ran to the stands and handed the small flag to a spectator. "I'm very proud to be an American citizen," Manny said later, adding, "Now they can't kick me out of the country."

The moment was poignant for the team's other Dominicans. "I was so proud of Manny," Pedro Martinez told the *Boston Globe*. "I was very happy Manny took that flag out, saying, 'Thank you, America, for giving me the chance.' Some people don't know Manny all that well, but Manny's really smart, and he knew what he was trying to say when he came out with that flag."

On May 29, he homered for the sixth time in nine games and led the league with 14. He had 35 RBIs and was batting .357 with a 1.114 OPS. The Sox were 30–19, a half game behind the Yankees. But soon the team stumbled after its hot start. They were 42–32 and 5.5 games behind the Yankees going into a key three-game set in New York. Manny had continued hitting well: 20 home runs, 59 RBIs, a .343 average, and a 1.102 OPS.

The Yankees series was a disaster. The Yankees swept it, increasing their lead to eight games and amassing a 50–26 record compared with the earthbound Sox at 42–35. One of the key moments in the series took place in the second game. With the game tied 2–2 in the bottom of the eighth, Garciaparra's throwing error allowed Kenny Lofton—now the Yankees' lead-off man and center fielder—to reach second on what should have been, at most, an infield single. Lofton ultimately scored and the game ended up a 4–2 Yankees victory.

Significantly, Garciaparra—who also went 0 for 4—sat out the next game, which the Red Sox lost 5–4 in thirteen innings. It was no secret Garciaparra was unhappy. As opposed to Manny, Garciaparra had not bounced back from the winter trade talks. He was hitting .235 and he and the Red Sox had not agreed in training camp on a contract extension. The shortstop would later say that he needed the game off because his Achilles tendon was sore but that he volunteered to pinch-hit in the late innings.

Manager Terry Francona, in his first year as Little's replacement, remembered it differently. According to *Feeding the Monster,* Garciaparra had asked Francona to let him sit out because he was upset with his defensive miscues the day before. Regardless, there was no disputing that Garciaparra had missed an important regular-season game.

By contrast, Derek Jeter appeared to be risking life and limb for the Yankees. With two outs and two runners in scoring position in the top of the twelfth and the game tied 4–4, Nixon came to the plate. He lifted a pop fly into shallow left field, not far from third base. The ball seemed destined to fall in fair territory and give the Sox the lead. But Jeter sprinted headlong toward the seats as the ball was landing and made a lunging catch, tumbling over the wall and into the third row after he'd snagged the ball in fair territory.

His chin and cheek were bleeding, his pinstripe uniform streaked red, when he emerged from the stands having recorded the third out. He was taken to nearby Columbia Presbyterian

Hospital for X-rays. Alex Rodriguez played shortstop in the top of the thirteenth, and the Yankees won the game in the bottom of the inning. Meanwhile, the Red Sox shortstop was sitting in the dugout. Reductive as it was to boil down either Jeter's or Garciaparra's career to this single game, the contrast between Jeter's grit and Garciaparra's inactivity was too clear for fans, sportswriters, and talk-show hosts to ignore. Garciaparra was only a few months removed from his superb 2003 season and postseason heroics, yet it looked like his days as a celebrated Red Sox player were drawing to a close.

Meanwhile, a transformed Manny was once again endearing himself with fans, and even the media, who got occasional quips. In a June 26 column, the *Herald*'s Tony Massarotti wrote, "It has been truly extraordinary to see Ramirez' popularity soar this season as he has allowed everyone a glimpse of his personality. Ramirez exchanged warm gestures with fans upon returning to left field after a sixth-inning double, and he made a curtain call after his catch in the seventh."

Manny even started making diving catches that brought him praise, although on one occasion he was a little too eager to catch the ball. On July 20, with Martinez pitching against the Orioles, Damon failed to haul in a deep fly ball off the wall in center. Damon chased down the ball and threw it toward the cutoff man Mark Bellhorn. But Manny, standing a mere twenty feet away, between Bellhorn and Damon, lunged quickly and intercepted Damon's throw, leading to an inside-the-park two-run home run. The play was a finalist for MLB.com's 2004 Blooper of the Year Award.

On August 1, the Red Sox were 56–47, meaning they were two games under .500 since starting 30–19. They were 9.5 games behind the Yankees and a game behind Texas (and tied with the Angels) in the wild card race. In a trade that rocked New

England, Garciaparra went to the Cubs as part of a four-team deal that brought Orlando Cabrera, the Expos' slick-fielding shortstop, and Doug Mientkiewicz, a Gold Glove–caliber first baseman, from the Twins.

Cabrera would never duplicate Garciaparra's offense, but the Sox were willing to trade homers for defense. Mientkiewicz, for his part, would serve as a first-rate defensive replacement. Nearly two weeks after the trade, the Sox caught fire. They went 28–7 between August 10 and September 16, including a ten-game winning streak and a sixteen-out-of-seventeen run. The team went from 60–50 to 88–57. It was enough for them to move ahead by 5.5 games over the Angels in the wild card race and to pull within 3.5 games of the Yankees going into a three-game series in the Bronx. A sweep would pull the Sox even with New York in the loss column.

The Red Sox won the opener, but the Yankees won the final two games of the series, effectively clinching the division. But the Sox' hot streak had iced the wild card, and they wound up heading to the playoffs with 98 regular-season wins. Their defense had improved dramatically because of Cabrera and Mientkiewicz. And all season long, even during the cold spells, the pitching had been better than it was in 2003, owing to the superb years of two off-season acquisitions: starter Curt Schilling (21–6, 3.26 ERA, 1.06 WHIP, 203 Ks) and closer Foulke (32 saves, 2.17 ERA), who'd been with the A's in the previous postseason. Manny finished the season batting .308 with 43 home runs, 130 RBIs, and a 1.010 OPS.

For the divisional series, the Red Sox drew the Anaheim Angels. Schilling and Martinez handled the Angels easily on the road in Games 1 and 2, though Schilling aggravated his right-ankle injury covering first base late in Game 1. Manny's three-run homer in the fourth broke open Game 1, vaulting the Sox to an 8–0 lead in a game the Red Sox won 9–3. Overall, Manny went 3 for 8 with 3 runs, 5 RBIs, and his key home run in the first two games.

The Red Sox won Game 3 at Fenway 8–6 and swept the series 3–0. They would face the Yankees in the ALCS for the second straight season.

Game 1 was Schilling against Mussina. It was like three games in one. The Red Sox fell behind 8–0 after six innings, rallied to make it 8–7 after seven and a half innings, and finally lost 10–7.

Schilling was clearly hobbled. He had taken the painkiller Marcaine before the game to minimize the effects of tendinitis in his right ankle. He was ineffective from the start, giving up six runs in three innings and leaving the game. Mussina, by contrast, was outstanding, no-hitting the Red Sox for the first six innings until the Red Sox mounted a furious rally, scoring five in the seventh and two in the eighth. But the Yankees slammed the door behind a two-run Williams double in the bottom of the eighth. Ortiz and Varitek were the offensive stars for the Red Sox, each with 2 hits and 2 RBIs. Manny went 1 for 4 and scored a run.

The Sox had the obvious advantage in Game 2, sending Martinez to the mound against Jon Lieber. But the Yankees won the pitchers' duel and took a 2–0 series lead with the series shifting to Boston. Manny was not a factor in the game, going 1 for 4, bringing him to 2 for 8 in the series with no RBIs.

In Game 3, the Yankees piled up twenty-two hits in a 19–8 rout, playing pinball off the Monster all night. The Red Sox led 4–3 after two innings and the game was tied 6–6 after three innings. But the Yankees blew it open in the middle innings, taking a 17–6 lead. The fans fell silent. No team in the history of Major League Baseball had ever rallied from a 3–0 series deficit. The possibility seemed especially farfetched given the Yankees' dominance in Game 3 and the historically lopsided rivalry. Though the Red Sox scored eight runs, Manny was quiet, going 1 for 4. He was now 3 for 12 in the series with no RBIs. Ortiz and Varitek were again the offensive stars for Boston. Each was now batting .500 in the series.

The match-up in Game 4 was Lowe against Orlando Hernandez. The Yankees led 4–3 after six innings and took the lead into the ninth when they summoned Rivera from the bullpen to close out the series and the Red Sox' season. But Boston tied the game off Rivera in dramatic fashion when pinch-runner Dave Roberts, an outfielder acquired for his speed in a late-season deal, stole second base and scored on a Mueller single.

The team rallied, improbably, off Rivera, but blew two chances to end it. The Red Sox mounted little offense in the tenth or eleventh, and staved off a bases-loaded New York threat in the eleventh.

In the twelfth, Manny led off with a sharp single to left. Ortiz then crushed a homer into the Yankee bullpen in right field. He rounded third, turned for home, and flicked his batting helmet into the air as his teammates waited to jump up and down around him at home plate. There would be a Game 5. And it would include a warmer Manny, who had gone 2 for 3 with three walks and one run. He was now batting .333 for the series, but it still seemed as if he had yet to hit his stride.

Game 5 was a battle between Martinez, who'd lost Game 2, and Mussina, who'd won Game 1. The score remained 2–1 Red Sox until the top of the sixth. On Martinez's one hundredth pitch of the night, Jeter lined a double down the right-field line, clearing the bases, giving the Yankees a 4–2 lead, and silencing Fenway.

The score stayed 4–2 until the Sox came to bat in the eighth. Ortiz led off the inning with a home run off Tom Gordon. Millar walked; again, Francona inserted Roberts as a pinch-runner. Nixon singled to center and Roberts went to third. That was when Rivera replaced Gordon. A Varitek sacrifice fly scored Roberts and the game was tied 4–4 before Rivera retired the next two batters.

It remained 4–4 through the night and into the next morning. But in the bottom of the fourteenth, nearly six hours after the first pitch had been thrown, Damon—2 for 24 in the series—worked a one-out walk off Loaiza. Cabrera struck out, and Manny, still without an RBI in the series, came to the plate with two outs. He earned a walk, setting the stage for Ortiz. Ortiz drew a 2–2 count, and then fouled off three straight pitches before hitting a soft liner into center field. It dropped, Damon raced home, and Boston, somehow, was going back to New York, now trailing 3–2 in the series but carrying the momentum with back-to-back extra-inning victories, both of which dented Rivera's air of invincibility.

The initial Game 6 drama was about whether Schilling would be available to pitch. The press had been floating stories that Schilling might wear a protective boot, but the Sox wondered about other ways to fix the dislocated tendon in his right ankle. The Sox doctors sutured the skin around the tendon into surrounding tissues. Blood seeped through Schilling's sock during the game, creating the most iconic image of the series.

Yet Schilling was magnificent, giving up only one run in seven innings on four hits. Lieber, pitching for the Yankees, gave up four runs in seven and one-third innings.

The Sox took a 4–2 lead into the ninth, and Foulke earned the save. It was on to Game 7.

Suddenly the Red Sox were back where they'd been one season earlier: a game away from their first World Series since 1986 and one game away from elimination. Boston had already become the first team in history to force a Game 7 after trailing a series 3–0. The deciding game pitted Lowe, coming off his quality start in the Red Sox' Game 4 win, against Kevin Brown, who'd gotten shelled but also earned a no decision in the Yankees' Game 3 victory.

Once again, Brown had nothing. The Red Sox won 10–3, advancing to the World Series and making baseball—and sports—history by coming back from an 0–3 deficit.

Manny was in the middle of several key rallies, but he had yet to strike a defining blow in the playoffs. He finished the ALCS 9 for 30 (.300) with 5 walks (.400 OBP), but he slugged just .333 and did not have an RBI. The ALCS belonged to Ortiz, Schilling, Varitek, Foulke, Damon, and Lowe. The World Series would belong to Manny.

CHAPTER 25

2004: World Series MVP

The St. Louis Cardinals won 105 games in the regular season, best in the majors, and they did not appear intimidated in Game 1 at Fenway. But they did appear outmatched. The Sox jumped ahead 4–0 in the first inning of Game 1. Ortiz started the scoring with a three-run blast off starter Woody Williams.

What ensued thereafter was a back-and-forth, topsy-turvy affair. The Cardinals scored once in the second and again in the third to make it 4–2 before the Red Sox extended their lead to 7–2 with a three-run third.

The Cardinals kept fighting. They closed the lead to 7–5 in the fourth, chasing Wakefield from the game. In the sixth, facing Arroyo, the Cardinals mounted a two-out rally.

That's when the game became a microcosm of Manny's career. In the seventh, with runners on first and second, Manny singled to right scoring Bellhorn and breaking the tie. Ortiz followed with a single, making it 9–7 Sox before the inning ended.

Just when the Red Sox were six outs away from winning Game 1, just when Manny was six outs away from having the game-winning RBI—his second RBI on a night when he went 3 for 5—Manny singlehandedly blew the newly formed lead with his shoddy play in the field. In the top of the eighth, with two runners on base, Renteria singled to left. Manny overran the ball, allowing pinch-runner Jason Marquis to score, just barely beating Manny's belated throw.

The next hitter, Larry Walker, lofted an easy fly to left. It should have been the second out. Manny could have caught the ball jogging but decided at the last minute to make a sliding catch. His spike caught in the grass and Manny dropped the ball. His cleat kicked up a divot. The ball rolled behind him. Roger Cedeno scored to tie the game, 9–9, and Walker ended up on second.

The game suddenly hung in the balance. But Foulke closed the inning, and Bellhorn smacked a two-run homer in the bottom of the eighth to give the Sox an 11–9 lead. Foulke made it stand up, and the Sox took Game 1.

All told, the Cardinals scored nine runs in Game 1. They would only score three more in the remaining three games. Two of them came in Game 2, when the Sox cruised to a 6–2 win behind Schilling. Schilling scattered four hits and yielded only one unearned run in six innings. The Cardinals foursome of Albert Pujols, Scott Rolen, Jim Edmonds, and Walker was silenced. Foulke pitched a perfect ninth and the Red Sox led the Series 2–0.

Offensively, Manny still hadn't done much: 1 for 4 with a single and a run scored. But he was batting .444 in the Series. Still, Foulke was easily the team's MVP after two games. If not Foulke, Bellhorn, whose two-run double gave the Sox a 4–2 lead in the fourth and gave Bellhorn 4 RBIs in two games, along with a team-leading .500 average and 1.792 OPS.

It was in Game 3 that Manny asserted himself as an MVP candidate. Martinez started the game for the Red Sox, facing Jeff Suppan for the first game in St. Louis. The Red Sox won 4–1, the Cardinals' only run coming when Walker hit a solo shot off Foulke in the ninth.

Manny ended up 2 for 4 with 2 RBIs and one run scored. His numbers were exceptional (.462 average, 1.225 OPS) and his 4

RBIs tied him with Bellhorn and Ortiz for the team lead. Mueller's percentages (.500 average, 1.315 OPS) were better, but Mueller had made three errors in Game 2, one of which had led to the Cardinals' only run. Manny had committed two gaffes in Game 1, but had atoned for them with strong defense in Game 3. Foulke had nailed down all three World Series wins with four innings in three games, but statistical rules did not credit him with a single save.

So the Series MVP was an open question heading into Game 4. In the Boston area, it was more hotly debated than the outcome of the Series. Lowe, last seen as the victor in Game 7 against the Yankees in the ALDS, started Game 4 against the Cardinals. Marquis was his opponent. Damon opened the game with a solo home run. Lowe needed no more support as he pitched seven shutout innings to bring the Sox their first World Series trophy in eighty-six years.

Manny had one hit during the 3–0 win, significant because it meant he had notched at least one hit in all fourteen playoff games. Dating back to 2003, he had a seventeen-game playoff hit streak—tied with Jeter and Hank Bauer for the all-time major league record. (The streak ended in the Sox' first playoff game in 2005.)

Overall in the playoffs, Manny hit .350 with 2 homers and 11 RBIs. His on-base percentage was .423. He was voted the World Series MVP, though his World Series numbers (.412, 1.088, 1 home run, 4 RBIs) were not much better than those of Mueller (.429, 1.127, no home runs, 2 RBIs), Ortiz (.308, 1.086, 1 home run, 4 RBIs), or Bellhorn (.300, 1.263, 1 home run, 4 RBIs). Then there was Foulke, who had nailed down all four games, but earned the statistical save only in Game 4.

Whether or not he deserved the MVP, no one could deny that Manny had performed when it mattered most, as opposed to

A-Rod, who—while hitting .258 with 2 home runs and 5 RBIs in seven games against the Red Sox—would not have even been in the debate for ALCS MVP, had the Yankees prevailed.

The two sluggers had nearly been traded for each other in the off-season, and in the aftermath of the Red Sox triumph, fans and the media reflected on the aborted A-Rod trade and the Red Sox' decision, before the season, to place Manny on waivers. "There was a time when the front office didn't think it could live with No. 24. In the end, how could it have lived without him? He was endearing, he was aggravating. He was clueless, he was clutch. He was Manny, the manchild who needed no last name," wrote John Powers in the *Globe*.

The MVP was one thing. Manny now had a ring, too, and with it he could refute any past or future claims that his attention deficits and defensive gaps had no place on a championship squad.

CHAPTER 26

2005: Inside the Monster

The Sox lost Derek Lowe and Pedro Martinez to free agency and replaced the popular Orlando Cabrera with Edgar Renteria. The team set its sights on repeating in 2005, hoping Renteria would upgrade Cabrera's offense and that the acquisitions of David Wells and pitcher Matt Clement would offset the losses of Lowe and Martinez.

As for Manny, he got off to a slow start, hitting .211 over the first ten games. The Boston press remained patient with him. They had learned his numbers would be there at the end.

But Manny continued to slump. His batting average was .230 on May 20, after forty-one games. His lone offensive highlight came May 15, when he became the thirty-ninth player in major league history to hit 400 homers. His 400th was an opposite-field blast off Mariners righty Gil Meche. At that point, only four players in history had reached 400 in fewer at-bats: Babe Ruth, Harmon Killebrew, Jim Thome, and Mark McGwire.

By June 26, Manny and the Sox were back in stride. His average was up to .271. He had 19 home runs and his 66 RBIs led the AL. His OPS was .913, below his career average but still elite. And the Sox (44–30) were in first place following a seven-game winning streak, 2.5 games ahead of the Orioles and 6.5 games ahead of the Yankees.

•   •   •

The drama in Manny's season started July 18, when he disappeared through a door in the Monster during a conference at the mound. He missed the first pitch of the next at-bat but came out in time for the second one—a good thing, because the ball was hit to him in left field. Francona later told the media that Manny "had to tinkle." It turned out not to be true. In September, the operator of the Monster's manual scoreboard told reporters Manny had come inside to chat. "He just popped in like he usually does," Christian Elias told the *Herald*. "And we started talking about this and that, the weather probably, and all of a sudden the phone started ringing and everything, and we were like, 'What?' And then Manny said, 'Oh, shoot,' and ran back out there." There wasn't even a bathroom inside the Monster, Elias said. He wasn't sure why Manny and Francona had floated the urination story.

Of course, Manny was known for advancing strange cover stories to reporters and for befriending stadium employees. Edward "Pookie" Jackson, the Red Sox home clubhouse attendant for almost fifteen years, talks about how Manny would sometimes try to toy with reporters. "I think the press sometimes takes him too seriously. Sometimes, he'd be joking, and they'd think he was for real. Like when he'd say, 'Get your story and get out!'" Jackson says. "He wouldn't say it with a smile, but when he went into the back of the clubhouse, he'd smile about it. He'd tell us [clubhouse employees], 'I'm going to say something to them and see if they write it.'"

Martinez still laughs about one of Manny's spoofs. "Manny calls the media, gets them all together and he says, 'Okay, wait, I'll be back in five minutes.' Well, he makes them all wait one hour. Finally, he comes back and he says, 'I'm going to give $5 million of my own money to sign Pedro back on the Red Sox.' Everybody took it seriously. He really got them to believe it."

But the stories that got the most attention rarely originated from Manny's sound bites.

On July 26, for example, *Sports Illustrated* delivered a bombshell: The magazine reported that Manny had, once again, asked management to trade him. The reported trade demand stunned the rest of the team. "It doesn't make sense to me," Ortiz told the *Herald,* saying he was close enough to Manny that they would have discussed any trade request.

What really happened? As Seth Mnookin detailed in *Feeding the Monster,* Manny sat down with Epstein, Lucchino, and co-owner Tom Werner in mid-July and explained why he needed to leave. "You guys are awesome," Manny told the executives. "The whole time I've been here, you guys have been awesome to me. But I can't take Boston anymore. I can't even take my kid to the park without being bothered. I need to get out of here." He suggested six teams he would play for.

The Boston press never reported the details of that meeting. Regardless, drama arrived for Manny not long after the *Sports Illustrated* story. Days earlier, Francona had promised Manny a day off on July 27. Then Nixon got a strained oblique July 26, forcing the Sox to put him on the disabled list. According to an anonymous source cited by Michael Silverman in the *Herald,* Francona had bench coach Brad Mills ask Manny if he still needed the day off, without reference to Nixon's unavailability. Manny said he still needed his off day.

Before Silverman's report, the mainstream belief of the press and the public was that Manny had denied a personal plea from Francona in the face of Nixon's injury. Even after Silverman's report, this belief held, and not without justification, since Silverman's source was anonymous. Regardless, the Sox had to play without Manny and Nixon, and they started an outfield of Damon, an out-of-position Millar, and rookie Adam Stern—and still beat Tampa Bay, 4–1. They moved to 56–45 and remained in first place, two games up on the Yankees.

The press pounced on Manny for his absence. "One day

someone within the Sox clubhouse or in the Yawkey Way offices will rise up and condemn him for his selfish indifference. That day has yet to come, mainly because his bosses and his teammates feel like Manny is, in essence, holding the team hostage. So the Sox mostly look the other way," wrote Edes in the *Globe*.

Silverman's source reported that Manny nearly came to blows with Schilling during an ugly locker-room exchange July 27, when Ortiz told Schilling that Tampa's scheduled starter, Seth McClung, had "nasty stuff." "Yeah, that's why Manny took the day off," Schilling replied. "Screw you," Manny shouted back. "I can hit anyone in baseball, including your ass." Ortiz had to separate the two of them.

Manny was out of the lineup July 31, fueling talk the Sox would complete a deal before the trade deadline passed that night. Reporters crowded into Francona's office for his pregame briefing. Millar burst into the office with Manny at his side. Millar announced he would be acting as Manny's translator for the press. Millar directed reporters to ask questions, and they naturally asked if Manny could ever be happy in Boston. "I'm strong. I'm just here to play and win—I'm a gangster," Manny said. "I'm still here. I'm here to win. I'm here to help this team win for 2005. I want to be with this team and win another World Series."

So the deal died, much ado about little, just like all the others before it. Regardless, in advance of a possible trade, Manny was held out of the lineup for the deadline-day game against the Twins, a game that marked the debut of Jonathan Papelbon, the Sox' best pitching prospect. Kapler, Millar, and Damon started in the outfield. With the game tied 3–3 in the eighth and Renteria on second after a clutch two-out double, the Twins walked Ortiz intentionally with Stern—Millar's defensive replacement—on deck. In the middle of the intentional pass, Manny popped out of the dugout and told Stern to go to the bench.

The crowd, which had booed Manny only two days earlier, roared as Manny strode to the on-deck circle. Manny stroked Juan Rincon's fifth pitch up the middle, scoring Renteria with what would become the winning run in a 4–3 victory. Fenway went berserk. "It's hard not to get chills when that stuff is happening," Francona told reporters after the game. "That's one of the most electric baseball atmospheres you'll ever see." Manny added his own commentary, using the phrase that had already become part of the Boston vernacular. "This is the place to be," Ramirez told a New England Sports Network reporter as he left the field. "Manny being Manny, it's great, man." The moment may have had a carryover effect for the team. The Sox went 9–2 in their next eleven games and, with a 68–47 mark after the games of August 13, opened a five-game lead over the Yankees.

The Sox were 82–57 and four games up on the Yankees entering a three-game series in the Bronx September 9. The Yankees took two of three in the series to pull within three games. The Sox, despite a 83–59 record, would have to fight the Yankees for the division.

But they lost three of their next five games to fall behind not only New York but also Cleveland for the wild card. After leading their division nearly the entire season, Boston was in danger of missing the playoffs. The good news, though, was that Manny was hot. He went 4 for 4 with 2 homers in a 15–2 victory over Tampa Bay September 20. He homered again in a loss the next day. He homered for a third straight game to open a series against Baltimore. The Sox swept the Orioles, with Manny homering again in the final game to key a 9–3 win. It was his forty-first. Manny had become only the second Red Sox hitter besides Carl Yastrzemski to have at least 40 in three seasons.

With seven games left, the Sox were tied with New York at 91–64. After splitting a four-game set with Toronto, the Sox were 93–66, one game behind New York.

In the final stretch of the season, Boston edged out Cleveland for the wild card spot. The team was slated to face the AL Central champion White Sox in the ALDS. Manny had carried them there. In Boston's final twelve games, he went 17 for 44 (.386) with 9 homers and 19 RBIs. He finished the season with 45 homers (third in the AL, tying his career high) and 144 RBIs (second), a .292 average and .982 OPS (fourth). After five seasons in Boston, Manny had 199 home runs and 610 RBIs.

The Red Sox were a shadow of themselves in the postseason and they fell to the White Sox 3–0.

Considering injuries to Schilling and Foulke, the losses of Lowe and Martinez, and the slumps of Millar and Bellhorn, the Red Sox had had a good year—ninety-five wins and a playoff berth—but they would not repeat. For what it was worth, Manny had turned around his playoff numbers with his superb Game 3, in which he went 2 for 3 with 2 home runs, 2 RBIs, 2 runs scored, and 2 walks. He wound up hitting .300 with a 1.317 OPS in 2005's three-game postseason.

The end of the 2005 season made Manny a so-called 10–5 player: he had played ten years in the majors and five with his current team, earning the right to veto any trade he didn't like. Trade rumors began swirling the day the season came to an end. And these rumors seemed more serious than the rumors of seasons past. One of Manny's agents, Greg Genske, met with Werner and Lucchino to outline possible deals. The group agreed "to work together on exploring trade options," Genske told Edes in the November 10 *Globe*. "We want to do what's in the best interests of the Red Sox and in the best interests of Manny." Lucchino said the talks were serious, and that the team was looking for "guidance" from Manny, since he could veto any trade. "We're not trying to make light of it," Lucchino said. "He has expressed from time to time a desire to explore this and we're going to go in good faith and actively explore it."

Manny wasn't the only outfielder potentially leaving town. Damon was a free agent. His agent, Scott Boras, was also meeting with the Red Sox brass.

CHAPTER 27

2006: 85 Days Without Theo; 27-Game Hitting Streak; 32 Games Missed

On October 31, hours before his contract as general manager expired, Epstein resigned. He and the team had not come to terms over a new deal. On November 1, the team began an eighty-five-day period of life without Epstein. So the off-season's various challenges now included a new management hierarchy within the Red Sox front office. Esptein's previous assistant, Josh Byrnes, had become the new GM of the Diamondbacks, meaning there was no heir apparent at Fenway.

Meanwhile, the Manny rumors continued. At various points in the off-season, Orlando Cabrera and Ortiz told the media that Manny would not return to Boston. In addition, Manny's home was placed on the market. In December, Red Sox senior advisor Bill Lajoie, one of the Sox officials picking up slack in Epstein's absence, commented directly on the prospect of trading Manny: "We're not going to get fair value in any shape or form [for Manny]," he told the *Boston Herald*. "This is an A-1 hitter. If you trade him, you are not going to get value, man for man. We will go as far as we can to satisfy him but we also have to satisfy the Red Sox."

On December 10, the *Globe*'s Chris Snow and Edes cited anonymous sources in reporting that the team had offered Manny to Baltimore for Miguel Tejada. The deal made sense. Both were dissatisfied, and the Sox needed a shortstop; the front office, in Epstein's absence, had shipped Renteria, whose acquisition had been a thorn in Epstein's side, to the Braves for prospect Andy Marte.

As usual, none of the Manny trades went through. But another one did, and it was a Thanksgiving-day blockbuster: The Red Sox traded elite shortstop prospect Hanley Ramirez (no relation), pitching prospect Anibal Sanchez, and two other prospects to the Marlins for starting pitcher Josh Beckett—only twenty-five but already a proven postseason performer—along with third baseman Mike Lowell.

Other significant moves occurred in Epstein's absence, too. The team traded Doug Mirabelli to the Padres for second baseman Mark Loretta, a proven starter who would be an upgrade over Bellhorn and Graffanino. Meanwhile, Damon signed with the Yankees, Mueller signed with the Dodgers, Millar signed with the Orioles, and John Olerud retired.

While Lowell could replace Mueller at third, the Red Sox still had holes at center field (Damon), shortstop (Renteria), and first (Olerud/Millar). But on January 25, the team no longer had a hole at GM. The thirty-two-year-old Epstein returned to the fold. In weeks, it would seem as if he had never left.

Manny and Macaco spent the off-season traveling through the Dominican Republic—courtesy of a three-month leave Manny had financed—capping it with a trip to Brazil. Manny loved his anonymity in Brazil, where the two men visited with Juliana's family, enjoyed the night life of Rio, and scoped out plots for a new, beachfront home. Manny returned to the States with an orange tint to his dreadlocks and a scraggly beard, sounding like a spokesperson for the Brazilian tourist bureau. Juliana had not gone to Brazil. She had remained in Weston, caring for their first son, two-year-old Manny Jr., and preparing for the birth of their second child, Lucas.

Perhaps it was his newborn; perhaps it was just the difficulty of mustering intensity for April baseball after three consecutive trips to the postseason, including a championship. But for one reason or another, Manny began the 2006 season in one of the worst power slumps of his career. After forty-two games, Manny was batting .294 with a .931 OPS—nothing dreadful there, but his power numbers told a different tale. He had 8 home runs and 22 RBIs. In the *Globe*, Edes pointed out that there were forty-eight big leaguers with more homers and ninety with more RBIs. But Edes also summarized the prevailing wisdom about Manny's slump, noting that previous New England panic attacks over Manny's slow starts had proven fruitless. Moreover, the Red Sox (26–16) were in first place, 2.5 games up on the Yankees (24–19).

As the season continued, Manny had a few moments of defensive excellence, especially at Fenway, where he had learned to play the difficult Monster. But he was also making alert plays on the road. In a June 6 game in the Bronx, Jorge Posada crushed a ball off the wall in center field. The ball caromed past Damon's replacement in center field, Coco Crisp. Under different circumstances, Posada might have had a triple, and a faster runner would have had a home run. But Manny had backed up the play smartly and held Posada to a double. Two batters later, Posada was stranded at second, and the Sox held on to their 1–0 lead behind rookie starter David Pauley, age twenty-two.

Two innings later, though—with the game tied 1–1 because of a Bernie Williams solo shot in the fifth—Manny committed a baserunning blunder by trying to stretch a one-out single into a double. Though he may have been simply trying to test Damon's weak arm, he was out easily, a key play in a game the Sox lost, 2–1, when Pauley started walking batters in the seventh. It was a typical Manny game—he went 2 for 3 with a walk and in the eighth he drove a ball over the wall in left only to be robbed of a homer by a leaping Melky Cabrera. Manny's batting average now stood, after fifty-six games, at .299, his OPS at .996. He had 14 home runs and 37 RBIs—more than respectable totals for a season just over one-third done. The Red Sox (33–23) fell 1.5 games behind the Yankees (35–22) with the loss but it was one loss in a still-young season.

On July 1, Manny homered to become the 241st player in big league history to amass 2,000 hits. The buzz surrounding him was overwhelmingly positive. He was the AL's leading vote-getter for the All-Star game, and his midseason numbers justified his popularity: He was hitting .306 with a 1.049 OPS, 24 home runs, and 65 RBIs. And the Red Sox (53–33) were in first place, three games up on the Yankees (50–36).

Manny announced he would skip the All-Star game to rest a sore knee. He had played until the All-Star break, so the decision to skip the game angered many in the press and baseball, including MLB commissioner Bud Selig. The team backed Manny, saying he needed to rest his knee.

Three days after the All-Star break, Manny started a career-best twenty-seven-game hitting streak that lifted his batting average to .325 and his OPS to 1.064. By the end of the streak, on August 12, Manny had 32 home runs and 93 RBIs. And the Red Sox (67–48) were in the thick of the race, trailing the Yankees (68–45) by two with forty-seven games remaining.

The Yankees came to Fenway for a five-game series, starting with a doubleheader August 18. By this time, the Sox still trailed by 1.5 games, meaning that the series gave them the chance to climb into first. Winning the division was paramount, because the defending champion White Sox held a two-game lead in the wild card standings.

But the Yankees swept the doubleheader, pounding Sox pitching in winning 12–4 and 14–11. After one day of baseball, the Yankees had increased their lead to 3.5 games.

In the third game, the Yankees destroyed Beckett, tagging him for nine runs in five and two-thirds innings in a 13–5 blowout. Manny homered again, a three-run shot off Randy Johnson that tied the game 3–3 in the fourth.

The Yankees walked Manny three times in game 4. Manny still went 2 for 2 with an RBI—his 100th on the season. Nonetheless, it was another Yankee win, this time 8–5 in ten innings. The Sox fell 5.5 games behind the Yankees and four behind the White Sox in the wild card race.

Their three-year playoff streak was in jeopardy. The Sox needed a win in the finale against New York, if only to stanch the bleeding, but they lost, 2–1, in a pitchers' duel between David Wells and Cory Lidle.

Manny walked twice and then left the game early because of what he said were cramps in his right hamstring. He did not play in the next game in Anaheim—another loss—until he pinch-hit in the ninth. The next night, Manny played, then said he felt sore-ness in his bothersome right knee after chasing a ball into the left-field corner. Francona lifted him after the fourth. An MRI the next day showed no structural damage but confirmed a case of patellar tendinitis, a condition in which the tendons around the kneecap become inflamed.

By the time Boston returned to Fenway August 31, they were out of the playoff race, eight games behind New York in the division and 7.5 behind the White Sox in the wild card. The team was 71–62, meaning they had gone 10–24 since reaching their high point of 61–38. Manny missed twenty-two of thirty games from late August through September as the Sox faded.

He had twenty-two at-bats between August 21 and September 24 and recorded just two hits.

The press was skeptical. The common belief was that Manny had quit on the team, now that the team had fallen from contention. Others, including Crisp and first baseman Kevin Youkilis, played hurt as the Sox floundered, but Manny had shown "a colossal indifference to the collective welfare of his team," Edes wrote in the *Globe*.

On his blog, *Feeding the Monster* author Mnookin wrote that he did not think Manny was faking an injury, and that "it's well known in baseball that Manny has a relatively low pain threshold. There does seem to be a consensus that he could play without serious risk of further injury, but that's something that's impossible to ever truly know."

Manny returned to the lineup for the second-to-last game of the season at Fenway September 30. There were scattered boos, but fans generally treated him warmly. Manny went 2 for 3 with a walk, a single, and a home run in the Red Sox 5–4 loss to the Orioles. After the homer, he was given a huge ovation. It was his 35th home run of the season. He also finished with 102 RBIs, terrific numbers considering he missed thirty-two games. He wound up batting .321 with a .439 OBP (best in the AL) and 1.058 OPS (second-best in the AL). So once again, the Hall of Fame player put up elite stats. But there was no postseason appearance this time around. Fans still loved him, because he was so good, so clutch, and so entertaining, but there were growing numbers who, right or wrong, had lost respect for him because he seemed so aloof, selfish, and soft.

CHAPTER 28

2007: Banner No. 2

While the rest of the team was starting to report to spring training, Manny was making plans to attend a high-class car auction in Atlantic City on February 24. The slugger planned to auction off his 1967 custom-built four-door blue Lincoln convertible. The New Jersey dealer, Tony Averso, said he had been in contact with Manny almost daily leading up to the auction and confirmed that Onelcida had undergone surgery, Manny's reason for not reporting to camp until March 1. Manny nixed his auction plans at the last minute.

In yet another amusing act of preseason goofiness, it appeared to many an internet surfer that Manny had posted an ad hawking a $4,000 grill on eBay.com. The ad featured a photo of Manny standing next to the grill. "Hi, I'm Manny Ramirez," the ad read. "I bought this AMAZING grill for about $4,000 and I used it once . . . But I never have the time to use it because I am always on the road. I would love to sell it and you will get an autographed ball signed by me. Enjoy it, Manny Ramirez."

As it turned out, the ad was posted by Manny's spirited fifteen-year-old-niece, Kathy, whom Juliana had enlisted to help sell the grill. Kathy asked her uncle to pose next to it. She wrote and posted the ad to her account, and then was amazed at the fallout. "I was in history class and this reporter calls my cell phone, and I was like, 'Hello?' and he was like, 'This is ESPN,' and I was like, 'Oh, my God!?'" she recalls.

The starting bid of $3,000 rose throughout the day, reaching $99,999,999 before being removed from the site Wednesday. Since the ad contained Kathy's contact information, not Manny's, it was deemed a violation of eBay policy. But the ad also started the *Globe*'s editorial writers wondering: "Is the peerless slugger consciously trying to play variations on the cartoon character he has become for most of Red Sox Nation, or is he merely a hardworking hitter whose carefree approach to the rest of life is the psychological secret of his success?"

Manny got off to another slow start, but the team hardly struggled without his production. After sixteen games, the Red Sox (11–5) were in first, having swept a two-game series at Fenway against the Yankees (8–8). He was hitting .193 with 1 homer and 8 RBIs. Ortiz, by comparison, had already mashed 6 homers and had 17 RBIs and was hitting .300. But it seemed as if Boston fans and media had finally learned not to read too much into Manny's early struggles. Besides, with a spate of new acquisitions (J. D. Drew, Japanese pitcher Daisuke Matsuzaka, and shortstop Julio Lugo), Beckett's resurgence, and Papelbon's emergence, the fans and media had novel complaints and fresher stories to tell.

Sure as summer's arrival, Manny's hot streak came. In a twenty-one-game stretch from late May to mid-June, he hit .400 (28 for 70) with 8 doubles, 13 runs, and 19 walks. He had just 9 RBIs in that period, though. His batting average on June 17 stood at an acceptable .290 with a low .860 OPS and only 9 home runs and 36 RBIs. Those were hardly pedestrian totals in a season that was one-third finished, but they were below Manny's standards. Still, the team was thrilled with his effort. Manny led the team in games played on July 1.

Manny's power emerged every now and then. On July 26, in a 14–9 victory over the Indians, he crushed two home runs, one of which he believed to be the longest of his career—a shot over the bushes beyond center field at Jacobs Field. Analysts measured it at 485 feet, shorter than the 501-foot blast Manny had slammed over the Monster in 2001, but impressive nonetheless. *Boston Herald* scribe Rob Bradford noted: "Just think, the night before Manny drew the attention of frustrated fans for failing to tell Coco Crisp to slide in a pivotal play at the plate. This was seemingly inexcusable. Well, last night he was excused."

The two blasts gave the thirty-five-year-old Manny 17 home runs and 64 RBIs after 102 games. Now there was some reason to believe Manny might not reach those benchmarks of excellence—30 home runs, 100 RBIs—that he had reached with ease in the nine previous seasons and in eleven of his twelve seasons as a major leaguer. Also, Manny was batting .303 with a .920 OPS, hardly poor, but hardly vintage Manny.

Regardless, the Sox were cruising toward their first AL East title since 1995, an accomplishment that would break the Yankees' decade-long grip on the division. After the July 26 win in Cleveland, they were 62–40, seven games ahead of the Yankees. Their lineup was full of patient hitters who worked counts and wore pitchers down. Youkilis, batting .308 after the July 26 win, had emerged as a reliable hitter in any spot in the order. Dustin Pedroia, after his slow start, was batting .315 and playing solid defense. Lowell led the team with 73 RBIs and served as crucial protection in the lineup for Ortiz and Manny. The team's two other outfielders, Crisp and Drew, were struggling at the plate, but their defensive prowess was evident. Beckett (13–4, 3.27 ERA) was a Cy Young candidate, while Matsuzaka (12–7, 3.79 ERA) was having a solid first major league season. Papelbon, the new closer, was like a young Mariano Rivera—he had 23 saves and a 1.72 ERA and seemed unhittable.

Entering a game in the Bronx on August 28, the Sox (80–51) were 7.5 games ahead of the Yankees (72–58) when Manny felt a stinging pain in his left side after swinging hard on a base hit in the sixth inning. Doctors concluded he had strained his left oblique, a muscle located on the side of the body between the navel and the chest muscles. Team doctor Larry Ronan believed Manny had been playing with the oblique strain for some time, but aggravated the injury on the swing.

Manny couldn't swing a bat for nearly two weeks. The Sox stayed afloat, going 6–6 in the first twelve games with Manny on the bench. His absence gave them the chance to work rookie Jacoby Ellsbury into left field. Ellsbury was a lightning-quick twenty-three-year-old left-handed hitter whom the Sox considered a key piece of their future.

Manny didn't take batting practice again until September 12. But he was still not ready to play. Some in the media wondered why Manny couldn't play when he looked so good in the cage. The Yankees (84–62) had crept to within 4.5 games of first, and they were coming to Boston (89–58) for a three-game set. Francona and the team took the long view. It was more important to have Manny for the playoffs than to push for the division title and risk aggravating the injury.

When Manny returned, on September 25, he hit second in the Sox lineup and went 1 for 2 with a walk and a run scored in a Sox win. He had missed twenty-four games. The Sox (93–64) went 12–12 without him. They clung to a three-game lead over the Yankees (90–67).

The Sox held on to win the division with a 96–66 record that tied Cleveland for the best in the league. Once again, they faced the Angels in the ALDS, perhaps a good omen, since the Sox had swept the Angels in the 2004 ALDS on their way to the title. In Game 1 at Fenway, Beckett showed he was ready to raise his game for the playoffs, just as he had in 2003 with

Florida. He dominated the Angels lineup, pitching a complete-game shutout, scattering four hits and striking out eight en route to a 4–0 Sox win.

In Game 2, the Angels scored three runs in the second, on their way to chasing Matsuzaka after four and two-thirds innings.

The Angels led 3-2 in the ninth, when Papelbon retired the Angels to give the middle of the Sox order a chance to win the game. Lugo had his biggest hit to date as a member of the Red Sox, leading off the inning with a single. Lugo moved to second on Pedroia's groundout, and in came reliever K-Rod to face Youkilis. Rodriguez struck out Youkilis on four pitches. Up came Ortiz. That gave Scioscia a choice: try to get Ortiz out or walk him and face Manny. At that point, Manny was 0 for 3 with 3 strikeouts and 2 walks. Scioscia chose to walk Ortiz, just as he had in the fifth inning.

To Manny, the message could not have been clearer: We fear Ortiz more than we fear you.

Rodriguez showed no fear of Manny. Perhaps he should have. After his first pitch missed, his second was almost right over the plate. Manny swung, and there was no doubt. The ball had just left his bat when he raised his arms above his head and stood still, admiring his shot as it sailed over the Monster. The Sox won, 6–3. Manny recognized the importance of the moment in the context of his below-average year. "It's been a long time since I've done something special like that," he told reporters. "But I haven't been right all year long. When you don't feel good and still get hits, that's when you know you're a bad man."

In Game 3 in Anaheim, nothing worked for the Angels. Schilling pitched seven shutout innings, guiding the Sox to a 9–1 rout and a series sweep. It was a scoreless game until the top of the fourth when Ortiz and Manny hit back-to-back homers off Angels starter Jered Weaver. It remained 2–0 Boston until the seventh, when the Sox blew it open with seven runs.

In the series, the Ruth-Gehrig caliber duo went 8 for 15 with 4 homers, 8 runs, 7 RBIs, and 11 walks. Manny reached base eight times in thirteen plate appearances. He batted .375 with a 1.740 OPS.

Cleveland defeated the Yankees in the other ALDS, meaning there would be no New York–Boston showdown in 2007. Not that facing the Indians was easy, given Cleveland's starting pitching. The Indians sent CC Sabathia—who edged Beckett for the Cy Young award—to the mound in Fenway for Game 1 against Beckett. In the first, Cleveland DH Travis Hafner homered off Beckett with two outs, giving the Indians a 1–0 lead before the Sox offense got a chance.

The Sox went on to win 10–3. Beckett got the win, yielding two runs in six innings. Manny went 2 for 2 with 3 RBIs, 2 runs, and 3 walks. He reached base in all five of his plate appearances, as did Ortiz. So far in the playoffs, they had been to the plate 36 times and reached base 29—Ortiz 16 of 18, Manny 13 of 18. Combined, it was an obscene .805 OBP.

In Game 2, the Indians struck back. On paper, it looked like a pitchers' duel, pitting Fausto Carmona (19–8, 3.06 ERA) against Schilling (9–8, 3.87 ERA). But neither pitcher made it through the fifth inning.

And, with an eventual 13–6 Indians' win, the 1–1 series headed to Cleveland, where the Indians won Game 3, 4–2, getting scoreless relief from Jensen Lewis, Rafael Betancourt, and Joe Borowski.

In Game 4, Wakefield took the mound against Paul Byrd. Initially, the pitchers held sway. It was a scoreless game after four innings. But the Indians lit up the Sox for seven runs in the fifth.

All three Red Sox runs came in the top of the sixth. It was an incredible display. Youkilis and Ortiz drilled back-to-back homers off Byrd. Indians' manager Eric Wedge replaced Byrd with Lewis. Lewis promptly gave up a solo shot to Manny.

Manny raised his arms and admired his shot, seemingly oblivious to the score—it was now 7–3, Indians—or the Sox' increasing chances of getting eliminated. Lewis settled in, retired the side, and along with Betancourt, shut out the Red Sox the rest of the way. The Indians led the series 3–1 and were on the verge of eliminating the Red Sox and advancing to their first World Series since 1997, when Manny was there.

Afterward, reporters asked Manny if he was concerned about losing the series. His response, which caused an uproar among baseball fans, was at once strange and predictable. "Why should we panic? We've got a great team. If it doesn't happen, good. We'll come next year and try to do it again. We're confident every day. It doesn't matter how things go for you. We're not going to give up. We're just going to play the game, like I've said, and move on. If it doesn't happen, so who cares? There's always next year. It's not like the end of the world or something."

Manny's statement captured the looseness of the squad. He'd spent a whole career cultivating a Zen philosophy of hitting; combined with the Sox' previous successes rallying from elimination in the playoffs, Manny was accurately depicting not just his own mind-set approaching Game 5, but that of the team, especially because their moneyman, Beckett, was taking the hill in a rematch of his Game 1 battle with Sabathia.

The result was the same. Beckett dominated, fanning eleven in eight innings and giving up only one run, in the first. Papelbon pitched a dominant ninth and the Sox won 7–1. Youkilis jump-started the Sox offense in the first with a one-out solo shot. Ortiz struck out and then Manny doubled—but he was thrown out at home to end the inning when he failed to slide on Lowell's single. Manny added an RBI single in the third on a shot to center field that looked like a home run—it looked like such a home run that Manny jogged to first. On television, Tim McCarver ripped him. Regardless, Ortiz had been sprinting all the way and scored to put Boston up 2–1. That was all Beckett needed. The Sox sealed the game with two runs in the seventh and three more in the eighth. Youkilis was the star, with 3 RBIs. Manny went 2 for 4 with 1 walk and his 1 RBI. For the series, he was batting .471 with a 1.491 OPS, both team highs, as were his 8 RBIs.

The Sox started Schilling against Carmona again in the must-win Game 6 at Fenway. Boston got to Carmona early, with a J. D. Drew grand slam. ESPN.com's Bill Simmons christened the homer "The $14 Million Grand Slam," a reference to the contract Scott Boras had secured for Drew, who hit .270 with 11 home runs and 64 RBIs in 466 at-bats in his first year as the Red Sox right fielder. His blast staked the Sox to a 4–0 lead as they cruised to a 12–2 win.

Game 7, at Fenway, pitted Matsuzaka against Jake Westbrook in another rematch of starters. This time, Westbrook was not as sharp as he'd been earlier in the series and by the bottom of the eighth, the Sox were pounding relievers Betancourt and Lewis. Fenway erupted as the game got out of hand and it became apparent that the Sox had overcome yet another series deficit to capture the AL pennant and return to the World Series.

All told, Manny hit .409 with a 1.260 OPS, 2 home runs, and 10 RBIs in the ALCS. He led the team in RBIs, and only Youkilis (.500 average, 1.505 OPS) outdid him in the percentages.

The Sox went on to face the Colorado Rockies in the World Series. The Rockies were hot, having swept both of their playoff series—3–0 over the Phillies, 4–0 over the Diamondbacks. The Rockies had also gone 13–1 to close out the regular season and force a one-game playoff for the wild card, which they won in thrilling, extra-inning-comeback fashion.

Game 1, in Boston, pitted Beckett against Jeff Francis. Beckett dominated, striking out nine and giving up only one run in seven innings. Manny went 3 for 4 with 3 runs and 2 RBIs in a 13–1 Sox victory. Ortiz finished 3 for 5 with 2 runs and 2 RBIs. Varitek, Drew, and Pedroia also had 2 RBIs in the demolition. The Sox also took Game 2 in Fenway with a 2–1 victory.

The Rockies did not threaten again. They vowed to come back in Colorado, but it seemed as if they had missed their chance to grab a win in Boston. The Red Sox dominated the Rockies in Game 3, 10–5, and edged them 4–3 in the Series finale to capture the team's second world championship in four years.

Lowell was awarded the World Series MVP. Manny—0 for 4 in Game 4—had hit only .250 in the World Series, but he finished the postseason hitting .348, with 16 hits, 11 runs, and a .508 OBP. He homered four times and had 16 RBIs in the team's fourteen playoff games. It was his finest postseason and, considering the stakes, arguably the finest sustained stretch of hitting brilliance of his career.

CHAPTER 29

2008: 500 Home Runs
in Dodger Blue

Manny was coming off perhaps his best month as a pro, but there was little time to enjoy it. He was entering the last guaranteed year of his contract, and to him it seemed unlikely the Sox front office would exercise its option to bring him back in 2009 for another $20 million. He would turn thirty-six in the coming season, he had missed chunks of the last two seasons with injuries, and he had just finished his worst statistical regular season since his rookie year. When healthy and motivated, he was still a great hitter, but the Sox had legitimate questions about how often both those conditions would be met going forward.

Aware of how pivotal the 2008 season would be for him, Manny joined Pedroia and Youkilis at Athletes' Performance, a training center in Tempe, Arizona. Garciaparra had trained there before, but Manny had never been interested in the center's tough regimen. In one of his more loquacious periods with the press, Manny was willing to discuss his contract status, leading to some hilariously inconsistent statements. It started in February, when reporters arrived at a charity event—Manny was donating his 1967 Lincoln Continental to the Franciscan Hospital for Children in Brighton, Massachusetts, the same car he had tried to auction in Atlantic City. Asked about the upcoming season, Manny replied: "It's going to be fun—I'm looking forward to 2009." It might have been an innocent slip, but Manny had skipped over the 2008 season and gone right to his potential (if the Sox declined his option) free agency.

Two weeks later, Manny fired Greg Genske and Gene Mato (who had worked for Moorad's agency) and signed with Scott Boras. The move had an obvious meaning. Boras was legendary for wringing the highest price from teams. He handed executives thick binders filled with optimistic statistical projections for his clients, who included Drew, Varitek, Matsuzaka, and Ellsbury. The tactic had worked often before, and it had worked for Boras's most famous client, A-Rod, who had landed the richest deal in history with Texas the same off-season Boston had signed Manny.

Meanwhile, Manny had started reading inspirational books, including *The Secret*, by Rhonda Byrne, the controversial but popular book that told readers they could change their lives for the better just by thinking positively. Macaco and Clara laughed off suggestions of Manny's scholarly side. "He keeps saying he's reading books; I've never seen him with a book," Clara says. "Maybe he'll read the one you're writing about him," joked Macaco.

Manny said that he had started doing Mantra yoga, a form involving prolonged meditation and chanting. His mother's cousin Rico had taught him in the off-season, and Manny believed it helped clear his head of negative thoughts. He was meditating February 27 when the rest of the Sox were meeting with President Bush for the usual champions' ceremony. Bush joked about Manny's absence. "I guess his grandmother died again," Bush said. Manny appreciated the joke. "The president is thinking about me. I like it. It makes me feel important to be mentioned," he told reporters.

The rest of his family was less amused. The eighty-year-old

Pura does, in fact, suffer from a chronic condition, amyloidosis, which causes abnormal deposits of proteins in her organs and tissues and required an extended hospitalization in March 2004.

Manny started the season on fire and stayed hot throughout April. That was crucial, because after a 4–3 win against the Yankees on April 12, Ortiz was batting .070. In the fourth, Manny homered off Mussina in yet another clash between the two marquee free agents the Sox had chased in 2000. When Manny came up again in the sixth with runners on second and third and two outs, everyone expected new Yankee manager Joe Girardi to walk him intentionally. Girardi's predecessor, Joe Torre, had done so twenty-three times in his tenure. But Girardi elected to have Mussina pitch to Manny instead. Manny stroked a two-run double to give Boston the lead for good.

Two days later, in Cleveland, Manny crushed a two-run, ninth-inning shot off Joe Borowski to break a 4–4 tie and give Boston another win. At that point, through fourteen games, Ramirez was hitting .309 (.974 OPS) with 3 homers and 14 RBIs. He homered twice more off Mussina on April 17, as if the Sox and Yankees needed any more confirmation of who had made the better signing in 2000. He now had 405 career homers and had just passed Ted Williams and Lou Gehrig on the all-time list.

But by mid-May, Manny was slowing down, and reporters questioned whether he was quaking under the pressure surrounding his 500th homer. By May 14, his average was down to .308 (.937 OPS) and he'd hit only two homers since April 26. But with one defensive play seldom seen in the game's history, Manny's drought was forgotten and he added to his odd legacy. With runners on first and second and one out in the fourth inning of a game at Camden Yards, Millar, the former Sox first baseman, lined a shot over Manny's head in left. Manny sprinted back to the wall. It appeared he would not reach the ball, and the runners began to advance.

But Manny stretched his left arm to the limit and snagged the ball on a dead sprint. His momentum took him running into the wall, and he jumped into it feet-first to bounce himself back onto the field. But as he jumped, he saw a lone Red Sox fan just over the wall. Manny reached up his right hand and high-fived the fan in midair. He landed, pivoted, and fired to the cutoff man, Pedroia, who in turn threw to first to double up Nick Markakis and end the inning. Manny grinned broadly as he ran back to the dugout, where he gathered around a television to watch replays. He re-enacted his high-five as teammates erupted in laughter. "It was fun," Manny said after the game. "I love it." The surreal play was fodder for sports highlights shows for days.

Manny had 498 home runs at this point, but the next two would be long in coming. As the days without a homer turned into a week, then nearly two weeks, reporters began asking whether Manny's "turn the page" attitude was faltering as the pressure of 500 built. He had hit only two homers between April 19 and May 20, a span of ninety-seven at-bats. He batted just .203 during that twenty-one-game span. "Maybe for the first time in a long time, Manny is feeling pressure as he approaches the milestone," wrote Sean McAdam of the *Providence Journal*.

He finally smacked number 499 on May 27, an opposite-field three-run homer in Seattle off Miguel Batista. He went homerless the next night, joking that he did so on purpose because the postgame press conference would have delayed the team's trip to Baltimore for their next series. Number 500 came in the second game at Camden Yards. Manny came up with the bases empty against a former teammate, side-armer Chad Bradford. He swung at Bradford's first pitch. It was classic Manny. He extended his arms to reach a ball on the outside part of the plate, made solid contact, and smoothly followed through, bringing the bat behind his head. It was, fittingly, a shot to right-center, the power alley that had always defined his greatness and made him so difficult for pitchers.

Ultimately, only seven players reached 500 home runs in fewer at-bats than Manny: McGwire, Ruth, Killebrew, Thome, Sosa, Foxx, and A-Rod. He admired the shot, then trotted around the bases at his usual pace, stepped on home, and pointed to heaven. Teammates circled around him, jumping and shouting, as he walked back to the dugout.

Juliana told the *Globe* of a "big weight lifted off his shoulders." Francona said the thing that made him happiest was watching Lugo, Ortiz, and Lowell crowd around Manny and celebrate with him. When Manny homered in each of the next two games, it looked as if he might be set to start hitting for power again. He was also spared playing the outfield, because Ortiz was out with a wrist injury—so Francona slotted Manny as the designated hitter and employed a defensively exquisite outfield of Ellsbury, Crisp, and Drew from left to right.

Manny homered against the Tampa Bay Rays on June 5—his 13th at the game 63 mark—and also had 5 RBIs (45 for the season). But there was an ominous sign: He said his hamstring hurt again. "It's weird because I haven't had my hamstring like this for how long, four years, three years?" he asked *Boston Herald* columnist Michael Silverman. "And now, with this one, every time I run, it bothers me." Manny sat out June 6 but came back the next day and homered again. At that point, he was hitting .303 with 14 homers and 47 RBIs.

But he homered just twice in the next nineteen games and sat out three of them because of what he claimed was lingering pain in his hamstring. Two troubling incidents that also took place around this time added fuel to speculation over whether the hamstring ailment was authentic. In the June 5 game, the Sox and Rays got into a bench-clearing brawl when Rays hurler James Shields hit Crisp on the right hip with a fastball. Crisp charged the mound; Shields wound up and threw a right hand that Crisp ducked before firing back with his own blows. Tampa's catcher, Dioner Navarro, sprinted after Crisp and tackled him. The dugouts and bullpens emptied.

Two innings later, cameras caught Manny in the dugout delivering a backhanded chop to Youkilis's head at the end of the fourth inning. Teammates rushed to separate them. Ortiz said it was the "first time" he'd ever seen anything like it.

Manny was one of many teammates frustrated with Youkilis's overreactions to poor at-bats, even when the team was winning. Youkilis tossed some equipment during an outburst in the dugout after he flew out to center in the fourth. According to Rob Bradford in the *Boston Herald*, Manny made his thoughts about Youkilis's behavior known. The two argued briefly before Manny backhanded him.

But the dugout altercation seemed like small beer after Manny's inexcusable behavior on June 28 in Houston. McAdam reported that Manny had asked Jack McCormick, the Sox traveling secretary, for complimentary tickets for family and friends to attend the game that day. McCormick, who was sixty-four at the time, balked, and, according to family members, insulted Manny, who shoved him to the ground and shouted, "Just do your job."

The incident was a blow to Manny's reputation among Boston fans. To this day there are fans who stand by him because of his productivity and because he has never gotten into any "serious" trouble—that is, crimes or steroid accusations. But after the McCormick incident it was harder for fans to dismiss Manny's immaturity as mere eccentricity. Once again Manny fell silent, providing none of the clarification or explanations that might have helped to at least attenuate the fallout.

Juliana explains that the request was for fewer tickets than reported and adds that "Jack's response was very rude. And Jack had a history of insulting Manny in front of the other players." Gene Mato concurs. "Jack disrespected Manny for many years, and on many occasions."

Of course, none of this excuses Manny's shoving the man, and fans ripped Manny on comment boards at ESPN.com and the Boston papers' websites, calling him a spoiled bully who demanded free tickets despite his $20 million salary. Then *Globe* columnist Gordon Edes noticed the sea change. As he recalls, "Fans were furious with me for questioning Manny in 2006. One even called my home. But by 2008 there was very little backlash." The reaction got worse when the team did nothing, at least publicly, to punish Manny. "When things happen with us, we take things very seriously and hopefully we deal with things respectfully to all parties," Francona told the press the next day. "But we also do it internally." Manny refused to talk about the incident. "Whatever happens in the clubhouse stays in the clubhouse," he told reporters. "I talked to [McCormick] and everything is fine. He's going to continue to be my friend. It's over with."

McCormick told reporters he couldn't remember the exact details of Manny's ticket request, but that he accepted Manny's apology. "I just want it to die," McCormick said. "It's over. He apologized. That's it. I just want us to get back to our winning ways." This did little to offset some fans' perceptions of Manny as a selfish, violent slugger allowed to run amok because of his prodigious talent. Rob Neyer, an ESPN.com baseball columnist, summed up a common reaction to the incident during an online chat. "What's that old saying?" he asked. "If you can hit a curveball you can get away with murder?"

CHAPTER 30

Mannywood

On the day Manny left Boston, the *Globe* posted a chart with his career numbers from 1993 through 2007: .312 average, .409 OBP, and 510 homers. Next to it was the headline: "Manny Deal Was Necessary."

On many levels, Manny's song never played well in the Boston market. Exasperation surfaced with every trade request, lack of hustle, injury, or gaffe. Millar once summed him up it the *Globe*: "He's got a good heart, a heart of gold. But there's also a gap there and he does things that [tick] people off. I don't know why he does it."

He does it, perhaps, because he lives in the moment, neither suffering regret nor calculating the consequences of his next move. Although his production rarely wavered in Boston, his comfort level did. The team morphed to reflect upper management's preference for low-maintenance professionals. Outliers—Damon, Martinez, Lowe, Millar, Tavarez—were weeded out. In their absence, Manny felt isolated. He remained close to Ortiz and Lugo, but never felt the same. At least that's how Macaco sees it. "Pedro, David, and Manny were like three legs of a stool," he says. "When Pedro left, things grew unstable."

Martinez agrees. "He was comfortable in Boston for a time. I was his closest friend. But once I left the team, things didn't seem to be the same. It wasn't the same group of guys, the same feeling, and that influenced Manny a lot."

None of which excuses Manny's meltdown in 2008. Still, he had reasons for his frustration. He had never come to grips with the intensity of the Red Sox fans. "I've got people waiting for me at 3:00 A.M. in my hallway," he complains. Trade discussions had arisen in four of the previous six years, but Manny and the Red Sox owners had never come to loggerheads. In anticipation of contract negotiations, Manny replaced Genske and Mato with the notoriously tough Boras. The Red Sox, buoyed by two championships, felt able to get him off the payroll without fan backlash, especially after the McCormick incident. "The team management didn't have his back," asserts Juliana. "They gave him up to the press instead of protecting one of their own players." Aware that his time with the team—and his teammates— was coming to an end, Manny was hard pressed to give his best to a team he knew was eager to cast him aside. He took 5.7 seconds to reach first on a hit in a game against the Angels and opted out of a Mariners game. In the coup de grace, he took himself out of the posted lineup against the Yankees.

Still, he seemed surprised by the backlash. On the Sunday before the trade, with his mother cooking in the kitchen and Macaco beside him, he sulked in his Boston penthouse apartment, gently tossing a soft baseball to Manny Jr. He had done his best to ignore the headlines, despite his mother's insistence on laying out the Boston papers each morning. Glancing away, he explained: "I'm private and I don't let nobody penetrate my space. I go play the game, go home, that's it. I don't read about what people are writing about me, that's not my style." He expressed feelings of betrayal by teammates who, in recent days, had distanced themselves from him. "When you've got a job in baseball, everybody's trying to cover their ass, you know. You're working for them. They're the ones that are sending out the checks. You're not going to put your hands in the fire for me. So you got to be careful who you trust. That's why I don't trust nobody. I go, play the game, and move on."

Is it possible that Boras's view influenced Manny into feeling mistreated by his teammates, unappreciated by management, and nervous about his financial future? No one but Manny knows. But Lowell has his hunches. "You know," he reflects, "guys go through a lot of things in a season and not all of it is on the field. A lot of times you can correlate bad patches with someone being sick or some family issue. And some of that gets lost in, you know, *SportsCenter*. I think the contract situation was something that was weighing heavy on his mind. I can't say how justified it is—for me, if his contract says they have the option, then they have the option—but it was weighing on him." Lowell and others have suggested that Boras's attitude may have sparked and then fanned the flames of Manny's anxiety.

Of course, Red Sox management did little to tamp out the problems, and may have added fuel to the fire. Manny's behavior had become reproachable, but hardly a radical departure from his ways of the past. This time, however, management seemed determined to use whatever means it had, including the local media, to sway opinion against him. On July 31, just one minute before the trade deadline, the Red Sox sent Manny to the Dodgers, agreeing to cover the remaining $7 million on his 2008 contract. Manny agreed to waive his no-trade clause and the Red Sox agreed to drop the two option years from his contract, rendering him a free agent in the fall. As part of the deal, the Sox surrendered two prospects and landed Jason Bay from the Pittsburgh Pirates, a solid player with an un-Manny-like persona in every way.

In the days following Manny's departure, management and the Boston media seemed bent on justifying the trade. As if he had just uncovered the next Watergate, *Globe* columnist Dan Shaughnessy broke the news that Selig had ordered an investigation into "the circumstances of Manny's final hours with the Red Sox," insinuating that Manny had forced the trade by "withholding services and playing at half-speed." Manny's production in July—a .347 average and 1.060 OPS—suggested otherwise, even if his reprehensible shove of McCormick and lack of hustle did not.

Manny and Los Angeles fell for each other like teenage lovers. He was enchanted by the city, especially its malls, but also its warm weather and the laid-back, multicultural fan base. Accustomed to celebrities, and hardly as diehard about their jocks as Bostonians, Southern Californians granted him relative privacy when he left the park. Manny rewarded Dodgers fans with gaudy numbers and a division title. In his fifty-three regular-season games with the team, Manny hit 17 homers and 53 RBIs, scoring 36 runs. He batted .396 and slugged .743, with a .489 on-base percentage. Dodgers fans, known for arriving fashionably late to ball games, suddenly couldn't miss the first inning. That would mean missing one of Manny's at-bats.

Attendance grew an average of forty-three hundred over the remainder of the regular season. Chants of "Maa-neey! Maa-neey!" filled Dodger Stadium. Little boys and grandmas alike slipped on dreadlock wigs—and they kept wearing them even after Manny trimmed his hair to shoulder-length. Dodger Stadium came alive.

And Manny embraced the attention at the ballpark. The night the Dodgers clinched the National League West title, Manny, drenched in champagne and red Gatorade, walked onto the diamond and addressed the adoring crowd: "Hey, what's up, L.A.?" he said. "Mannywood!"

The clubhouse underwent a transformation, too. The stiffness of a team trying too hard to meet expectations dissolved when Manny, on only his second day with the team, turned up the volume dial on his speaker-connected iPod, disregarding a rule prohibiting music in the clubhouse. Younger players began feeling more at ease. They walked around the clubhouse bobbing their heads and singing favorite Manny tunes. Some wore T-shirts that said "We love Manny being Manny." In more serious moments, they turned to Manny for advice on his approach to the game.

Manny had tried to mentor younger Boston players on occasion. "Manny helped me develop as a player here," says Ellsbury. When Pedroia earned Rookie of the Year honors for 2007, Manny bought him a Rolex watch and attached a congratulatory note. Manny had also bought the diminutive scrapper designer suits during his rookie season, just as older players had given him gifts when he was with Cleveland. But in Los Angeles, Manny seemed to, perhaps for the first time in his career, embrace the role of leader, even if in his quirky way. Players tried to emulate him, and felt awe watching him swing the bat.

"He's pretty much the most unbelievable thing I've ever seen on a baseball field," young Dodgers pitcher Clayton Kershaw told the *New York Times*.

Manny's dominance continued into the playoffs. He batted .500 with 2 home runs and 3 RBIs in the Dodgers' (84–78) wild card sweep of the favored Cubs (97–64). His OBP was .643, his OPS was an obscene 1.743.

In the NLCS, the Dodgers faced the Philadelphia Phillies, who also had a powerful offense, featuring slugging first baseman Ryan Howard and second baseman Chase Utley. The Phillies' starting pitching also had an X-factor, ace Cole Hamels, a six-three lefty who was only twenty-four and could beat anyone when he was on. In addition, the Phillies' bullpen boasted fireballer Brad Lidge, who had not blown a save all season long. The series also marked a reunion of sorts for Manny and Phillies manager Charlie Manuel, who'd managed Manny with the Indians and in the minors.

Meanwhile, in the AL, the Red Sox had advanced to face the Tampa Bay Rays in the ALCS, so dreams of a Red Sox–Dodgers World Series loomed large. In Boston, mouths watered at the prospect of opposing Manny—not to mention Dodgers starting pitcher Derek Lowe and backup infielder Nomar Garciaparra and former Yankees manager Joe Torre—on baseball's largest stage.

Game 1 of the NLCS ended 3–2, with Lidge slamming the door on the Dodgers in the top of the ninth. Manny was 2 for 4 in the game, with 1 RBI. In Game 2, the Phillies abused Chad Billingsley, scoring four runs in the second and four in the third to open an 8–2 lead. With two outs and two on in the top of the fourth, Manny hit a three-run shot, trimming the lead to 8–5. But zeros filled the scoreboard from the fifth inning on.

The scene shifted back to Los Angeles for Game 3. On the verge of elimination, the Dodgers needed another Game 3 gem from pitcher Hiroki Kuroda, and they got it. He limited the Phillies to two earned runs in six innings. The Dodgers won 7–2, and Manny went 1 for 2 with 2 walks, 2 runs, and 1 RBI. He was now batting .400 for the series with a 1.338 OPS.

Game 4 was the Dodgers' chance to tie the series 2–2. Lowe yielded two runs in five innings of work. But in the top of the sixth the Phillies tied the game and exposed the Dodgers' middle relief. It was 7–5 Phillies when Lidge entered the game with two outs in the bottom of the eighth. The first batter Lidge faced was Manny. Manny doubled to center. Dodger Stadium exploded. Four outs away from trailing 3–1 in the series, now it seemed possible the Dodgers could tie the series 2–2. But Lidge retired the side. Hamels awaited the Dodgers in Game 5.

Some 56,800 people filled Dodger Stadium for Game 5, and Manny's potential last game there. Manny did not let the fans down, even though Hamels was masterful, limiting the Dodgers to one run in seven innings. Manny walked and was stranded in the first and grounded out in the fourth. When he came to bat in the sixth, the Dodgers trailed 5–0, with the Phillies having their way with Billingsley and celebrity reliever Greg Maddux. With two outs and no one on, Manny homered to deep right off Hamels. Again, it was the magic third at-bat. The Dodgers wound up losing 5–1, but Manny acquitted himself well, going 2 for 3 with 1 walk and 1 RBI. For the series, he hit .533 with a 1.749 OPS. He also had 2 home runs and 7 RBIs. If the Dodgers had won the series, he would have been its MVP, indisputably.

More than that, Manny was living proof that Hamels was mortal. Manny's ability, at age thirty-six, to hit Hamels was evidence that his bat was not slowing down, and that he could still perform in pressure-packed, postseason situations. But where would Manny play in 2009? Would he stay in the NL, whose pitching he dominated as if it was batting practice? Or would he go to the AL, where he could play DH into his forties?

Hoping to recapture the magic of their 2008 season, the Dodgers came to the general managers' meetings with a two-year guaranteed offer worth $45 million. Boras declined to respond and the offer was withdrawn. The Yankees and Mets, both with new stadiums, both with large payrolls, and both missing the previous postseason, appeared to have every incentive to give Manny the four- or five-year deal at $25 million a year he desired. But a lot depended on where some other free agents went to play. Angels first baseman Mark Teixeira, another Boras client but only twenty-eight, signed an eight-year, $180 million contract with the Yankees. The Yankees also signed pitcher CC Sabathia for $161 million over seven years. "Gas is up and so am I," Manny had declared shortly after the 2008 season. But as the price of gas went down, the economy contracted, and the few teams that could afford him signed other stars, his options in the languid free agent market grew limited. In the days leading up to spring training, one of the greatest hitters in Major League Baseball history remained without a contract.

And what did Manny have to say about his potential destination? "You think now that I hit another home run I can get a six-year deal?" he joked with reporters after Game 2 of the Phillies series. But when the series ended, Manny had little to say. "I'm done talking," he told reporters on the day he cleaned out his locker. "See you next year."

"In Los Angeles?" the reporters asked.

"I don't know," Manny said. He tried in vain to escape reporters before leaving the clubhouse that day, according to Jill Painter of the *Los Angeles Daily News*. Reporters kept asking him about his plans. Manny kept saying, "I don't know," or saying nothing at all. "He stood looking up at the elevator waiting for the doors to open, which would've been a good commercial for Southwest Airlines' 'Wanna Get Away' campaign," wrote Painter.

In Manny's locker there remained a few hangers and a fortune from Panda Express taped to his nameplate. It read: "Don't look back. Always look ahead."

CHAPTER 31

There's Something About Manny

There is no denying Manny's gravitational pull. He may be reviled or loved, but he is seldom ignored. Some of the allure lies in his extraordinary talent, and of course, the fact that his ascendance as a consistent power hitter coincided with the so-called steroids era. Unlike sluggers whose numbers grew precipitately with their physiques, Manny's performance has followed a steady trajectory. Only twice in his career has he hit fewer than 30 home runs or 100 RBIs in a season. And Manny's swing just *looks* natural, as if his power is derived from technique more than muscle.

But the source of the sports world's fascination with Manny is also his unconventional style and what can seem like dual personalities inside and outside the batter's box. His talent with a bat is supernatural. And yet his very mortal weaknesses and his idiosyncrasies outside the batter's box, along with his apparent indifference to them, make him one of the most interesting personalities in professional sports. After all, many of today's sports stars are cut from the same sheer cloth. Their statements convey the virtues of teamwork, accessibility, and modesty, even when their actions on the playing field or behind closed locker-room doors indicate quite the opposite. Manny has never bothered much with self-image, declining to protest when his flaws are revealed or his actions are misinterpreted. He has repeated several times in his career that he just wants to "play the game and go home," and yet, he acknowledges that the other parts of the baseball machine must continue to turn and screech and whistle and spit around him. His view of the media is an example.

"You can't blame the press," he says with the same kind of apparent indifference with which he might greet a bases-loaded strikeout. "If I worked in the press, and I always had to go to the stadium, if I had to go looking for people to ask them questions, I would do it, too. But sometimes people have to understand that there are people who don't like to talk much, that don't like to give their opinion. People who just want to play the game."

In one sense, and perhaps only one, Manny is a throwback to a time when baseball players had less fear of being themselves, for better or worse, a time when they did not have to worry about their marketability and when their salaries were not the measure of a player's responsibility to engage in the extras that make baseball good business. For many fans, that can be both refreshing and amusing. Manny's stripped-down approach to professional baseball can even sound philosophical at times, even if unintentionally. "Why do people want to know what I think?" he asked a *Boston Herald* reporter in 2007, perhaps a silly question given his star status, but also a question worth considering when we ask ourselves a more fundamental question about what we should expect from our star athletes.

Of course, Manny is also intriguing because he is so mystifying, a walking contradiction. He commits to something before he has made up his mind. He practices harder than anyone on the team, but then he can't seem to muster the energy to run out a pop fly. He downplays his physical and mental preparation, instead of calling attention to an aspect of his work ethic that would offset much of the media's criticism. He seems indifferent to the material world, but is intensely protective of his wealth. He is considered by many to be humble and modest, yet strikes Rocky poses in response to his own home runs and calls himself "a bad man." He is what his former minor league coach Dave Keller described as "one of the simplest, most complex men I've ever known."

Each of us brings our own recipe to the table—a particular brew of genetics, family dynamics, social ecologies, and luck that to a large extent, determines who we are. But as our lives flow from childhood to adulthood, our quirky edges get smoothed over. Most ballplayers are contoured by their parents' and teachers' demands for mainstream conformity and achievement. In Manny's world, the primary shape-shifters were his coaches. Other athletes (such as Manny's pal Julian Tavarez) remain unpolished, but public interest in their quirks is only proportional to their achievements.

And, yes, like most dominant athletes, Manny as a young man had more power, wealth, adoration, women, and fewer checks on his behavior than most boys from his neighborhood. These conditions enabled his baseball skills to flourish, while everyday wisdom and maturity were left relatively undeveloped. Running through any explanation of Manny has to be a recognition of the license his talent has granted him.

His entry into the world of professional sports amplified the license and peculiarities that, under everyday circumstances, would have been subject to constraints. His planetary system of managers, coaches, agents, friends, employees, and, to a certain extent, Macaco, have abetted this process with their hesitancy to ever call him on his lapses.

Ted Williams once asserted, "I've found that you don't need to wear a necktie if you can hit." The truth of this statement holds true for Manny. During formative teenage and early adult years, an unnatural alignment of youth and power led him to develop into someone who is slightly more oblivious to the people and events around him and less schooled in manners, obligations, and constraints than most of us. Psychologists have referred to this as *acquired situational narcissism,* a sort of clinical self-absorption that can sometimes afflict the rich and famous.

It would have been nearly impossible for him to escape these strong currents. His talent and drive carried him across the river so briskly and with so few correctives that he arrived on the other side unscathed.

In some ways, this simplifies the task of deciphering him. Manny was also born with a particular temperament—socially anxious, but good-natured and active—that enchanted those around him. A basic mistrust—triggered by a shy temperament, a fair-weather father, and immigration to Washington Heights—also influenced his character development. At crucial points in his career this distrust has been ignited and has sent him into a defensive, retreating mode.

But there was also an abundance of love in his early childhood years, providing a secure base from which he could focus his energies and talents exclusively on baseball. There was no need to prove himself to a prodding parent or to overcome self-doubt, and there were abundant opportunities to hone his talent.

His passion and drive were further fueled in Washington Heights where, almost from the start, he was recognized as a prodigy. As far back as his coaches and teammates can remember, his physical gifts and work ethic set him apart. At the plate, he has always been as attuned as an orchestra conductor. There's no sense of urgency or panic. He approaches the plate in the same relaxed state whether the bases are empty or loaded. He never lets one at-bat affect another. Each time he comes up it's with a clean slate—a mind as oblivious to a previous home run as it is to a slump.

To be gunning for a game-saving hit, to be irritated by a drunken fan, to be psyched out by a pitcher's mind games is also to be prevented from fully relaxing. Released from such concerns, Manny routinely enters what psychologist Mihly Cskszentmihlyi calls "flow," a state of deep concentration, sharp focus, and, paradoxically, deep relaxation that enables peak performance. This experience can be so engrossing and exhilarating that it becomes its own reward, a vital source of happiness, and a driving force for achieving greatness in life.

It is this process of the body and the mind performing at the limits of their capacity so effortlessly that eventually produces total absorption—the merging of action and awareness. Flow manifests itself in different ways—for baseball players, the bat becomes an extension of their arms, the arc of the ball an extension of their mind and will.

Manny put it like this to the *Miami Herald*: "When I'm doing everything right, it doesn't matter, I have no fear. It's like there's no pitcher out there. And when I'm not all right, all pitchers are tough. You could get me out. My sister could strike me out." This parallels what is going on within the brain, where the most challenging tasks are done with a minimal expenditure of mental energy. Neuroscientists have discovered that while the brain can absorb millions of pieces of information in a split second, only a small fraction can be processed. When people are engaged in their craft, there is less brain arousal and conscious interference and, ultimately, better performance. This allows Manny to master one of the most challenging tasks in professional sports: not just hitting, but hitting consistently.

Dan O'Dowd and others use the term "savant" to describe Manny: "Manny is like a hitting savant. He may not be able to get from his apartment to the ballpark. I mean, if you want him to show up for something, you're unlikely to get him to show up for it. But when he gets into that forum—from the on-deck circle to the batter's box—there is perhaps no one who can better handle the challenges of it, and no one who has better instincts and adaptability." From this perspective, Manny isn't different from an absentminded professor, whose mind is so specialized and consumed by his craft that he is as helpless as a lamb outside the lab. What we chalk up to brilliance in one context looks like deficiency in another.

That is what scout Mickey White meant when he invoked the phrase "Manny being Manny" more than fifteen years ago, before it ever appeared in print. As White recalls, the Indians were playing the Mariners and Manny was facing Randy Johnson for his first at-bat of the night. Manny powered a double off the wall. "I was in the press box and the writers were commenting about how he made all these mistakes in the minors. I told them to give him a chance, just to watch his swing. 'Okay,' they said, 'but why does he act like he's so out of it?' Without really thinking I just said, 'Well, that's just Manny being Manny.' What I was trying to convey is that hey, Einstein would walk into rooms with his fly open. Why? Because he was thinking about equations. Well, with Manny it's the same thing, only he's thinking about hitting."

Or in Manny's words: "Once I get out of the game I put my brain in park. Boop," he says, rolling his eyes up, with his hands motioning beside his ears, "and I move on." Mike Lowell is more analytical. "I have a theory on Manny. He has a mentality, and I don't know exactly what it is. But I believe all pro baseball players have some case of either ADD or OCD. You almost have to be hyperfocused, right? I think he turns all his focus into the batting cage. So sometimes he's not as focused defensively as he is in the batter's box. He kind of lets it go and I think that's what people like to see."

In essence, Manny's relaxed, playful attitude is his greatest gift. His uncanny ability to enter his own private, relaxed, and focused universe in the batter's box is a form of intelligence. Researchers have, in fact, noted that several of the psychological skills known to enhance athletic performance, including the ability to relax, positive thought control, self-regulation, concentration, and energy control, are forms of emotional intelligence. The best athletes learn to recognize their own ideal performance states and to develop the skills needed to manage their emotions. From this perspective, the rest of the world—reporters, his biographers, his relatives, fans, even the president of the United States—can seem like they're all conspiring to pull him from this special place. Mark Shapiro nailed it when he said, "What accounts for his Manny moments is that he doesn't care or get caught up in things that other people have neuroses about."

It's the same reason Manny consistently compiled incredible hitting statistics in Boston, despite his intermittent bouts of discontent.

Simply put, Manny's brain on baseball is more relaxed, efficient, and focused than just about anyone's anywhere. And his state of mind enables him to go so deeply into his swing that he seems to transcend the known world. Flow creates a feeling of invincibility, liberating him from self-doubt and instilling in him a sense of power, confidence, and calm.

But this sort of absorption is only possible when people feel they have the skills to meet the challenge, when every ounce of their attention is focused on the one task at hand, and actions become intuitive. To perfect this edge, Manny has developed an insatiable appetite for videos. Billy Broadbent, Fenway's video man, would occasionally hear Manny pounding on his locked door during the snowy off-season. Manny studies not just the starting pitchers, but the relief pitchers that he faces when a game is on the line. "Intellectually he's a very good player," says Jeff Moorad. "Manny was always somewhat unique, quirky, nontraditional, whatever you want to call it. Mostly though I know that he is as a serious student of the game as there is."

Others who have watched Manny have proffered theories likening him to a wily enchanter who will decline to swing at pitches he can hit or intentionally miss in order to induce that pitch later, when he can do the most damage. Bill James, Red Sox advisor and Sabermetrician, believes Manny will purposely get into a full count when a teammate is on first base so that the runner will take off with the pitch, making it more likely he will score a run on a hit. Another Red Sox consultant, Allard Baird, told *Kansas City Star* columnist Joe Posnanski that he believes Manny will swing and miss at a pitch in April so that the pitcher will throw him the same pitch in September. "When it comes to hitting, the guy's mind works on a whole other level," Baird said. Some of Manny's teammates thought so, too. And when, on September 6, 2008, Manny struck out with the bases loaded against the Arizona Diamondbacks' starter in the third inning of a game for the division lead, he followed that with a three-run homer and a two-run double in his next two at-bats against the same pitcher. Of the third-inning strikeout, Dodgers catcher Russell Martin said after the game, "He was just setting them up right there. He got them the next time around."

Younger players on the Dodgers were in awe of his ability to win mind games with pitchers. "I learned that he's one of the smartest guys I've ever been around," first baseman James Loney told the *Los Angeles Times* after the Dodgers won a spot in the 2008 playoffs.

By getting a fix on pitchers' tendencies, hitters can better anticipate the play, ultimately shifting the advantage their way. Visualizing ahead of time can help focus the mind on clear goals and act as a blueprint for what is about to unfold. It creates moment-by-moment awareness of what one wants to achieve and helps set the stage for that flow experience. Zitter describes how, even in his earliest years, Manny approached the plate with a plan. "He would come to me before every at-bat and he would describe what he thought the pitcher was going to do with each pitch, and what his plan was. Then he would follow that plan."

Other players and managers also talk about Manny's rigorous mental preparations, and his capacity to keep a great deal of information in his head. Frank Mancini recalls how he and Manny would talk about pitchers. "He'd say something like, 'I'm having trouble with breaking pitches at this location, and this guy has a tendency to do this, so let's work on that.' I mean, just the last time he was here, we were talking about Fausto Carmona. And I said, 'He's got some great stuff.' And Manny said, 'Yeah, but he can't throw his breaking ball for a strike. So, if I see a breaking pitch, I'm just going to let it go by.' And he'd know what kind of pitch each pitcher would throw, given the count. So it's those little things that he would pick up about every single pitcher in the game, and mentally store, that was so absolutely amazing. A lot of guys might have the same amount of talent as Manny, but they're not able to put it all together to get to that point of anticipating each and every pitch."

As Manny described in Spanish to *USA Today*, "You have to constantly hone your talent. It's all muscle memory. You have to input all that stuff into the computer [brain], so you don't have to think about it when you get to the plate." Such mental rigor, although extremely specialized, also suggests that Manny's brain is alive and well. It just happens to be singularly focused on what he does best.

Of course, getting to such an experienced and transcendent state also takes practice. A lot of practice. As with any skill, well-rehearsed moves require less effort than those that are fresh or challenging. Through practice, the motions of the swing become more like breathing, spontaneous and part of a seamless, automatic process that requires little conscious effort. A consistent theme since Manny's high school days, described by his teammates and coaches, is his almost superhuman drive. He routinely arrives earlier for practices and subjects himself to more punishing and intense workouts than any other player in the clubhouse.

Dave Page, the Red Sox' strength and conditioning coach, told the *Boston Herald,* "I've been in baseball for nine years in the major leagues, and by far, Manny is the most consistent and most intense workout guy I've ever had." On game days, Manny arrives at the stadium at 8:00 A.M., takes at least sixty swings in the indoor batting cage, and lifts weights, before returning home for lunch. He then returns two hours before he's required to be in uniform so that he can take even more batting practice.

This work ethic often comes as a surprise to fans and announcers. As Mike Lowell observes, "I think everyone likes to see the long hair, the baggy pants, but then he puts up forty home runs every year. I mean, no one just steps into the box and does that. I believe that mechanically he has one of the best swings I've ever seen. I mean, if I had that swing I'd probably take just as many swings as I needed to maintain that perfect swing. I wouldn't be trying to improve something that I thought was perfect. And from the outside point of view it really does look perfect. But he's always searching for that perfect thing to make it better."

Manny's work ethic also made an impression on David Ortiz soon after they became teammates. "Believe me, coming here and watching Manny, the way he works, he teach me a lesson. I came up through the Twins, and when I got here I thought, 'I'm gonna watch the superstars, see how they work,' and Manny was the one that I watched. He showed me how he worked, and I started working with him and believe me, my whole career changed. It was a lot of work. I never worked like that before in my life. I got my ass kicked. Manny is an animal. He works like you're not going to believe."

As with other legendary players, it is this commitment to constant practice that makes the difference. Ted Williams chafed at suggestions that exceptional vision accounted for his hitting prowess. "My eyesight is 20/15. Half the major leaguers have eyes as good as that. It isn't eyesight that makes a hitter; it's practice. Conscientious practice. I say that Williams has hit more balls than any guy living, except maybe Ty Cobb. I don't say it to brag; I just state it as a fact. From the time I was eleven years old, I've taken every possible opportunity to swing at a ball. I've swung and I've swung and I've swung."

Of course, no amount of swinging would put a player on the path to the Hall of Fame if he didn't also have natural ability. Here again, Manny has an edge. In addition to power, he has an exceptional eye for the ball and amazingly quick hands, which grant him slightly more time to decide whether to swing at a ball. Because of his blinding bat speed, he can allow the ball to come to him before he unleashes his swing. And when he connects, he's able to drive the ball in every direction. As Lowell says, "He's balanced, he's strong, and he hits the ball all over the field. And there's only a choice set of guys who can do that."

"Only God knows why Manny is so good," says Pedro Martinez. "He simply has God-given abilities. He is one of the best, most balanced hitters I've ever seen."

"He's got the fastest bat speed in the major leagues," remarks pitcher Paul Byrd. "When you have a good eye and your bat speed is extremely quick, you can afford to wait on pitches longer. His swing is harder than anybody else's and faster. That, in and of itself, is intimidating. You don't have to be David Ortiz stature to intimidate the pitcher. When the hitter swings so fast you can feel yourself come out of your shoes, that's intimidating." Indeed, it takes less than half a second for a fastball to reach home plate, and it is what Manny does with that time that seems to set him apart.

Chance and circumstance also played a part in Manny's success. Indeed, no amount of effort and talent, however breathtaking, can be fully realized without a certain amount of blind luck. How might Manny have fared had he been born into an earlier generation, or in a different country (including Haiti, just one hundred miles west), or to a less nurturing family? Even less obvious factors proved fortunate—his early childhood move from a cramped, sequestered apartment to a young neighborhood with an open field across the street, and his later immigration to baseball-obsessed, mentor-rich New York, for example. Suppose he had never met Mel Zitter, who met and raised Manny's intensity and laid claim to countless hours of practice? Of course, Manny was not the passive recipient of these opportunities—he had the strength and drive to seize them and to cultivate the relationships they provided.

This final ingredient, Manny's ability to attract and draw guidance from coaches, managers, and other caring adults, has been as persistent as his work ethic. These adults, who have served as beacons, provided opportunities and training, and ensured a safe passage along the way, are central to understanding Manny's character development. And certainly having Macaco by his side has made him a happier man. "Macaco means so much to us. Manny would do anything for him," says Juliana, glancing warmly toward Macaco before looking out onto the field. "And I'll tell you this—if it weren't for Macaco, Manny wouldn't be out there playing."

Mentors are a gift and salvation to the lucky few who find them. Even the most brilliant potential has crashed and burned in the absence of dedicated mentoring. Who knows how Darryl Strawberry, Brien Taylor, Josh Hamilton, and countless other tragic figures might have fared with Macaco by their side. But it would be a mistake to assume that Manny would have inevitably failed without his mentors. They have eased his journey and enriched his life, but Manny was born with a spark, an exquisite natural talent, and an indomitable drive and passion for baseball. "I grew up in a neighborhood with drugs, everything else, and I said no to all that," Manny says. "I wanted it. I wanted it more. I wanted it my whole life. And when I am done with baseball, I will enjoy my life and my family. I will spend more time with my kids. I will never look back, never think about the game."

Manny Ramirez's Major League Baseball Statistics

SEASON	TEAM	G	AB	R	H	2B	3B	HR	RBI	TB	BB	SO	SB	CS	OBP	SLG	AVG	OPS
1993	Cleveland Indians	22	53	5	9	1	0	2	5	16	2	8	0	0	.200	.302	.170	.502
1994	Cleveland Indians	91	290	51	78	22	0	17	60	151	42	72	4	2	.357	.521	.269	.878
1995	Cleveland Indians	137	484	85	149	26	1	31	107	270	75	112	6	6	.402	.558	.308	.960
1996	Cleveland Indians	152	550	94	170	45	3	33	112	320	85	104	8	5	.399	.582	.309	.981
1997	Cleveland Indians	150	561	99	184	40	0	26	88	302	79	115	2	3	.415	.538	.328	.953
1998	Cleveland Indians	150	571	108	168	35	2	45	145	342	76	121	5	3	.377	.599	.294	.976
1999	Cleveland Indians	147	522	131	174	34	3	44	165	346	96	131	2	4	.442	.663	.333	1.105
2000	Cleveland Indians	118	439	92	154	34	2	38	122	306	86	117	1	1	.457	.697	.351	1.154
2001	Boston Red Sox	142	529	93	162	33	2	41	125	322	81	147	0	1	.405	.609	.306	1.014
2002	Boston Red Sox	120	436	84	152	31	0	33	107	282	73	85	0	0	.450	.647	.349	1.097
2003	Boston Red Sox	154	569	117	185	36	1	37	104	334	97	94	3	1	.427	.587	.325	1.014
2004	Boston Red Sox	152	568	108	175	44	0	43	130	348	82	124	2	4	.397	.613	.308	1.009
2005	Boston Red Sox	152	554	112	162	30	1	45	144	329	80	119	1	0	.388	.594	.292	.982
2006	Boston Red Sox	130	449	79	144	27	1	35	102	278	100	102	0	1	.439	.619	.321	1.058
2007	Boston Red Sox	133	483	84	143	33	1	20	88	238	71	92	0	0	.388	.493	.296	.881
2008	Boston Red Sox	100	365	66	109	22	1	20	68	193	52	86	1	0	.398	.529	.299	.926
2008	Los Angeles Dodgers	53	187	36	74	14	0	17	53	139	35	38	2	0	.489	.743	.396	1.232
Career totals		2103	7610	1444	2392	507	18	527	1725	4516	1212	1667	37	31	.411	.593	.341	1.004

Acknowledgments

An authorized biography of the elusive Manny Ramirez? It seemed a difficult-bordering-on-impossible proposition at the outset. But we found critical help in the three people who hold sway over Manny Ramirez—his mother, his wife, and his Little League coach, Carlos "Macaco" Ferreira. We are deeply grateful to them for making this project possible.

We owe the greatest thanks to Macaco. A father figure and a trusted advisor to Manny, he introduced the idea of the book—and us—to Manny and advised him to participate in the project. Manny obliged. Macaco saw the book as a way of motivating others to invest in the lives of urban youth. Manny saw the book as a way of giving back to the man who mentored him. And what began as a series of conversations with Manny in 2005—at his home in Florida, his apartment in Boston, at spring training, and at Fenway Park, expanded into this book. We also spent countless hours with Macaco, who still lives in an austere Washington Heights public housing unit. Arranging interviews with Manny and Macaco was not without its frustrations and setbacks—last-minute cancellations and abrupt changes in plans were all too frequent in the beginning stages of the project. But as we got to know Macaco and Manny, and learned to adopt their Zen-like perspective, they and their families welcomed us into their homes and lives with warmth, sincerity, and openness. We are deeply grateful.

The close circle of women that encompasses Manny's life—his wife and mother, but also his grandmother, three sisters, and nieces—provided sympathetic perspectives on Manny's sometimes undecipherable behavior and insightful stories from his childhood. Manny's wife, Juliana, his primary gatekeeper, facilitated access to Manny, who may be one of the most difficult people on earth to contact. (He changes his cellular phone number every few weeks and only provides the new number to a trusted few.) But Juliana relayed messages, helped set up interviews, and generously provided her own perspectives on her husband.

Manny's mother, Onelcida, and grandmother, Pura, were also instrumental, opening their hearts, their kitchens, and their photo albums to us. We also appreciate the candor and generosity of Manny's three older sisters, Clara, Evelyn, and Rossy with whom we exchanged frequent phone calls. The calls began with conversation about Manny, but most often ended with both prosaic and pressing concerns—their teenage children, college applications, marriages, jobs, and the everyday stuff of life. Over time, the Ramirez women became more like extended family members, enabling us to see Manny as the husband, son, uncle, and especially, younger brother he is.

We spoke with scores of other people for this project, all of whom were generous with their time. The list includes Manny's former coaches and managers. Mel Zitter sits at the top—as does Steve Mandl—but the list also includes Dave Keller, Brian Graham, Charlie Manuel, Mark Shapiro, Dan O'Dowd, Mike Hargrove, Mark Schuster, North Johnson, and Rod Carew. We appreciate the perspectives of Joe DeLuca and Mickey White, both of whom were deeply involved in bringing Manny to Cleveland. We are also extremely grateful to Manny's former agents, Luis Valdez, Jaime Torres, Jeffrey Moorad, and Gene Mato, as well as his former major league teammates, Pedro Martinez, Paul Byrd, Trot Nixon, David Ortiz, Julio Lugo, Mike Lowell, Jacoby Ellsbury, Tony Peña, and Omar Ramirez. Manny's childhood friends and teammates also were generous with their time and their memories of life and baseball in Washington Heights. They include: Carlos Puello, Edwin Diaz, Jose Mateo, Trovin "Kiki" Valdez, Nestor Cruz, Nestor Payano, and Richard Lopez. We are also thankful for stories shared by Rose and Bill Quayle, Sherry Magee, Frank Mancini, Winston Llenas, Bud Brutzman, Charles Maher, Frank Mancini, Carl Long, Maria Balbuena, Ino Guerrero, Edward "Pookie" Jackson, Angel Grullon, Jeffrey Ruiz, and Lissette Leonor. Thanks also to Jerome Kagan, Ruben Rumbault, Carola and Marcelo Suarez-Orozco, Patsy Powers, Robert Jackall, and Mary Waters for sharing their expertise.

We are indebted to the great Leigh Montville for his example and advice on how to tell great stories and for his wonderful introduction to this book. Other gifted sportswriters, including Seth Mnookin and Gordon Edes, were also influential in this process. Zachary Lowe made a sizable and important contribution to this book, expertly researching and writing about Manny's years with the Cleveland Indians and Red Sox. We are also indebted to Ilan Mochari, Melody Fischer, and, of course, Brant Rumble, who carefully edited the manuscript. Sara Thynne, a Burlington, North Carolina, librarian; the poet Dick Flavin; David Shapiro; and George Mitrovich. The MENTOR/National Mentoring Partnership, especially Gail Manza, provided generous support during the writing of this book. A portion of its profits will help to support the organization and its important work.

And finally, our deepest thanks go to our families and friends. Jean Rhodes thanks Dane, Audrey, Ian, and Thomas Wittrup;

Acknowledgments

Nancy McNamara; Edith Rhodes; Juliet Schor; Nancy Rappaport; Marc Zwetchkenbaum; Niobe Way; and Kristen Lucken for their love and support. Shawn Boburg is grateful to Carlos and Betty Boburg, for their love and guidance; to Stephanie Akin, for her patience, her encouragement, and her suggestions; to Cristobal Pera, for his endless enthusiasm and his advice; and Elizabeth Boburg, for her ideas, her edits, and her loving support.

About the Authors

Jean Rhodes, Ph.D., is professor of psychology at the University of Massachusetts in Boston, is considered the nation's leading expert on youth mentoring. She has published op-eds about mentoring in the *New York Times* and the *Boston Globe*.

Shawn Boburg is a reporter at *The Record* in Bergen County, New Jersey. He has written and contributed to several national award-winning stories, including the 2003 Pulitzer Prize–winning coverage of the tragic drowning of four young Dominican boys in the Merrimack River in Lawrence, Massachusetts.